Liberty, Equality, Democracy

Liberty, Equality, Democracy

Edited by Eduardo Nolla

NEW YORK UNIVERSITY PRESS
New York and London

Library of Congress Cataloging-in-Publication Data
Liberty, equality, democracy / edited by Eduardo Nolla
     p.   cm.
    Papers presented at a conference held at Yale University in April 1990.
    Includes bibliographical references and index.
    ISBN 0-8147-5774-X (cl)
    1. Tocqueville, Alexis de, 1805-1859--Contributions in political science--
Congresses. 2. Democracy--Congresses. 3. Liberty--Congresses. 4. Equality--
Congresses. I. Nolla, Eduardo.
JC229. T8L47   1992
321.8'0973--dc20
                                            92-6456
                                             CIP

New York University Press Books are printed on acid-free paper,
and their binding materials are chosen for strength and durability.

To George W. Pierson

Contents

THE PROBLEM OF THE TWO *DEMOCRACIES*

Preface

This book contains some of the papers given at an international conference held at Yale University in April 1990 commemorating the 150th anniversary of the publication of Alexis de Tocqueville's *Democracy in America*.The conference was sponsored by the Whitney Humanities Center and the Beinecke Rare Book and Manuscript Library, with the participation of the Social Thought and Ethics Program at Yale and the generous support of the Georges Lurcy Charitable and Educational Trust.

The editor would like to thank Yale University for permission to quote from the Yale Tocqueville Collection at the Beinecke Rare Book and Manuscript Library.

Abbreviations

Editions of Democracy in America

Tocqueville scholars have long discussed the merits and defects of the English translations of *Democracy in America*. There seems to be agreement only on the need for a new translation. The two standard English editions are used in this book.

The French version used is the critical edition published by Eduardo Nolla in 1990. It contains a large number of previously unpublished materials from Tocqueville's drafts, notes, correspondence and manuscript of *Democracy in America*.

DA [B]   *Democracy in America*. The Henry Reeve text as revised by Francis Bowen now further corrected and edited... by Phillips Bradley (New York: Vintage Books, 1945). 2 v.

DA [M-L]   *Democracy in America*. Edited by J. P. Mayer. A new translation by George Lawrence (Garden City, N.Y.: Anchor Books, 1969).

DA [N]   *De la Démocratie en Amérique*. First critical edition, revised and augmented, by Eduardo Nolla (Paris: Librairie Philosophique J. Vrin, 1990). 2 v.

Tocqueville's complete works

OCB   *Oeuvres complètes*. This is the first edition of Tocqueville's complete works, edited by his friend Gustave de Beaumont (Paris: Michel Lévy Frères, 1864-78).

    I-III. *De la Démocratie en Amérique*.
    IV. *L'Ancien Régime et la Révolution*.
    V. *Correspondance et œuvres posthumes*.
    VI. *Correspondance d'Alexis de Tocqueville*.
    VII. *Nouvelle correspondance*.
    VIII. *Mélanges, fragments historiques et notes sur l'Ancien Régime et la Révolution*.
    IX. *Etudes économiques, politiques et littéraires*.

OC   *Oeuvres complètes.* The new but as yet unfinished edition of Tocqueville's complete works. (Paris: Gallimard, 1950-   ).

        I. *De la Démocratie en Amérique.* Introduction by Harold J. Laski. Preliminary note by J.-P. Mayer. 2 v. (1951)

        II:1. *L'Ancien Régime et la Révolution.* Introduction by Georges Lefebvre, preliminary note by J.-P. Mayer. (1952)

        II:2. *L'Ancien Régime et la Révolution. Fragments et notes inédites sur la Révolution.* Edited and annotated by André Jardin. (1953)

        III:1. *Ecrits et discours politiques.* Edited and annotated by André Jardin. Introduction by J.-J. Chevallier and André Jardin. (1962)

        III:2. *Ecrits et discours politiques.* Edited and annotated by André Jardin. Introduction by André Jardin. (1985)

        III:3. *Ecrits et discours politiques.* Edited and annotated by André Jardin. Introduction by André Jardin. (1990)

        IV. *Ecrits sur le système pénitentiaire en France et à l'étranger.* Edited by Michelle Perrot. 2 v. (1985)

        V:1. *Voyages en Sicile et aux Etats-Unis.* Edited and prefaced by J.-P. Mayer. (1957)

        V:2. *Voyages en Angleterre, Irlande, Suisse et Algérie.* Edited and annotated by J.-P. Mayer and André Jardin. (1958)

        VI:1. *Correspondance anglaise. Correspondance d'Alexis de Tocqueville avec Henry Reeve et John Stuart Mill.* Introduction by J.-P. Mayer. Edited and annotated by J.-P. Mayer and Gustave Rudler. (1954)

        VI:2. *Correspondance anglaise. Correspondance et conversations d'Alexis de Tocqueville et Nassau William Senior.* Edited and annotated by H. Brogan and A. P. Kerr. Notes by J. -P. Mayer. Preface by Lord Roll. Introduction by H. Brogan. (1991)

        VII. *Correspondances étrangère d'Alexis de Tocqueville.* Edited by Françoise Mélonio, Lise Queffélec and Anthony Pleasance. (1986)

        VIII. *Correspondance d'Alexis de Tocqueville et de Gustave de Beaumont.* Edited, annotated and introduced by André Jardin. 3 v. (1967)

        IX. *Correspondance d'Alexis de Tocqueville et d'Arthur de Gobineau.* Edited and annotated by M. Degros. Introduction by J.-J. Chevallier. (1959)

        XI. *Correspondance d'Alexis de Tocqueville et de Pierre-Paul Royer-Collard. Correspondance d'Alexis de Tocqueville et de Jean-Jacques Ampère.* Introduced, edited, and annotated by André Jardin. (1970)

        XII. *Souvenirs.* Introduced, edited, and annotated by Luc Monnier. (1964)

        XIII. *Correspondance d'Alexis de Tocqueville et de Louis de Kergorlay.* Edited by André Jardin. Introduction and notes by Jean-Alain Lesourd. 2 v. (1977)

        XV. *Correspondance d'Alexis de Tocqueville et de Francisque de Corcelle. Correspondance d'Alexis de Tocqueville et de Madame Swetchine.* Edited by Pierre Gibert. 2 vols. (1983)

        XVI. *Mélanges.* Edited by Françoise Mélonio. (1989)

        XVIII. *Correspondance d'Alexis de Tocqueville avec Adolphe de Circourt et Madame de Circourt.* Edited by A. P. Kerr. Revised by Louis Girard and Douglas Johnson. (1984)

YTC   The Yale Tocqueville Collection at the Beinecke Rare Book and Manuscript Library, Yale University.

Introduction

Eduardo Nolla

> "Colloque: s. m., de *cum loqui*, parler ensemble. Conférence où l'on dispute sur des points de religion; et parce qu'ordinairement on se quitte sans changer d'opinion, on nomme *colloque* tout entretien qui ne termine rien." Condillac, *Dictionnaire des synonymes*, in *Oeuvres complètes de Condillac* (Paris: Presses Universitaires de France, 1951), III, 131.

Tocqueville would have said that there is no better way to deal with his thought than through a collective work containing different and frequently opposed points of view. But surprisingly Tocqueville scholars have rarely met in international conferences or in the pages of books.[1] In fact, a quick glance at the most important works of Tocquevillian scholarship suggests a kind of oscillation between the United States and Europe, as if only through a great effort could interest in Tocqueville exist simultaneously on both sides of the Atlantic.

And even when a certain amount of intellectual contact has taken place,[2] it has always been clear that the European Tocqueville is generally not the American Tocqueville. American scholars still smile to remember Raymond

---

1. The most notable exception is the 1959 commemoration of Alexis de Tocqueville's death, and the publication of the papers read at the Paris international meeting: *Alexis de Tocqueville. Livre du centenaire, 1859-1959* (Paris: Centre National de la Recherche Scientifique, 1960).
2. Only during the last few years have a certain number of European works been available in English translation. Recent translations include the following authors: André Jardin, Jean-Claude Lamberti, Michael Hereth, and Tocqueville's texts translated by Roger Boesche. Also a number of articles by Wilhelm Hennis, Jean-Claude Lamberti, Raymond Aron and François Furet can be read in English now.

Aron's "rediscovery" of Tocqueville in 1979,[3] and their European colleagues are, for their part, surprised by American neglect of the second part of *Democracy in America*, which remains at the center of European scholarship on Tocqueville.[4] But for several reasons this situation of intellectual distance and sometimes studied ignorance is rapidly changing.

The renaissance of Tocqueville studies in the early twentieth century started with a number of biographical and textual works.[5] Since then, much effort has been and is still devoted to the publication of the Tocqueville papers,[6] their inaccessibility unfortunately having slowed down and thwarted no small number of research projects.

The approaching completion of Tocqueville's *Oeuvres complètes* has evidently been one of the main factors that has helped to expand Tocquevillian scholarship. André Jardin's definitive biography, an excellent work of scholarship, has solved many problems related to Tocqueville's life. It has had at the same time the perhaps unintended but remarkable result of assuring many a scholar that the remaining unpublished Tocqueville manuscripts will force no radical changes in his scholarship.

But an entirely new orientation has been the most symptomatic of the recent changes in Tocqueville studies. As more and more texts have become available, and as this availability has coincided with the emergence of the new set of problems of western society generally grouped under the term "postmodernity," the study of Tocqueville has moved away from the historical and biographical towards the theoretical and philosophical.[7]

This change is not unrelated to the discovery that the unpublished papers of Tocqueville have come in many cases to shake the foundations of what had until recently been accepted as the standard explanation of Tocqueville.[8]

---

3. Raymond Aron, "Tocqueville retrouvé," *Tocqueville Review*, 1 (1979), 8-23.
4. We should partly exclude France from this position. The French scholars have for obvious reasons been intrigued more by Tocqueville as historian of the French Revolution.
5. The works of Antoine Rédier and Roland-Pierre Marcel included new unpublished materials, as did George Pierson's book.
6. I refer not only to the efforts of the international commission in charge of the publication of his works but also to the efforts of many scholars (James T. Schleifer, Roger Boesche, Eduardo Nolla,...) to publicize previously unpublished manuscripts.
7. This is proven, among other facts, by the final abandonment of the principle of the prophetic vision of Tocqueville, i.e. the idea that his theories are a product of a sixth sense or intuition but have no sound philosophical or theoretical grounding. Few things have slowed the study of Tocqueville more than this attempt to see in him a political prophet but not a philosopher.
8. The best evidence of a philosopher's status as a "classic" of the history of thought is perhaps not the amount of scholarship produced on his work or the number of new editions, but rather the realization that Tocqueville is not yet fully understood.

And when a certain postmodern malaise started to appear in political and philosophical theories, Tocqueville scholars discovered that their author possessed a difficult and original "philosophy" that seemed particularly pertinent to the present.[9]

This does not mean in any way that political theorists had not already dealt with Tocqueville, but rather that their present interests are more theoretical and philosophical. This also means, paradoxically, that Tocqueville's thought has become more timely and practical than before.

For example, fewer and fewer contemporary studies center on the question of Montesquieu or Mill's influence on Tocqueville,[10] in an attempt to make him fit in the classical tradition of liberal thought, while more and more pages are written on Tocqueville as a Pascalian and Roussonian thinker.[11]

It seems somehow appropriate that an age which praises itself for living in the void[12] will turn its eyes to a Pascalian Tocqueville. It is known that Pascal was always afraid of a large abyss that seemed to open to the left of his table while he was working. and that to reassure himself he put a chair to his left.[13]

Tocqueville speaks about not one but two abysses, to his right and to his left. This metaphor is so appropriate—not only to aristocratic and democratic times, pre- and post- Revolution, but also to modernity and postmodernity, West and East,—that it is not surprising to find that contemporary authors read *Democracy in America* as a new *Pensées* more than as a kind of *Spirit of the Laws in the United States*.

Ortega liked to say that all new philosophy is produced with the help of bricks and boards taken from the fallen structure of previous philosophies. Today the constructive abilities of philosophy are said to be exhausted and

9. This use of Tocqueville in relation to contemporary questions is evident in authors as distant from each other as Jean Baudrillard, Robert Nisbet or Gilles Lipovetsky. In a postmodern vein it could be said that Tocqueville is one of the first authors who rejects the "big narratives."

10. This had been an accepted assumption since the first appearance of the first part of *Democracy in America*. Luis Díez del Corral has masterfully exposed the shaky ground on which most of these studies were based. It must also be noted that Díez del Corral was the first to point out the Pascalian element of Tocqueville's thought, more than thirty years ago. See his *El pensamiento político de Tocqueville* (Madrid: Alianza Universidad, 1898), especially chapter III.

11. Tocqueville's liberalism is now considered to be strange (Roger Boesche) or elusive (Peter A. Lawler). In any case, very different from classic liberalism.

12. See Gilles Lipovetsky, *L'ère du vide* (Paris: Gallimard, 1983).

13. See Luis Díez del Corral, *El pensamiento político de Tocqueville* (Madrid: Alianza Universidad, 1989), 246-247.

Alain Rénaut has put Ortega's words in a modern perspective by speaking of the need of philosophers to become thieves.

Whatever constructive, destructive or de-constructive view of philosophy is taken, it is equally true that at present Tocqueville is a prized object of thievery.

There is probably no other place where the interest in Tocqueville is more evident than in Eastern Europe. Like Western Europe, the countries of the East are discovering in Tocqueville[14] a critic and defender of democracy who has the advantage of not using psychoanalytical, linguistic or Marxist terminology, and who offers the possibility of being read as a philosopher (like Pascal) who dislikes and mistrusts philosophy. Tocqueville spoke of philosophy as the "essence of all gibberish,"[15] "voluntary torment that man consents [...] to inflict on himself."[16] One thing is clear from the beginning of the introduction to the *Democracy*. "The author of this work," reads a draft, "set out to write a book on politics and not a book of philosophy."[17]

But is precisely in Eastern Europe that Tocqueville today runs the greatest risks. He is presented as the author of a non-Marxist Bible for contemporary societies, and there is always the temptation of reading him as the countries of Eastern Europe have been used to read Marx, as an author who offers answers, solutions, recipes, forgetting that the real interest of Tocqueville's message is that books need to be written and read but not obeyed or followed.[18]

Tocqueville, following the steps of Plato, disliked books. He did not like books of philosophy and especially books of political philosophy, because, for him, the existence of political philosophy resulted from a failure of politics, an absence of political practice[19]. Political philosophers who lack contact with political life, as the *philosophes*, create an orderly, uniform, just, simple, intellectual nation where they retire.

---

14.   A large number of conferences and meetings on Tocqueville are presently taking place in Eastern Europe (in Yugoslavia in 1991, in Czechoslovakia, Bulgaria and Rumania in 1992)
15.   Draft of a letter to Le Peletier d'Aunay, November 8, 1831. YTC [Yale Tocqueville Collection], BIa2. All of the documents of the Beinecke Rare Book and Manuscript Library are cited with the kind permission of Yale University.
16.   Letter to Charles Stoffels, October 22, 1831, YTC, BIa1, and *OCB*, VII, 83-84. See *OCB*, VI, 370.
17.   YTC, CVk, 1, 73.
18.   See Eduardo Nolla, *Democratia (sau) Cartea Inchisa*, 22, 40 (1991), 10-11.
19.   "True enlightenment comes, for the most part, from experience." *DA* [N], I, 236. The Enlightenment is "the exercise of thought completely abstracted from active practice," *DA* [N], II, 31, note c.

Order, prediction, transparency, perfection belong to theory and not to reality. "There is no subject that does not broaden the more one immerses oneself in it," Tocqueville wrote to Chabrol, "neither fact nor observation at the bottom of which one cannot discover doubt. All of the objects in this life appear to us, as through a veil, like certain decorations at the opera, whose contours one cannot grasp with precision. There are people who enjoy living in this perpetual twilight; as for me, it tires and depresses me; I would like to hold the political and moral truths the way I hold my pen."

The most important element of the contemporary vision of Tocqueville is precisely the realization that Tocqueville retains his attraction for us today because he successfully sustains contradictions, simultaneously embracing knowledge and ignorance, theory and practice, thought and action.

Tocqueville mocks the philosophy of the Enlightenment for not having direct links to reality, for being literary and above all individualistic; he, on the other hand, is continually in motion, in constant intellectual effervescence. He cannot stop himself from thinking, from being what he likes to call an "examining machine," "a reasoning machine; a kind of syllogism incarnate."

In a note he once exclaimed: "The only truth that I acknowledge as absolute is that there is no absolute truth."[20]

The process of thought, then, resembles a syllogism always in search of a conclusion. For Tocqueville, life takes place in the doubt between randomness, on the one hand, and causes beyond calculation on the other. For man, the world is a closed book, empty of truths and of absolute systems.[21]

This is precisely why one must avoid what can be observed in the United States, where "everyone closes himself off... completely, and claims from this vantage point to be able to judge the world.... When they see that they can solve all of the small difficulties with which they are presented in their practical lives, without outside help," Tocqueville remarks about the

---

20. YTC, BIIb.
21. "When I began to reflect, I believed that the world was full of proven truths; that one only had to look hard in order to see them. However, when I applied myself to the consideration of objects, I could only perceive inextricable doubt [...] I convinced myself in the end that the search for absolute, *demonstrable*, truth, like the search for perfect happiness, was a quest for the impossible. It is not that there are no truths that merit the *complete conviction* of man; but, rest assured, they are very few and far between. For the great majority of things that it is important for us to know, we have but likenesses, approximations. To despair because it is this way is to despair of man; for this is one of the inflexible laws of our nature." Letter to Charles Stoffels, October 22, 1831, YTC, BIa1 and *OCB*, VII, 82-82.

Americans, "they thus conclude, easily enough, that the world is explainable, and that nothing escapes the boundaries of intelligence."[22]

To live in doubt and contradiction is to live in democracy and to be fully human.

> One could perhaps compare democracy to the sun that produces light by rolling impetuously over itself and in ceaselessly agitating all of the molecules of which [it is made up].[23]

It is only in the action of man and in his conflicting ideas that the human spirit develops:[24] only in everyday commotion, in the small disturbances of public freedom does democracy survive.[25]

> You have to admit... that there is not one single intellectual truth that can be demonstrated, and that the centuries of enlightenment are centuries of doubt and discussion.[26]

It follows that the surest way of avoiding absolute ideas and excessive generalities, of avoiding the excesses of political theory as one avoids total confidence in books, is by forcing each man to engage with ideas, to think, to fight against reality, to contest, to search for an identity.[27]

In other words, for Tocqueville the aim of thought must be to create doubt, to maintain man in uncertainty, to move him away from systems and absolute truths, away, precisely, from a life of books and theories.

Perhaps the most important effect of the recent publication of previously unpublished manuscripts has been to show a Tocqueville who is more of an aristocrat and a conservative that had been thought up to now.[28]

---

22. *DA* [N] II, 14.
23. YTC, CVa, 9.
24. "Feelings and ideas do not renew themselves, the heart does not grow and the human spirit does not develop but by the reciprocal actions of men against each other." *DA* [N] II, 105.
25. *L'Ancien Régime et la Révolution, OC*, II:1, 197.
26. Letter to Charles Stoffels, April 21, 1830, in *DA* [N], II, 323.
27. "When, tired of searching for what motivates one's fellow man, he [man] strives at least to distinguish what motivates himself, he does not yet know what to believe. He searches the universe, and he doubts. He returns finally to himself, and the obscurity seems to increase the closer he comes and wants to know himself." *DA* [N] II, 77, note v.
28. Roland-Pierre Marcel spoke of Tocqueville as a "conservative-liberal".
    Hugh Brogan sees in him an aristocrat convinced of the success of democracy. Harold Laski, Phillip Bradley, Wydham Lewis, John Lukacs, Antoine Rédier and Robert Nisbet think of him as an aristocrat who hates democracy.
    Jacob-Peter Mayer and Albert Salomon have spoken of a "liberal of a new kind". Russell Kirk qualified Tocqueville as "liberal à la Burke". Maxime Leroy wrote about Tocqueville, the "liberal-conservative".

It may be enough to show that in the drafts of *Democracy in America* Tocqueville is perfectly convinced that aristocracy is necessary for the development of humanity, that "it is under an aristocracy or a prince that men that were half savage have obtained the several notions that will later allow them to be cultivated, equal and free."[29] Is it necessary to add that the author of *Democracy in America* confesses that he would not free the American slaves?[30]

But as the scholar advances in the study of the manuscripts, he discovers that Tocqueville is, more than one could have supposed, a convinced liberal, and that far from hoping to stop the movement towards democracy, he "wishes to produce it."[31]

When a reviewer of the *Ancien Régime et la Révolution* describes him as an aristocrat Tocqueville takes his pen and writes:

> You seem to think of me as a friend of the old regime that the force of truth has forced to give reasons to the enemies of that regime. That is, Sir, totally wrong. There has been no person that has better brought to light the vices, the excesses, the faults of that old regime; even if I think that in the midst of all the bad institutions that it contained there were several things that it would have been desirable to keep. No one, I dare to say, has ever described the evil that the spirit and prejudices of class, class divisions and the bad government of royalty have produced in France. No one has shown the part of responsibility that the royalty, the nobility and the bourgeoisie have had in the violence of the Revolution. How could you, Sir, put in doubt in one phrase my sympathy for the people, when a large part of my work has been dedicated to show under a new, true, sharper light the peculiar kind of oppression that they suffer and their miseries, and to understand how the bad education that the royalty and the high classes have given to them explain their violence?... I am a sincere and ardent friend of what you yourself consider the main conquests of the Revolution: political liberty and all the individual liberties that this expression contains, the abolition of all caste privileges, equality before the law, total religious liberty, simple legislation,...[32]

Richard Bendix, Seymour Lipset, Jack Lively and Raymond Aron have their doubts about Tocqueville's liberalism but see in him mainly a weapon against Marxism.

29. *DA* [N], II, 96, note g.
"If nations had started with a democratic government I doubt that they would have ever been civilized", *DA* [N], I, 160.
30. "I confess that if I had the misfortune of living in a country where slavery had been introduced and that if I hold in my hand the liberty of the Blacks I would not open it", *DA* [N]I, 276, note f.
31. *DA* [N], II, 8, note h.
32. In a letter of July 31, 1856. Quoted with the kind permission of the Bibliothèque de Versailles.

One of the most important lessons of Tocqueville's manuscripts is, to say it simply and quickly, to show a Tocqueville who is at the same time more of an aristocrat and more of a democrat.[33]

Is this a contradiction? Not in the case of Tocqueville. Tocqueville's liberalism can only be understood if one gives its full force to the disjunction between aristocracy and democracy, centralization and decentralization, unity and plurality, liberty and equality,... He requires from us to be simultaneously democratic and aristocratic, conservative and liberal, pre and post-revolutionary.[34] The early nineteenth century was not capable of avoiding this opposition. The late twentieth century finds itself in a similar situation.

Tocqueville knew well that this was at the origin of his thought.

> I was in such a balance between past and future that I didn't feel instinctively attracted towards one or the other and I didn't have to make great efforts to glance to each side with calmness.[35]

Tocqueville exaggerated the tranquillity and lack of interest with which he watched both sides but he was sincere: history made it difficult for him to be an ultra or a liberal. With his usual perspicacity, he predicted that the major historical division between pre-revolution and post-revolution would always prevent readers from appropriately understanding his *Democracy in America*, and he wrote to a friend in these terms: "Some will find that I do not like democracy and that I am too severe with it, others will think that I dangerously promote its development."[36]

The contemporary scholars of Tocqueville are beginning to find themselves more and more in a similar situation. They need to chose between modern or postmodern, reason or passion, liberty or equality, and

---

33. I have dealt with this problem in some detail in, *Autour de l'autre Démocratie*, Naples, 1990.
34. Not only did Tocqueville propose that the powerful legislative power be balanced with a permanent executive, which recalls Montesquieu, but there is also in all his work a confrontation between concentration and diffusion of power. The first chamber is to be elected by universal suffrage, the second by limited suffrage. If political power must be concentrated, the administration should be decentralized. The jury is effective only when directed by the judge. The oppositions and interplay of different principles are multiplied in the work until Tocqueville ends up presenting to us a democratic regime that is only and properly democratic if it contains a certain number of non-democratic elements or, using Tocqueville's word, a certain amount of aristocracy.
35. To Henry Reeve, *OC*, VI: 1, 37-38.
36. Letter published in *OC*, XIII:1, 374, but maybe not sent to Louis de Kergorlay.

they find in Tocqueville the only theory that attempts to maintain the best from a system of opposition.[37]

It should not be surprising then that this book contains many different and frequently opposed views on Tocqueville, that it offers an image of the author of *Democracy in America* that is never totally and permanently clear, but that changes from page to page.

When speaking and writing about Tocqueville using his own methodological tools there can be no clear answer, no definitive result, only a permanent intellectual search. It is only by the constant attempt to decipher the meaning of democracy and democratic times and the simultaneous awareness of the impossibility of the task that we can fulfill Tocqueville's own theory and pay tribute to his great book.

As he himself put it:

> The books which have made men reflect the most, and have had the greatest influence on their opinions and their acts are those in which the author did not seek to dictate dogmatically what it was proper to think, but rather where he pointed them in the direction of truths for them to find, as if of themselves.[38]

37. It can be said that part of the present attraction of Tocqueville rests in the fact of his use of a two-speed "asynthetical" dialectical system that avoids the Hegelian-Marxist three-speed "synthetical" historical engine.
38. Letter to Francisque de Corcelle, September 17, 1853, *OC*, XV:2, 80.

THE ANGEL AND THE BEAST

[1]

The Human Condition: Tocqueville's Debt to Rousseau and Pascal

Peter Augustine Lawler

Alexis de Tocqueville is widely admired for his distinctive moderation, political astuteness, and genuine devotion to human liberty. He is studied seriously today primarily for his political analysis, and less so for his provocative and perceptive observations concerning the psychological effects of democratic conditions. There has been remarkably little serious discussion of Tocqueville's comprehensive reflections on the human condition, although they inform all of his work.

Despite his many admirable qualities, Tocqueville is usually regarded as a derivative thinker. He is generally viewed as a student of the political philosophers Jean-Jacques Rousseau and Charles de Secondat Montesquieu, and not quite their intellectual equal.[1] My contention is that Tocqueville's understanding of the fundamental human questions is not inferior to that of the political philosophers, and that his primary but hardly uncritical debt is

---

1.   Two outstanding recent sources which view Tocqueville as a student of Rousseau are John Koritansky, *Alexis de Tocqueville and the New Science of Politics* (Durham, N.C.: Carolina Academic Press, 1987) and Wilhelm Hennis, "Tocqueville's Perspective," *Interpretation*, 16 (1988), 61-86. Two which interpret Tocqueville in light of Montesquieu are Anne M. Cohler, *Montesquieu's Comparative Politics and the Spirit of American Constitutionalism* (Lawrence: University of Kansas Press, 1987), 170-190 and Jean-Claude Lamberti, *Tocqueville and the Two "Democracies"*, Arthur Goldhammer trans. (Cambridge, Mass.: Harvard University Press, 1989). I assess the recent literature on Tocqueville in "Tocqueville's Elusive Moderation," *Polity*, 22 (1989), 181-189.

to Pascal, whom he regards as the most radical of thinkers[2]. Tocqueville understands Rousseau's thought to be a Pascalian derivative.

Tocqueville, as is often noted, called himself a "new kind" of liberal. Scholars now generally recognize that the liberal Tocqueville meant to stand apart not only from the reactionaries and radicals, but also from the apolitical liberals of his time. But they see far more clearly what Tocqueville is not than what he is. The foundation and character of his innovative liberalism remain obscure.[3]

My purpose here is to come to terms with the distinctiveness of Tocqueville's thought and partisanship by showing how they are rooted in his Pascalian understanding of the human condition. I want to show the depth of his affirmation of human liberty. I also want to show, using Tocqueville, what features of the human condition are responsible for the greatness of and our dissatisfaction with modern liberal democracy. The extent to which Tocqueville saw human liberty as a problem, rooted in the paradoxical character of the human condition, has not yet really been appreciated.

Tocqueville was fundamentally a partisan of human liberty. All of his political analysis is written from that perspective. He understood with what he believed to be unprecedented clarity how problematic that partisanship is. Human liberty cannot exist without considerable self-consciousness, but it is not simply self-consciousness. It is both a response to and a diversion from the self-consciousness of the mortal, from his experience of the truth about his condition.

The Human Condition

In the second volume of *Democracy*, near the end of his account of the democratic or skeptical destruction of the poetic propensity of human beings to idealize reality, Tocqueville describes the core of human existence. What

2.   Tocqueville's biographer, André Jardin, makes any number of penetrating observations concerning Tocqueville's fundamental experiences in light of Pascal, but he does very little to connect them to his political analysis. André Jardin, *Tocqueville: A Biography*, translated by Lydia Davis with Robert Hemenway (New York: Farrar, Strauss, Giroux, 1988).
3.   Tocqueville called himself a "new kind" of liberal in a letter to Eugène Stoffels (July 24, 1836). Roger Boesche's is the most recent and perhaps the most comprehensive effort to determine what kind of liberal that is. He does well in describing what Tocqueville is not, but he fails to get to the root of the distinctiveness of his thought. *The Strange Liberalism of Alexis de Tocqueville* (Ithaca, N.Y.: Cornell University Press, 1987).

human beings can know about themselves when they are freed from illusion or diversion or idealism is that they are time-bound beings existing contingently between "two abysses."[4] The human being comes mysteriously from nothing and returns there. There is no natural or divine support for human existence.

This self-knowledge produces "incomprehensible miseries." The miserably self-conscious mortal is the wondrous, terrible beast with the angel in him, full "of contrasts of infinite greatness and littleness." This being knows something of himself, but he cannot grasp himself as a whole. All he knows, and can ever know, Tocqueville says, are "his passions, his doubts, and his unexpected good fortune."[5] He knows himself as a doubtful, incoherent, and contingent being who passionately desires to be something else. He wishes to be a beast or an angel, but he is miserable as a man.[6]

The human condition is one of paradoxical discontent, or discontent with the paradoxes that constitute that condition. Human beings long to know the infinite, but cannot. They desire that impossible knowledge because they long to understand themselves, but cannot. Human beings understand themselves as parts of a whole, and they know that the part cannot be understood without understanding the whole. But the human parts do not even begin to know why they are distinguished, and know it, from the whole. All human beings know that they exist, and they cannot rest content with that anxious and frightening knowledge by itself. They long "for peace of mind and moderation of desires," but cannot find them. Human beings cannot help, in their anxious uncertainty, but attempt to articulate the whole. But their theoretical efforts are always either distorted by partiality or pride or are excessively general or self-denying. They know, when they are genuinely self-conscious, that only God can see the relation between the parts and the whole. Hence only God can know how and why human particularity or self-conscious mortality exists.[7]

Human beings seek certainty and stability, but they cannot find them. When seeing their limitations, they are filled with doubtful anxiety. So terrible is that truthful experience that they spend most of their lives in flight

---

4. *DA* [M-L], 487.
5. *Ibid.*, 487.
6. *Ibid.*, 546. Cf. Tocqueville's comments about the human condition, especially his condition, in his letter to Kergorlay (July 6, 1835) in Alexis de Tocqueville, *Selected Letters on Politics and Society*, Roger Boesche ed., James Toupin and Roger Boesche trans. (Berkeley, Cal.: University of California Press, 1985), 103 and in his letter to Pierre-Paul Royer-Collard (August 15, 1840), 143.
7. *DA* [M-L], 294, 436, 444. Letter to Edouard de Tocqueville (November 2, 1840) in *Selected Letters*, 148-149.

from it. By "instinct" (or irrational natural inclination) they seek rest, but, by reason, or to the extent they are self-conscious, they cannot find it. Tocqueville's account of the miserable anxiety of the self-conscious mortal existing contingently in the infinite universe is Pascal's.[8]

Prideful Belief

Tocqueville continues to follow Pascal by observing that it is natural for human beings to believe, to divert themselves through the imagination from the miserable isolation of doubt. Unbelief, Tocqueville says, is "an accident," "a sort of intellectual aberration," and an unfortunate one.[9] The unbeliever is miserable, and he cannot live well. As Pascal said in general and Tocqueville said about himself, such a being is most deserving of our pity.[10]

Human beings by "instinct" and "passion" are led away from the misery of doubt to prideful belief, to "sublime" illusions that give purpose, direction, and dignity to their mysterious distinctiveness or liberty.[11] They do not want to know that their existence is accidental or unsupported by nature. Hence they complete or make sense out of or idealize their distinctiveness through their imaginations. Human beings, in other words, are usually inclined to understand themselves poetically. They are led, usually rather unconsciously, to the conclusion that too much self-consciousness or doubtful anxiety is destructive of life. They do not want to be needlessly miserable.[12]

Unbelief is an accident, a mysterious defeat of nature or instinct. By making life too restless and miserable, it cannot help but be destructive of life. Paradoxically enough, too much self-consciousness tends to have the effect of destroying self-consciousness. Unbelief is the accident which overcomes the accident of human distinctiveness or liberty. Tocqueville's Pascal, distinctive in the purity of his effort to think radically without pride, is presented as literally having thought himself to death in an extreme effort to free his mind or soul from the limitations of his embodiment. Pascal's pure

8.   One outstanding political thinker who does see something of the debt of Tocqueville's political analysis to Pascal is Pierre Manent, *Tocqueville et la nature de la démocratie* (Paris: Julliard, 1982), 80-95. Compare my discussion of the restless Americans below with Manent's, and with Pascal, *Pensées*, F. Trotter trans. (New York: Dutton, 1958), "The Misery of Man without God," fragments 60-183, especially 100. On the paradoxes that constitute the human condition, see also fragments 434-437.
9.   *DA* [M-L], 297.
10.   See letter to Edouard de Tocqueville (November 2, 1840), in *Selected Letters*, 149.
11.   *DA* [M-L], 296, 545.
12.   *Ibid.*, 483, 542-545. Cf. Pascal, *Pensées*, fragments 82-83, 100.

devotion to the truth is the most "extraordinary" of accidents.[13] In its extremism or its purity, it cannot help but be misanthropic.

Belief is not a total suppression of self-consciousness, but a response to it. Unbelief or excessive doubt, Tocqueville says, is dizzying and paralyzing, whereas the passion that leads to belief is a source of human strength. If all human beings perceive is "constant restlessness," if everything is in flux, then nothing in particular seems possible. Belief makes human liberty or action possible.[14]

"Sublime" or prideful, spiritual or soul-based doctrines, Tocqueville observes, usually find support in human instinct or passion. Hence they have the tendency to be self-fulfilling prophecies. The belief that human beings somehow or another transcend time, that they have "an immaterial and immortal principle" that is only "for a time united to matter" he calls "indispensable to man's greatness." If human beings believe that they are more than time-bound beings, they will produce accomplishments that endure the ravages of time.[15]

But human beings know, when they do not distract themselves from genuine self-contemplation through the imaginative generation of prideful belief, that they do not transcend time. The greatest of human accomplishments are nothing in the light of eternity. Tocqueville calls the doctrine of "Socrates and his school," as well as its derivatives such as Christianity (which Tocqueville interprets as a sort of Platonism for the people, the American's "most precious inheritance from aristocratic times") "sublime" and salutary, but really "childish," even "ridiculous" as theory.[16] More generally, he sides theoretically with Pascal against all the philosophers who hold that contemplation is in some sense or another pleasurable and the highest good for human beings. All such experience and all the metaphysical doctrine it generates is distorted by prideful belief and imagination.[17]

---

13. *Ibid.*, 461.
14. *Ibid.*, 434-436. See letter to Jean-Jacques Ampère (August 10, 1841) in *Selected Letters*, 152-153, on the "strength of the "passions" as the antidote to paralyzing "doubt" or "philosophical malaise."
    For another attempt to see the Pascalian foundation of Tocqueville's thought, see my "The Restless Mind," in *Tocqueville's Defense of Human Liberty*, Peter A. Lawler and Joseph Alulis eds. (Garland Publishers, forthcoming).
15. *DA* [M-L], 544-545.
16. *Ibid.*, 544-545. Cf. letter to Louis de Kergorlay (August 8, 1838) in Gustave de Beaumont ed., *Memoir, Letters, and Remains of Alexis de Tocqueville*, (London: Macmillan, 1861), I, 343-347, and letter to Beaumont (April 22, 1838) in *Selected Letters*, 130. See my "Tocqueville on Religion and Human Excellence," *Southeastern Political Review*, 11 (1983), 139-160.
17. I develop Tocqueville's criticism of the philosophers in my "Was Tocqueville a Philosopher?" *Interpretation*, 17 (1990), 401-414. See Pascal, *Pensées*, on the

Contrary to the philosophers, Tocqueville holds that the genuine affirmation of human liberty must be despite or because of doubt, anxiety, and error. There are, in Tocqueville's work, all sorts of tensions and contradictions flowing from his decision to put human liberty before openness to the truth, while acknowledging that the former is not possible without a considerable amount of the latter.[18] To avoid misanthropy, or the fate of Pascal, Tocqueville affirmed the paradoxical inconsistencies of human liberty, and devoted himself to their perpetuation.

Tocqueville says that free human beings must think about "the greatest problems of human destiny," but must not "despair" about reaching solutions for them. When too much "doubt invades the highest faculties of the mind," human beings "ignobly" give up thinking about their fundamental problems.[19] The extremely self-conscious and doubtful Americans "have little time for thinking," because they self-consciously avoid it. Tocqueville predicts that, in their language, "metaphysics and theology will slowly lose ground."[20]

The perpetuation of human liberty depends upon thought, and the perpetuation of thought depends upon belief. The human condition, in other words, must not ordinarily appear to the mind as problematic as it really is. Metaphysics and theology must seem possible. The "ideal [or poetic] world" they describe must really seem to exist. Platonism and Christianity are salutary restraints on the mind that make contemplation, including self-contemplation, endurable.[21]

Tocqueville himself was not certain that human liberty even exists. He granted in a letter to Arthur de Gobineau that no one could be certain that fatalistic determinism is untrue. He only knew that, from the perception of his partisanship, it was "pernicious."[22] Tocqueville had to suspend doubt, to some extent, to make the decision to defend human liberty. But his doubt or theoretical uncertainty was an indispensable part of the nobility or human

deceit of the imagination, which is greatest for "the wisest men." See also on the self-deception of philosophers, fragments 150 and 152.

18. Both Michael Hereth, *Alexis de Tocqueville: Threats to Freedom in a Democracy* (Durham: Duke University Press, 1986), 161-171, and Larry E. Shiner, *The Secret Mirror: Literary Form and History in Tocqueville's "Recollections"* (Ithaca, N.Y.: Cornell University Press, 1988) do a good job of exploring these contradictions. They also both underestimate Tocqueville's own awareness of them.

19. *DA* [M-L], 444.

20. *DA* [M-L], 441, 479.

21. *DA* [M-L], 434, 544-545.

22. Letter to Gobineau (December 20, 1843), in John Lukacs, *The European Revolution and Correspondence with Gobineau* (Westport, Conn.: Greenwood Press, 1959), 227. See the use of "pernicious" in Tocqueville, *DA* [M-L], 543.

liberty of his project. Devotion to a cause that may or may not succeed is distinctively human liberty. Such devotion is neither reactionary nor radical, nor is it apolitical.[23]

For Tocqueville, human liberty is necessarily a mixture of the truth and error. It is a mixture of the reason, passion, and instinct that constitutes human life.[24] Tocqueville's distinctive moderation, as some of his philosophic critics complain, is not that of a harmoniously ordered soul. It is an affirmation of the tensions, contradictions, and paradoxes of the incoherent mixture of body and soul. Tocqueville asserted emphatically that human liberty is not a product of reason, nor of the instinct human beings have to seek happiness or contentment. It is a mixture of passion and self-consciousness which eludes reason and resists contentment.[25]

Tocqueville's Paradoxes

Tocqueville understood himself, most fundamentally, to be a political actor rather than a theorist or writer. He wrote only when circumstances denied him a place on the political stage and then only on behalf of the restoration or perpetuation of political liberty.[26] Yet he knew he was extraordinarily detached or theoretical and hence doubtful and anxious for an actor. This doubtful detachment produced an indecisiveness which limited the effectiveness of his action. But it was also the source of the unrivaled quality of his political judgment and his political integrity.[27] He knew that action was an only partly successful diversion from his anxiety, but it was enough of one for him not to doubt life's seriousness or experience disgust for it.[28]

---

23. See David Epstein, *The Political Theory of "The Federalist"* (Chicago: University of Chicago Press, 1984), 111-125.
24. Socratic partisans such as Koritansky and Hereth criticize Tocqueville for not having a harmoniously ordered soul and for not simply accepting, in some sense or another, what Nietzsche called Socrates' "bizarre" equation of reason, virtue, and happiness (*The Twilight of the Idols*, "The Problem of Socrates").
25. See Tocqueville, *The Old Regime and the French Revolution*, Stuart Gilbert trans. (New York: Anchor Books, 1955), 169.
26. See Tocqueville, *Recollections: The French Revolution of 1848*, George Lawrence trans., Jacob-Peter Mayer and Anne P. Kerr eds. (New Brunswick, N.J.: Transaction Books, 1987), 1-4. Cf. letter to Louis de Kergorlay (December 13, 1850), *Selected Letters*, 252-253, and Hereth, *Alexis de Tocqueville*, 19, 83.
27. *Recollections*, 82-85, 230-231.
28. See Jardin, *Tocqueville*, 384. Tocqueville, *Recollections*, 82-85, 230-231.

Political life was not enough of a diversion for Tocqueville to insure his happiness or contentment.[29] Yet he preferred it to what seems to others to be the fortunate circumstances of domestic contentment, the indolence of which sometimes made him miserable over "nothing".[30] Tocqueville says in his *Souvenirs* that the coming of the revolution of 1848 made France and most Frenchmen miserable. He also says it made him happy. It freed him from the doubtful, isolated anxiety he experienced in the bourgeois or middle class world. In that world, there was no diversion weighty enough to engage his attention. As a result, Tocqueville was too indecisive to choose from the many similar and not very political choices. The revolution was a great diversion. With its coming, "one could no longer make a mistake about the path to follow."[31]

In his letters and his *Souvenirs*, Tocqueville attempts to come to terms with the tensions and contradictions that constituted his own existence, which he understood as an extreme example of the paradoxical mixture that is the beast with an angel in him. He viewed himself as extremely self-conscious and when undiverted, extremely miserable. His "great pride," he acknowledged, "was as nervous and restless as the mind itself." The "sad story" of "the anxious and restless soul," he also wrote, "is a little bit the story of all men, but of some more than others, and of myself more than anyone I know."[32] The same paradoxes he found in himself he found in history, the record of the development of human self-consciousness.

The most famous of these is his most well-known contribution to contemporary social science, the so-called "revolution of rising expectations." In the *Old Regime and the Revolution*, Tocqueville notes that "popular discontent" increases when material conditions improve. When conditions improve most rapidly, revolution is most likely. He says that "this may seem illogical—but history is full of such paradoxes."[33] History, in other words, resembles and is the product of the beast with the angel in him.

The movement of the history of the West, for Tocqueville, is from instinct to calculation, sublime illusion to realistic selfishness, material poverty and weakness to prosperity and power, political oppression to liberty, and

29. See, for example, the letter to Kergorlay (October 25, 1842) in *Memoir,* I, 252, and the letter to Madame Swetchine (January 7, 1856) in *Memoir*, II, 319-320.
30. See letter to Edouard de Tocqueville (November 2, 1840), *Selected Letters*, 149, and the letter to Madame Swetchine (February 11, 1857), *Selected Letters*, 349. Jardin notes, about Tocqueville, that "there was something a little pathological about his irritability in domestic life" (Jardin, *Tocqueville*, 373).
31. *Recollections*, 46-47, 84-85, 193.
32. *Ibid.*, 84. Letter to Edouard de Tocqueville (November 2, 1840) in *Selected Letters*, 149.
33. *The Old Regime*, 176.

contentment to misery. The movement is, at the most general level, from aristocracy to democracy through the mind's skeptical or doubtful destruction of the prideful beliefs that support human distinctions. Tocqueville seems to follow Rousseau in showing that human beings, over time, become more human or historical or self-conscious and less natural or subordinated to instinct or merely brutish desire. They also limit self-consciousness through prideful belief, but, over time, they even free themselves from most of that. The paradox articulated by Rousseau is that progress toward prosperity, self-consciousness, and liberty is accompanied by a decline in virtue and happiness or contentment. Human history is the destruction of illusion and the growth of misery.[34]

Pascal and Rousseau

Tocqueville's debt to Rousseau for his understanding of history does not reduce his more fundamental reliance on Pascal. It brings to mind the close similarity of much of the analysis of the human condition in Pascal and Rousseau. Both agree that human self-consciousness produces an anxious and restless misery which, if immoderated, becomes unendurable. They both agree that the human condition, at least what human beings can know about themselves without faith, is an unfortunate accident. The human being is and knows himself to be a miserable error.[35]

Those self-conscious mortals who are aware of their condition, and who do not have faith, are to be pitied. Rousseau, who did not have faith, was still able to find a way of existing that was not pitiable, but only because he was able to negate his human self-consciousness, his consciousness of time. His most enjoyable and choiceworthy condition was not contemplation, especially contemplation of the human condition, but his forgetfulness of that condition in an atemporal "reverie." The latter condition, in which Rousseau was aware of his existence but not his "troubles," brought him close, at least, to the pre-historical or pre-human instinctual or natural experience of contentment or the goodness of existence. Given that self-consciousness makes

---

34. Rousseau presents this history in his *Discourse on Inequality*. It is this very theoretical Rousseau who is presented here, not the Rousseau of, say, *The Social Contract*. Jardin says that this Rousseau influenced the second volume of *Democracy*, but not the first (*op. cit.*, 244). I would say that his influence becomes much greater and more fundamental in the second volume, as does the influence of the very theoretical Pascal. The second volume is a much more profound book than the first.
35. Cf. Pascal, *Pensées*, fragments 83, 100, 139, 151. See Rousseau, *Discourse on Inequality*, note i.

one miserable and anxious, even the philosopher becomes a "dreamer" who prefers "pleasurable fancies" or "fictions" to the truth.[36] The project of history in Rousseau's light is to bring history or self-consciousness to an end, because history is nothing but a misery-producing error.[37]

Tocqueville views Rousseau's history as presupposing the authenticity of Pascal's experience of being a self-conscious mortal. As the human being becomes more human or historical, he comes to know and experience more of what was always true about the contingency of his particular existence. From Tocqueville's perspective, Rousseau appears as fundamentally a derivative thinker. Pascal had already known everything fundamental that he knew.[38]

History and Misery

The historical observation that human progress increases self-consciousness and discontent and hence leads to revolution or some other form of misanthropic self-destructiveness is accounted for most completely by Tocqueville in at least three ways. The first is his analysis of the emergence of the misery of the European industrial worker in his very theoretical "Memoir on Pauperism," which is instructively supplemented by parts of the *Souvenirs*.[39] The second is his chapter in the second volume of *Democracy* on the restlessness of Americans in the midst of prosperity. Finally, there is his history of Western thought which informs all of this work at least from the beginning of the second volume. This intellectual history begins with the proud, sublime illusions of the Socratics and ends with Pascal's self-destructive ef-

---

36. Rousseau, *Reveries of a Solitary Walker*, fifth walk.
37. Rousseau, *Reveries* considered in light of the *Discourse on Inequality*. Marx's debt to Rousseau is clear here, as is the source of the often-noted similarities in Marx's and Tocqueville's historical analysis. Tocqueville, of course, sees with Rousseau, but against Marx and other optimistic socialists, that the end of history would be the end of humanity.
38. If Tocqueville is right about this, then Allan Bloom's account of the philosophical tradition as, most radically, a whole from Socrates to at least Rousseau must be substantially revised. See my "Bloom's Idiosyncratic History of the University," *Teaching Political Science*, 16 (1989), 174-179.
39. Alexis de Tocqueville, "Memoir on Pauperism," *Tocqueville and Beaumont on Social Reform*, Seymour Drescher ed. (New York: Harper and Row, 1968). For the relationship between the "Memoir" and the *Souvenirs* see my "Tocqueville and Revolution in his *Souvenirs*," paper presented to the 1989 meeting of the American Political Science Association.

fort to think radically without pride.[40] In each case the cause of human destruction is the misery caused by an excessively heightened self-consciousness, too much awareness of the truth, and not enough dependence on instinct and diversion or illusion or prideful belief. Human liberty comes to be experienced as unendurable.

I will limit myself here to discussing enough of the "Memoir on Pauperism" to reveal some of the principles of Tocqueville's theoretical analysis and to show its obvious structural similarity to the chapter in *Democracy*. I will then explain how the Americans' perverse or paradoxical condition illuminates, for Tocqueville, the problem of human liberty.

Tocqueville begins the "Memoir" with the observation that in medieval times everyone was relatively content because no one, by modern standards, had comfort. The people, in particular, "enjoyed a kind of vegetative happiness." They were "limited in their desires as well as their powers, without anxiety about a present or future that was not theirs to choose."[41] Their contentment was possible because of their lack of self-consciousness or reflection about their condition. They thought very little about time. They did not have what we regard as comfort because their desires had not been expanded much by mixture with self-consciousness. Only from our civilized perspective does their poverty seem unfortunate, and even we can recognize, with some prideful condescension, their good fortune in lacking anxiety.

But "each century," Tocqueville goes on, "extends the range of thought" and "increases the desires and powers of man."[42] Human beings, as they progress, become more powerful and knowledgeable, more anxious and dissatisfied, and, on the whole, more miserable. They labor to conquer nature or chance, to reduce their contingency by increasing their control. In so doing, they distance themselves from nature or instinct or unself-conscious contentment. They also, in truth, make themselves more subject to fortune or chance.

Tocqueville says that "civilized man is... infinitely more exposed to the vicissitudes of nature than savage man." Because "he has expanded the range of his needs," he "leaves himself open to the hazards of fortune."[43] Natural existence is governed by impersonal necessity. Human or historical existence is accidental, that which is not governed by instinct or impersonal

---

40. On this intellectual history, see my "Was Tocqueville a Philosopher?" For an earlier formulation, which appreciates insufficiently Tocqueville's debt to Pascal, see my "Democracy and Pantheism," *Interpreting Tocqueville's "Democracy in America,"* Ken Masugi ed. (Savage, Md.: Rowman and Littlefield, 1991).
41. Tocqueville, "Memoir," 6.
42. *Ibid.*, 7-10.
43. *Ibid.*, 10.

necessity. Human beings labor to overcome the contingency of their existences which they, inexplicably, come to experience through their self-consciousness. By so doing, they heighten their self-consciousnesses or make
themselves feel more contingent. They expand their needs by mixing brutish
desire with anxious self-consciousness.[44] They actually make their existence
more subject to chance. Human beings, the paradox goes, make themselves
more miserable in response to their misery.

The Restless Americans

For Tocqueville, the most instructive example of this paradox is the
American one. It shows that human misery has little to do with poverty or
political oppression. That Americans "are so often restless in the midst of
prosperity" shows that human misery increases with enlightenment—or the
replacement of instinct by selfish calculation—and the resulting improvement in material and political conditions.

In the chapters immediately preceding the one describing this restlessness
Tocqueville says that the American theory is "that in order to gain happiness
in this world a man resists all his instinctive impulses and deliberately calcu-
lates every action of life." On its basis "he habitually sacrifices the pleasures
of the moment for the lasting interests of his life."[45] This "enlightened self-
love" or "self-interest properly understood" exists at a great distance from
and opposes extremely the "blind instinct" of egoism.[46]

It seems at first glance that Tocqueville understands self-interest rightly
understood to be a correction to both "egoism" and "individualism," two
more primitive or less self-conscious forms of human selfishness. But a
closer examination of the progression in the text shows enlightened self-interest actually to be more in error than its predecessors. Tocqueville begins
by saying that egoism is given by nature. It is, in other words, not an historical acquisition. It is not part of the accident or error that is human distinctiveness. Tocqueville calls individualism, a somewhat calculated form of
selfish withdrawal, a "misguided judgement" or error. Individualism appears
at some point in history.

Tocqueville then makes it clear that enlightened self-interest appears at a
late stage of history, among a very self-conscious people. It is a more comprehensive and calculating kind of error, an extreme form of the one that fu-

---

44. Cf. the "Memoir" with *DA* [M-L], 546-547.
45. *Ibid.*, 529.
46. *Ibid.*, 528-529. Cf. 506-507.

els human or historical development. Its fundamental assumption is that happiness is simply the product of the negation of instinct and the extreme resistance to "pleasures of the moment." It also holds that it is in the self-interest properly understood of human beings to adhere to a comprehensive belief that is "not at all... sublime," that, in other words, dispenses with pride altogether.[47]

The American inability to acknowledge dependence on instinct or even belief for happiness results in misery. What Tocqueville calls "self-interest properly understood," it turns out, is not that at all. The pride Americans take in their comprehensive devotion to calculation is a diversion from the miserable awareness of their mortality, which is perversely heightened by calculation. Americans extend the spirit of calculation even to their acquisition of "eternal felicity" in an effort to bring even that under their control. They are, however, sometimes aware of the futility and even absurdity of that effort. Hence Americans are at times vulnerable, Tocqueville says, to religious enthusiasm or "madness," to what can occur when human beings become intensely aware that they have no control over their fate.[48]

Paradoxically, Americans assert that they can control everything, but sometimes they feel they can control nothing at all. Their self-consciousness drives them to self-destructive excesses. They do not know a humanly appropriate mixture or moderation.[49] Tocqueville's description of the extreme restlessness of Americans comes as no surprise to readers of the preceding chapters.

Tocqueville begins his description the way he begins the "Memoir," not with restlessness, but with rest or contentment. He begins, by way of contrast, with a much earlier point in the development of history or humanity. He describes the inhabitants of "certain remote corners of the Old World... which have stayed still while all around them moved." These people "are mostly very ignorant and very poor," and "often oppress[ed]." History, through some accident, has passed them by. They are, obviously, still feudal people. They do not share in the modern world's liberty, prosperity, and enlightenment. They are, as a result, content or even happy. "They do not," Tocqueville observes, "give a moment's thought to the ills they endure."[50] They do not reflect on the limitations of their condition.

---

47. *Ibid.*, 507. Cf. 526.
48. *Ibid.*, 530.
49. *Ibid.*, 534-535. Cf. Delba Winthrop, "Tocqueville's American Woman and the True Conception of Democratic Progress," *Political Theory*, 14 (1986), 249.
50. *DA* [M-L], 535-536.

Tocqueville moves from the restful circumstances of these thoughtless people to that which causes the Americans to be extremely restless or discontent. As a result of their labor to bring everything under their calculation or control, Americans are "the freest and best educated of men in the circumstances the happiest to be found in the world." Despite or because of these circumstances, however, these "lucky men" seem, in contrast to their Old World ancestors, "serious, almost sad." Despite their comprehensive affirmation of calculation, their activity seems anything but calm and methodical. They pursue and acquire material enjoyments with a "feverish ardor," but these material enjoyments do not make them happy. The most powerful effect of Americans' enjoyment is to call attention to others they have not had. They reflect on the limits of their condition and act with the resulting dissatisfaction in mind. Tocqueville observes that "in democratic times... *minds* are more anxious and on edge."[51] The most remarkable characteristic of the Americans, for Tocqueville, is that their experiences show that what he regarded as extraordinary mental restlessness had become common.

The Americans' feverish pursuit of enjoyment or happiness is meant to divert them from the misery they experience at rest or leisure. Tocqueville himself knows by experience that "calm and easy circumstances" can give one "a disgust for life." He observes that, when presented with a vacation, the Americans will "travel five hundred miles in a few days as a distraction from his happiness."[52] Americans are constantly on the move even when there seems to be no material need. Despite their acquisition of prosperity they perceive their environment as hostile and they continue to struggle against it.[53] Tocqueville's chapter readily calls to mind Pascal's conclusion that "men who naturally understand their own condition avoid nothing so much as rest."[54]

Tocqueville's Americans feel with extraordinary intensity the constraints of their existence, including "the shortness of life." They "cleave to the good things of the world" in a futile search for assurance against death. But Americans cannot escape enough from their consciousness of time ever truly to enjoy life. To divert themselves from the knowledge that they cannot be happy, they pursue happiness. It is "remembrance of the shortness of life,"

---

51. *Ibid.*, 536-538, emphasis added.
52. *Ibid.*, 536, 538.
53. See *Ibid.*, 532 on "hostile fate" and Pascal, *Pensées*, fragment 139: "Thus passes away all man's life. Men seek rest in a struggle against difficulties; and when they have conquered these, they become insufferable."
54. Pascal, *Pensées*, fragment 139.

Tocqueville says, that "constantly goads them on."[55] Through the pursuit of material enjoyment, Americans distract themselves from their souls' insatiable longings for certainty and stability. They are miserable because their diversions do not work particularly well. Tocqueville says "whatever pains are taken to distract it [the soul] from itself, it soon grows bored, restless, and anxious amid the pleasures of the senses."[56]

Americans, by instinct or nature, seek happiness but they cannot find it through selfish calculation. Their human liberty is manifest in the distinctively human misery of this paradoxical situation. They are, despite their seemingly petty materialism, not simply beasts, but beasts with angels in them. From the human perspective described by Pascal, the Americans' refusal or inability to be simply decent and contented materialists is a sign of their greatness.[57] They are to some extent proud of their misery and not wholly without reason.

Most decisively, however, pity or compassion is becoming more fundamental than pride for them. They are miserable because they perceive their existence as unfortunate. They think of themselves and their fellow enlightened democrats, despite or because of their fortunate material circumstances, as particularly deserving of compassion. Compassion overwhelms pride as Americans perceive themselves, with growing clarity, as victims of a historical process beyond their control.[58]

The American Faith

The Americans are unfortunate because they live at such a late stage of historical progress. Less historical beings, Tocqueville observes, have less miserable and accidental existences. But all human beings seem to be unable to live completely without faith. The Americans believe that history, which has produced their misery, will also somehow liberate them from it. Unlike the industrial workers of France whom Tocqueville describes in the *Souvenirs*[59], Americans do not hope for revolution because they are still able to take some pride in the perception that their misery is based on their choice.

Americans have faith in egalitarian progress. They are progressives, not revolutionaries. They hope that the process of destruction of prideful distinc-

---

55. *DA* [M-L], 536-537.
56. *Ibid.*, 535.
57. *Ibid.*, 534.
58. *Ibid.*, 564-565, and 493-496.
59. On the industrial workers, see my "Tocqueville and Revolution."

tions, which has brought them so much prosperity and so much misery, will eventually locate a resting place in which they can find satisfaction. Thus far, equality has mainly liberated desire while making one increasingly aware of one's limitations. The gulf between desires and the means to satisfy them widens.[60] But, perhaps with the achievement of "complete equality," a point will be reached where all are satisfied equally and without anxiety.

On this point instinct or natural inclination seems to make Americans unreasonable. Their faith in history or egalitarian progress is an opiate, dulling the misery of their self-consciousness. They cannot help but believe sometimes that there must be some connection between historical progress and happiness, that history and the human condition are not simply perverse or paradoxical. The achievement of comprehensive equality will eradicate the contradictions that make them miserable.

Americans, Tocqueville shows, tend to identify the pursuit of "complete felicity" with the pursuit of "complete equality." But they achieve neither. Tocqueville writes of the American's "futile pursuit of... complete felicity which always escapes him."[61] In just the same way wholly satisfactory equality "is always slipping through people's fingers, the more when they think to grasp it, fleeing, as Pascal says, in eternal flight."[62] Perhaps this rare explicit reference to Pascal is meant to underscore that it is the pursuit rather than the achievement that genuinely attracts Americans.

But Tocqueville also says that Americans become increasingly anxious about equality. They seem to do so because they come to suspect, in their growing self-consciousnesses, that it cannot do what they hope it will do. The pursuit of equality seems to become less effective, over time, as a diversion. The egalitarians, to remain diverted, become more fanatical.

Egalitarian idealism seems unreasonable as a project for human beings. They would be miserable, bored beyond belief or without escape from the pain of self-contemplation, in a society characterized by what Tocqueville calls "absolute dead level" equality. The coming of such a society, he says, would be yet another "misfortune."[63] The paradox here is that the coming of the society to which egalitarian idealism points, a response to or a diversion from the unfortunate misery of extreme human self-consciousness, might be the greatest of misfortunes for self-conscious mortals. This society other the-

---

60. *DA* [M-L], 537.
61. *Ibid.*, 536.
62. *Ibid.*, 198. Almost the same words are repeated on 538, without the mention of Pascal's name. See Pascal, *Pensées*, fragments 135, 139.
63. *DA* [M-L], 538.

orists call the end of history.[64] To live in such a place, one without even the possibility for revolution or greatness, Tocqueville certainly regarded as the greatest misfortune for himself. "Men," he concludes, "will never establish an equality which will content them."[65]

He also suggests, however, that the hidden but real goal of egalitarian idealism is the destruction of self-consciousness or humanity itself. Contentment will exist in the absence of men. Such a destruction, by definition, would bring history unproblematically to an end.[66] Tocqueville seems uncertain on the reasonableness or possibility of this goal. Sometimes he contends that such a destruction is impossible. But for the most part it seems to be his primary fear. His most precise thought seems to be that the misery of self-consciousness is an indispensable component of human nature or the human condition, but there is no guarantee that the existence of human beings will last forever.

Tocqueville says in the *Souvenirs* that he cannot be certain that socialist revolution will always fail in eradicating property or individuality, but he views that possibility as most unlikely. Revolution will probably not achieve its misanthropic intention.[67] In *Democracy*, he foresees as rather likely the possibility that Americans might surrender their intense consciousness of time and their anxious concern for the future. They might well lapse into a sort of apathetic imbecility, "into a complete and brutish indifference about the future."[68] They would, in other words, move toward the contentment of feudal people and beyond. In a letter expressing what his biographer calls "the idea which is the key to" *Democracy*, Tocqueville writes that the most dangerous tendency of democracy is "a steady lowering of the intellectual level of society with no conceivable limit."[69] Excessive self-consciousness destroys self-consciousness. Extreme restlessness produces extreme passivity. The extreme attempt to negate instinct and illusion through calculation culminates in a decisive victory for instinct.

64. The idea of the end of history calls to mind Hegel, Marx, and Alexandre Kojève. See the instantly famous essay of Francis Fukuyama, "The End of History?," *The National Interest*, 16 (Summer 1989), 3-18 for the most recent expression of Kojève's version of the Hegelian argument that history has come to an end.
65. *DA* [M-L], 537, 640-645. Cf. Jardin, *Alexis de Tocqueville*, 373, 451.
66. Tocqueville, for example, says that "pantheism" is the philosophical system "most fitted to seduce the mind in democratic ages," because "it destroys human individuality." His conclusion is that "all those who still appreciate the true nature of man's greatness should combine in the struggle against it" (*DA* [M-L], 452). See, generally, my "Democracy and Pantheism."
67. *Recollections*, 76.
68. *DA* [M-L], 548, 690-695, 735-736, note BB.
69. Jardin, *Alexis de Tocqueville*, 273. This quote is from the draft of a letter that may never have been sent.

The American Problem

In another paradoxical way perhaps the deepest problem with the Americans is that their response to self-consciousness or the truth about their condition is unreasonable. Tocqueville says that their reason gives way before their will.[70] Their restlessness, of course, is willful opposition to the truth that they cannot fundamentally transform their condition. Their comprehensive doctrine of calculation is a willful diversion from that which they cannot bring under their rational control. It is also unreasonable to resist happiness or contentment, to be self-conscious simply because it is unreasonable to be needlessly miserable. Most fundamentally, it is unreasonable to be a partisan of an accidental exception to impersonal necessity, the reasonable laws that govern nature. Human will opposes reason's desire for consistency or uniformity. The negation of instinct through willful calculation is bound to produce unreasonable behavior.[71]

Why should the unfortunate accident not will self-destruction in the name of reason and contentment? Americans know they cannot answer this question well. Human beings, Tocqueville believes, cannot answer it without pride, and the Americans do not believe enough or do enough justice to their souls' longings to answer it with enough pride.

The Moderation of Misery

The extreme form of the error of the American Tocqueville calls "individualism," which is an expression of the apolitical liberalism of the state of nature doctrine of Thomas Hobbes and John Locke.[72] That liberty is too extreme or unmixed to be human. Human liberty, in truth, cannot come into existence or sustain itself apart from the political and other communities of prideful belief. The liberty affirmed by the liberal philosophers is liberty

70. *DA* [M-L], 538.
71. *Ibid.*, 544, 548.
72. This insight informs much of analysis in Manent, *Tocqueville*. See also Lamberti, *Tocqueville and the Two "Democracies"*, especially 169-190. Lamberti distinguishes well between Rousseau and Tocqueville: "Rousseau... sacrificed the individual to the citizen. Better than anyone else, Tocqueville posed the central problem of modern philosophy: how to respect the individual while preserving the citizen" (188). To perpetuate human liberty or greatness means to perpetuate tensions and paradoxes, even with misery and anxiety.

for the apolitical, unendurable experience of miserable anxiety described by Pascal, one that is experienced with growing intensity as the liberal project to achieve unprecedented liberty and prosperity succeeds. On this point Tocqueville affirms Rousseau's criticism of liberalism. But Tocqueville rejects Rousseau's radically democratic correction to the error of apolitical liberalism. Rousseau's state of nature doctrine, which shows the goodness of unself-consciousness contentment, points to the destruction of human distinctiveness, the last distinction to be destroyed by the democratic or doubt-filled movement in thought. The two state of nature doctrines represent, for Tocqueville, the two apolitical extremes.

Tocqueville believed he had Pascal's experience of miserable isolation and still was able to affirm his human liberty. It is with his own experience that he rejects the misanthropic extremism of Rousseau and Pascal. Tocqueville thought himself fortunate to be so extraordinarily proud.[73] Even his pride needed some support from belief. Americans must be led from some of their experience of lonely isolation with more prideful involvement in politics to remain free, and with the perpetuation of their endangered (by doubt) religious or metaphysical belief. They must also be led to recognize that, even in their extreme self-consciousness, they are more dependent upon instinct and prideful belief than they admit.[74] They should be led to follow Tocqueville's own example, and, when in doubt, choose the more prideful alternative. Tocqueville, the political actor, diverted himself from the apolitical anxious misery of Pascal. His diversion, however, was not completely successful, and he was even proud of his misery.

Tocqueville wanted a similar sort of mixture for the Americans and other extremely self-conscious modern people. He did not want the Americans to be either simply citizens or Christians. He did not follow the Rousseau of *The Social Contract* in reducing religion to simply civil religion, which cannot do justice to the anxious longings in the soul of the self-conscious mortal. The modern attempt to reduce the self-conscious individual to the citizen, found in Rousseau and certain forms of socialism, is also misanthropic in its extreme hostility to individuality or self-consciousness.[75] But Tocqueville also criticized the apolitical tendency of Christian theology, which culminates in Pascal's description of the miserable loneliness of the

73. See my "Tocqueville on Metaphysics and Human Excellence," *Teaching Political Science*, 14 (1987), 87-88.
74. *DA* [M-L], 526.
75. Consider that there is no way Koritansky's analysis, which does tend to reduce Tocqueville's political teaching to that of *The Social Contract*, and hence his teaching on religion to civil religion, can do justice to Tocqueville's analysis of religion with reference to the individual (*DA* [M-L], 542-545).

human being in the absence of a personal God.[76] The moderation appropriate to the beast with an angel in him includes a mixture of citizenship and Christianity.

Tocqueville's goal was to promote the movement from the extremism of extreme self-consciousness, through the leadership of extraordinarily proud statesmen, to a more humanly appropriate mixture of extremes, to human liberty. Tocqueville remained, to the end, uncertain concerning the prospects of this movement. He rejected decisively the fatalistic determinism of radicals and reactionaries while seeing that the movement of history, immoderated by statesmanship, might reveal the truth of such theory. It is part of his human liberty, which included doubtful anxiety, that he was sometimes quite confident, but at other times quite doubtful concerning the possibility of his success. The matter, of course, is still in doubt.

76. See Jardin, *Tocqueville*, 61-64, on the misery Tocqueville felt when he, as an adolescent, ceased to believe in the personal God, a misery which he felt, to some extent, his whole life. Jardin sees clearly that Tocqueville understood himself to have entered political life as a passionate diversion from this misery.

[2]

The Role of Religion in Preserving American Liberty — Tocqueville's Analysis 150 Years Later

Catherine H. Zuckert

More than 150 years ago, Alexis de Tocqueville came to America to study the future of the world. The conditions in which human beings lived were everywhere becoming more and more equal, he observed; but egalitarian conditions did not always or necessarily give rise to political liberty. On the contrary, as people became more equal, individuals became less able to act on their own behalf and were, therefore, more vulnerable to oppression by others. Perceiving the danger, Tocqueville travelled to the United States to discover how a nation could preserve the liberty of its inhabitants under egalitarian conditions. Americans had been able to maintain their freedom, he concluded, as a result of the interaction of three related factors: the "peculiar and accidental situation in which Providence ha[d] placed the Americans," their laws or political institutions, and their "habits and mores."[1] Of the three, habits and mores were most important; and the specific habits and mores that worked to preserve American independence were, moreover, primarily religious.

A century and a half later we cannot but wonder whether Tocqueville's analysis continues to hold. To decide whether his analysis was, much less continues to be, tenable, it is obviously necessary, first, to determine exactly what he claimed the role of religion was in preserving liberty in America. In the second part I will then investigate the extent to which the increased ethnic, racial and cultural diversity of the American population, the

1.   *DA* [M-L], 277.

"revolution" in sexual mores that followed the widespread availability and use of birth control, and the changes in American law have affected that place.

Religion in America Circa 1840

Tocqueville's argument about the role of religion in maintaining liberal democracy in the United States has itself been the subject of a good deal of scholarly controversy. There have, indeed, been three major sources or kinds of criticism. First, some critics have pointed out that Tocqueville's description of democracy in the United States was, at best, partial.[2] Tocqueville himself admitted as much. He came to the United States to discover what it could teach his compatriots. He did not set out to show Americans how their nation worked or how to preserve it. He did not include a consideration of race in his general analysis of democracy in America in the first volume, but segregated it in the last chapter, because that problem was not particularly relevant to France.

Second, some commentators have argued that Tocqueville's emphasis on the social utility of religion undermined the very beliefs he argued were salutary by suggesting that they were more beneficial than true[3]. Such objections ignore Tocqueville's emphasis on the natural roots of religion, I believe, as well as his insistence that the range and effect of religious beliefs in democratic times cannot extend far beyond their natural foundation.

Finally, however, Tocqueville himself was responsible for some of the confusion and consequent criticism of his analysis of the role of religion in preserving liberty under egalitarian conditions. In the five years between the publication of the two volumes of his masterpiece, he changed his mind about the applicability of the American example to French circumstances— particularly with regard to religion. As a result, the advice he gave European legislators concerning the necessary beliefs and the means of preserving them in the second volume differed from that he had offered in the first volume.

2.   Sean Wilentz, "On Tocqueville and Jacksonian America," in Abraham S. Eisenstadt ed., *Reconsidering Tocqueville's "Democracy in America"* (New Brunswick, N.J.: Rutgers University Press, 1988), 209-210.
3.   Jack Lively, *The Social and Political Thought of Alexis de Tocqueville* (Oxford: Oxford University Press, 1962), 96-97; Marvin Zetterbaum, *Tocqueville and the Problem of Democracy* (Stanford, Cal.: Stanford University Press, 1967), 120-124, 147. For a fuller response, see Catherine H. Zuckert, "Not by Preaching: Tocqueville on the Role of Religion," *Review of Politics*, 43 (1981), 259-280.

Tocqueville's Analysis in the First Volume

In the first volume Tocqueville suggested that religion had a pre-eminent role in maintaining a democratic republic in the United States. That role was, however, not merely primarily, but necessarily indirect.

In a chapter entitled, "Religion Considered as a Political Institution and How it Powerfully Contributes to the Maintenance of a Democratic Republic Among the Americans," he took note of what has since come to be called "American Civil Religion."[4] In contrast to France at his time, he observed, no religious group publicly and directly opposed the liberal egalitarian political principles of the regime, not even the Catholic church. On the contrary, in America priests as well as Protestant ministers explicitly and frequently prayed to God not merely to support democracy at home but to spread its principles and institutions abroad.

Nevertheless, Tocqueville insisted, the "indirect influence of religious beliefs upon political society in the United States" was much greater than the direct effects of such explicit preaching. It was, indeed, "just when it is not speaking of freedom at all that [religion] best teaches the Americans the art of being free."[5]

As many political theorists have pointed out, the preservation of independence or free government has a moral prerequisite. People who are not able to control themselves will inevitably find themselves controlled by others. No one can be independent or self-governed who is not self-controlled. The kind of self-control or restraint Tocqueville thought religion has fostered in America was, however, severely limited. In both volumes he insisted that no set of beliefs could check or oppose the materialistic desires of human beings living under democratic conditions. At most, he suggested, religious beliefs could be combined with extremely worldly, economic concerns to produce two politically desirable results.

First, religion contributed powerfully to the development of the stringent, if not literally "Puritanic" views of individual morality, especially with regard to sexual relations, characteristic of nineteenth-century America.

> In the United States... religion is often powerless to restrain men in the midst of innumerable temptations which fortune offers. It cannot moderate their eagerness

---

4. Cf. Robert Bellah, *The Broken Covenant: American Civil Religion* (New York: Seabury Press, 1975), and Russell E. Richey and Donald G. Jones eds., *American Civil Religion* (New York: Harper and Row, 1974).
5. *DA* [M-L], 290.

to enrich themselves... but it reigns supreme in the souls of the women, and it is women who shape mores. Certainly of all countries in the world America is the one in which the marriage tie is most respected and where the highest and truest conception of conjugal happiness has been conceived.[6]

Their religious beliefs did not make Americans more generous and high-minded, less calculating and self-seeking in their public affairs than they might otherwise have been. On the contrary, the respect for the marriage tie inculcated by religion fostered the tendency Americans had on economic grounds as well to attend more to their own private affairs than to public concerns. Europeans sought to divert, if not to satisfy their strongest passions through political action, Tocqueville suggested, because they were unhappy at home. Able to satisfy their desires simply and naturally at home, Americans were much less attracted by the excitement of public life; "and as the regularity of life brings [them] happiness, [they] easily form the habit of regulating [their] opinions as well as [their] tastes."[7]

The second beneficial indirect effect nineteenth-century American religious beliefs had on their political "mores," according to Tocqueville, was, indeed, to restrain not only their engagement in, but also their expectations with regard to the possible results of, political action.

Nature and circumstances have made the inhabitant of the United States a bold man, as is sufficiently attested by the enterprising spirit with which he seeks his fortune. If the spirit of the Americans were free of all impediment, one would soon find among them the boldest innovators and the most implacable logicians in the world. But American revolutionaries are obliged ostensibly to profess a certain respect for Christian morality and equity, and that does not allow them easily to break the laws when those are opposed to the executions of their designs; nor would they find it easy to surmount the scruples of their partisans even if they were able to get over their own. *Up to now no one in the United States has dared to profess the maxim that everything is allowed in the interests of society.*[8]

Like their respect for marriage vows, Tocqueville indicated, American resistance to revolutionary political ideas and innovations was not simply or strictly religious in origin.

Their practical experience, in both political and economic endeavors, also made Americans much more skeptical about the basis and validity of abstract theories and generalizations than less experienced Frenchmen.

The combined effect on American political "mores" was, nevertheless, of decisive importance. Having read the Constitution, Tocqueville recognized that in the United States a sufficiently large majority could legally do what-

6.   *Ibid.,* 291.
7.   *Idem.*
8.   *DA* [M-L], 292. My emphasis.

ever it wanted. The much vaunted protections of freedom of speech, religion and assembly in the First Amendment could themselves be destroyed by amendment. "Thus," he concluded, "while the law allows the American people to do everything, there are things which religion prevents them from imagining and forbids them to dare."

Individual liberty can be preserved only where government is limited; and government would remain limited under egalitarian conditions only so long as the vast majority of the people thought that it should. Insofar as their religion convinced Americans that human aspirations and achievements not only were but should always be limited, religion constituted the fundamental support or foundation for the preservation of constitutional democracy. "Religion, which never intervenes directly in the government of American society, should therefore be considered as the first of their political institutions."[9]

Tocqueville devoted the remainder of his discussion of the role of religion in preserving free government in the first volume to convincing his French readers that religion retained the influence it did in American politics, ironically enough, precisely because it kept itself and its practitioners strictly separate from the state. Eighteenth-century French rationalists had predicted that religious zeal would disappear with the spread of enlightenment and freedom; America was living disproof of their claims. Religion was alive and well in America, because religion had a natural source, and American democratic political institutions were more firmly based on nature than the aristocratic European arrangements that had preceded them.[10]

Acting purely on the basis of their natural inclinations, human beings would both imagine and desire an afterlife.

> The short space of sixty years can never shut in the whole of man's imagination; the incomplete joys of this world will never satisfy his heart. Alone among all created beings, man shows a natural disgust for existence and an immense longing to exist.... These different instincts constantly drive his soul toward contemplation of the next world.... Religion, therefore, is only one particular form of hope, and it is as natural to the human heart as hope itself.

9. *Idem.*
10. Tocqueville concluded the first volume of *Democracy in America* by observing: "An aristocratic body is composed of a certain number of citizens who, without being elevated very far above the mass of the citizens, are nevertheless permanently stationed above them.... *One can conceive of nothing more contrary to nature and to the secret instincts of the human heart than subjection of this sort.... An aristocracy cannot last unless it is founded on an accepted principle of inequality,* legalized in advance and introduce into the family as well as into the rest of society—*all things violently repugnant to natural equity* that only constraint will make men submit to them." *DA* [M-L], 399. My emphasis.

People could, indeed, "detach themselves from religious beliefs" only "by a sort of intellectual aberration, and in a way, by doing moral violence to their own nature."[11]

If religions founded their influence solely on the longing for immortality native to all human beings, there would be no way to deny or stifle the appeal. When religions sought to increase their influence by exercising temporal power, however, they brought the purity of their concern for the afterlife into question and aroused opposition on grounds of political interest as opposed to questions of faith. The price to be paid for linking church and state might not have been evident when monarchies appeared to be permanent. As human beings became more equal, however, governments would change more frequently and ecclesiastical officials who identified their own concerns too closely with temporal authorities would undermine the credibility of their claims to be concerned primarily, if not solely with the eternal. By allying themselves with a particular political party, churchmen would also provoke hostility on purely secular grounds.

If Europeans followed the American example and established a strict separation of church and state, he urged, they could preserve the natural seeds and manifestations of religious sentiments among their populace as well and enjoy the beneficent political effects.

The Change in the Second Volume

By the time he wrote the second volume, however, Tocqueville no longer believed it would be possible to preserve Christian beliefs in Europe the way they had been maintained in America.

The intellectual habits of people living under equal conditions did not favor religion, he observed. People who thought they were equal to all others did not easily accede to authority. They believed that they ought to be able to decide matters on the basis of their own experience. Finding that they were able to solve the minor problems that arose in daily life, they tended to conclude that everything in the world was explicable. As a result they acquired "an almost invincible distaste for the supernatural."[12] It would, therefore, be virtually impossible to establish a new religion in democratic times; it would, indeed, be difficult to preserve inherited beliefs.

Religion had persisted in the United States despite rather than because of the egalitarian conditions that prevailed there as a result of two historical cir-

---

11. *DA* [M-L], 296-297.
12. *Ibid.*, 430.

cumstances peculiar to that nation. First, because the colonies had originally been established in America to secure religious liberty, religion had become associated in the minds of Americans with the founding of their nation and so had become part of their patriotic sentiments. Second, the Christian beliefs the immigrants brought with them to the New World had survived unchallenged, because America had not experienced a democratic revolution.

"Every revolution must shake ancient beliefs, sap authority, and cloud shared ideas."[13] In a nation like France where equality had been established only after a prolonged and violent struggle among the classes, religious faith could not, therefore, be preserved the way it had been in America merely through separation of church and state. Because of the past association of the church with an aristocratic order, partisans of democracy were apt to be hostile to Christianity, unless they could be convinced that its preservation would serve their own secular ends. The Christian religion would also have to take a distinctly democratic form.

In the second volume Tocqueville concentrated, therefore, on persuading his democratic countrymen of the utility of preserving a few simple, nevertheless fundamental religious tenets. First, he pointed out, no individual or people could actually live solely on the basis of critically examined empirically "verified" truths. In order to get through an ordinary day people had to take a host of propositions on faith. If they tried to act only on the basis of what they knew without a doubt, they would be paralyzed. This was particularly true in the case of the most fundamental, but also most perplexing questions concerning the existence of God, immortality of the soul, and obligations human beings owed others. If the greatest human intellects had addressed these questions for centuries without coming to satisfactory answers, much less agreeing on them, ordinary people certainly could not. To prevent the industry of the nation from being stymied, it was thus highly desirable to have a widespread, though non-enforced consensus on the answers to these fundamental questions.

A consensus on fundamental principles or basic articles of faith is necessary to maintain any society, Tocqueville observed. But widespread religious beliefs have special advantages in democracies as well. They counter the two tendencies of people living under equal conditions which most threaten to destroy their liberty—their tendency to become isolated from others and to think only of themselves, and their tendency to become inordinately fond of material pleasure.

13.   *DA* [M-L], 432.

Precisely because religion generally works counter to the strongest tendencies of people living in democratic times, however, religion itself would be destroyed, if it remained simply in opposition. Religious faith might have a natural source in the human desire for immortality, but that desire was not strong enough to counter the more immediate attraction of physical pleasure or material gain. The only way religion could be preserved and exercise a salutary effect on morals—both individual and social—in democratic times was to combine it, as in America, with economic calculation in public opinion.

Although past religious beliefs had, like all others, been thrown into question by the revolution, it would be possible to foster a consensus on a few religious principles. Democratic circumstances are not antagonistic to all tenets of faith. On the contrary, people "who are alike and on the same level in this world easily conceive the idea of a single God who imposes the same laws on each man and grants him future happiness at the same price."[14] They also feel the desire for immortality from which religious sentiments naturally develop. Although people who think they are the equal of all others believe that they ought to be able to decide all questions for themselves on the basis of their own experience, they find, particularly in the case of the most fundamental questions, that they cannot. Unwilling to admit the superior insight or knowledge of a few, democratic peoples reason that if all are equal, the greatest number must be right. Once formed, Tocqueville thus concluded, public consensus in democratic times would have more influence on individual belief than any tyrant's decree had in the past.

If religious beliefs were to be propagated and preserved by such a public consensus, however, both the doctrinaire and formal aspects antagonistic to democratic tastes would have to be minimized. It would not suffice, in other words, merely to separate church and state. The content and form of religious services had to be adapted to democratic conditions. Religious leaders would also have to work at achieving a synthesis of secular and sacred beliefs. Rather than stressing the ways in which concern for their eternal salvation stood in opposition to the material interests of their congregations, preachers needed to recognize the dominance of public opinion and explicitly align themselves with it in an emphatically nonpartisan way.

The public consensus Tocqueville urged his French readers to foster was not, moreover, largely or even fundamentally religious. On the contrary, he suggested, the only effective way to counter the isolating tendencies of the primarily materialistic drives and interests of people living under egalitarian

14.   *Ibid.*, 445.

conditions was to appeal to those materialistic drives and interests them-selves. Americans did not do justice to their own generous impulses when they attributed all their charitable deeds to "self-interest, properly under-stood." Nevertheless, he insisted, the American notion that individuals served their greater, long-run self-interest by postponing some present plea-sures and contributing some of their present gains to cooperative social en-deavors provided the most effective basis for both individual and political morality under democratic conditions. This doctrine served, indeed, pre-cisely the two functions for which Tocqueville had praised religion. Although it did not destroy the materialist desires of democratic people, "self-interest, properly understood" did make them pursue those interests honestly. It also worked to overcome the "individualism" or isolation solely economic pursuits tended to foster.

Convincing people that it was in their long-run interest to discipline their immediate desires could not only make them act in a more "socially con-scious" manner, Tocqueville argued; it could also make them more religious.

> If the doctrine of self-interest properly understood were concerned with this world only, that would not be nearly enough. For there are a great many sacrifices which can only be rewarded in the next. However hard one may try to prove that virtue is useful, it will always be difficult to make a man live well if he will not face death. One therefore wants to know whether this doctrine can easily be reconciled with religious beliefs.

The founders of virtually all religions had, in fact, used the same kind of rea-soning to convince people "that lasting happiness can not be won except at the cost of a thousand ephemeral pleasures, and finally, that one must con-tinually master oneself in order to serve oneself better."[15] The goal was simply further away. Even if people in democratic times were not entirely convinced that there was a God, an immortal soul, or an afterlife, they could be persuaded to act as if they did. If the doctrinaire and formal requirements of religion were minimized, people would not have to act much differently on grounds of faith than they would on grounds of interest. They were used to calculating the relation between short-run sacrifice and long-run advan-tage; and as Pascal had pointed out, the immediate cost of professing belief or even, perhaps, attending church services, was small compared to the pos-sible long-run gain (or loss).

If religion survived in modern egalitarian societies, Tocqueville con-cluded, it would be as a result of such self-interested calculations made gen-erally effective through the force of public opinion. The specifically

15. *Ibid.*, 528.

religious content of self-interest properly understood was minimal, but irreplaceable. To convince individuals to risk their lives for the sake of the common good, belief in God and judgment in the afterlife were extremely helpful, if not indispensable. The necessary beliefs were few, simple, and, we should note, not distinctively Christian. Indeed, when he turned to discuss the basis of individual morality per se (as opposed to the basis and performance of obligations to others), Tocqueville suggested, even belief in divine retribution or punishment was not essential. "Most religions are only general, simple and practical means of teaching men that the soul is immortal."[16] That function could have and had been performed by the ridiculous doctrine of metempsychosis as well as by Platonic philosophy. What was essential was for people to see that there was more to human life than the goods of the body, to maintain a more elevated view of the potential of human life, and hence to set themselves higher and more distant goals.[17]

Although he himself was most concerned about maintaining the spiritual qualities that distinguished human beings from animals, Tocqueville thought materialistic concerns would remain dominant under democratic conditions.[18] Rather than appeal to higher, but rarer human inclinations and desires, he thus consistently couched his analysis in terms of interest. He concluded his comments on the importance of maintaining religious beliefs in democratic times by observing that without an elevated conception of human potential and correspondingly distant goals, human industry and hence prosperity would itself eventually suffer.

"It is easy to see that it is particularly important in democratic times to make spiritual conceptions prevail, but it is far from easy to say what those who govern democratic peoples should do to make them prevail."[19] Because democratic peoples resisted authority and judged on the basis of their own experience, no attempt to prescribe a public creed was apt to succeed. "The only effective means which governments can use to make the doctrine of the immortality of the soul respected," he thus concluded, "is daily to act as if they believed it themselves."[20] What cannot be taught by precept may be fostered by example.

16. *DA* [M-L], 544.
17. This is the place or respect in which Tocqueville foreshadows Nietzsche most closely. Unlike Nietzsche, however, Tocqueville remained a democrat on grounds of natural right.
18. Because the human soul could never be completely satisfied with the material, he predicted that there would be sporadic outbreaks of extreme spiritualism, including religious revivals. He nevertheless thought that such events and groups would remain the exception and never become the rule.
19. *DA* [M-L], 545.
20. *Ibid.*, 546.

Because people in democratic times trusted their own experience much more than anything they were told, the most effective, if not the only way of shaping their opinions was to affect their experience. And the primary way of shaping the experience of people living under egalitarian conditions in a politically, indeed, a humanly salutary manner that Tocqueville recommended was to decentralize as many political processes and decisions as possible. People who became active in politics quickly learned the need to join with others in order to achieve their own goals. Having learned both the techniques and advantages of organization in politics, Americans had not only applied them to promoting their economic interests but had also used them to support a variety of opinions about moral and intellectual questions. In other words, their decentralized political institutions had provided Americans with the experience that had given rise to general belief in the doctrine of "self-interest properly understood" upon which, Tocqueville suggested, the preservation of religious sentiments also depended.

Contrary to the impression he left in his analysis of *Democracy in America* in the first volume, in the second volume Tocqueville showed that neither the individual self-restraint (or morality) nor the limitations on political experimentation (or "imagination") which preserved limited government and thereby individual freedom in the United States were primarily results of religious belief. On the contrary, he indicated, religious beliefs were and would continue to be held under democratic conditions primarily as a result of self-interested calculation. The limitations on the American "imagination" in the arts resulted from their special historical relation to England, as a result of which they did not feel a particular need to develop their own literature. American resistance to general theories advocating radical experimentation in politics resulted from the practical experience afforded by decentralized political institutions. And finally, he admitted, the severe "mores" he had observed in American women resulted more from democratic social conditions, which made it hard for a man to convince a woman he loved her if he was not willing to marry her, and economic circumstances, which generally kept married men and women separate from one another, than they did from religious beliefs, strictly speaking.

In the five years which had intervened between his writing the two volumes, Tocqueville finally explained, he had come to understand the threat to the preservation of individual liberty in democratic times somewhat differently. It was not so much that the majority would impose its will politically or intellectually on the minority, as he had originally feared. The danger was, rather, that the effects of ever more centralized political authority and economic organization would gradually erode the grounds of all individual initiative and independence. The obvious, though by no means easy, way of countering this danger was to institute and preserve as many decentralized institutions as possible.

As a result of this new understanding, Tocqueville was able, moreover, to avoid the contradiction at the root of his analysis of democracy in America in the first volume. As he first presented it, the preservation of American political liberty in the form of limited government depended upon the exercise of what he himself dubbed the "tyranny of the majority" in the realm of public opinion. Religion was his main example. By linking religious belief first, foremost, and, indeed, almost exclusively with the individual's natural desire to prolong his own existence and only secondarily and indirectly with the rule of public opinion, in the second volume Tocqueville not only minimized the always problematic public aspect of religion in democratic conditions but also associated it more closely with the freedom of thought and depth of soul he himself most wanted to preserve.

150 Years Later

Life in the United States has changed a great deal in the 150 years since Tocqueville wrote his classic study. As a result of the waves of immigration, white Anglo-Saxon Protestants no longer constitute a majority of the population. Most people now live in urban areas; both the economy and the government have become primarily national. There has, moreover, been a "revolution" in American "mores." The cohabitation of unmarried couples is now not merely tolerated, but legally protected; the divorce rate and the number of illegitimate births are very high.

Religious beliefs nevertheless appear to exercise just the kind of limited influence Tocqueville attributed to them in the second volume. According to current public opinion polls, 94% of all Americans believe in God; 73% believe in some form of life after death.[21] 65% of the American public say they belong to a church or synagogue; 40% attend services every week.[22]

The propagation of these beliefs is not a result of public inculcation or even the sort of informal social pressure Tocqueville found so tyrannous in Jacksonian America. Since World War II the Supreme Court has drawn the lines between church and state much more rigidly than they were drawn in the early nineteenth century, first, by declaring publicly required professions of faith, in the form of the pledge of allegiance to the flag or as an oath of

21. *Gallup Poll*, October 1988.
22. *Public Opinion*, October/November 1984.

office, to be unconstitutional infringements of the freedom of religion protected by the First Amendment and, second, by proscribing prayers and Bible reading in the public schools as an unconstitutional "establishment."[23] In explaining their decisions, the justices repeatedly stated that they were trying to protect dissenters from exactly the kind of informal social pressure Tocqueville had described as the "tyranny of the majority" which, he had also observed, was exercised particularly with regard to religion.

Aside from the tax relief accorded to charitable organizations in general, the major form of political support for religion would thus appear to be the power of example. The chief officials of the American national government appear to be even more religious than their constituents. Whereas 65% of the American public claimed to belong to a church or synagogue, 94% of the members of the current Congress identify themselves as members of a specific religious denomination.[24] As Robert Bellah has observed, American presidents regularly appeal to popular American beliefs in God and the immortality of the soul in their inaugural addresses; both houses of Congress as well as the United States Supreme Court also begin their sessions with a prayer. Rather than constitute a constitutionally proscribed form of "civil religion," as Bellah argues, I would suggest in light of the Court's current interpretation of the meaning of the "religion" clauses, these observances ought rather to be understood primarily as public officials acting as if they themselves believed. (These ceremonies are constitutionally permissible, because each branch of government has the right to regulate its own internal procedures.) Such public professions of faith might well be politically motivated. Religious faith would not last under democratic circumstances, Tocqueville argued, unless it became a part of a public dogma concerning "self-interest, properly understood."

Religious beliefs alone would not suffice, Tocqueville predicted, to keep people in democratic conditions honest or sexually restrained. As the repeated investigations of Congressional "ethics" in the last two decades have demonstrated, church-going is by no means a guarantee of personal or political morality, particularly with regard to pecuniary gain and sexual adventures. In the first volume of *Democracy in America* Tocqueville had argued that men of the highest character would be unwilling to submit themselves to the vulgarities of democratic electioneering. Nor did he think religious belief

---

23. *West Virginian Board of Education v. Barnette*, 319 U.S. 624; *Torasco v. Watkins*, 367 U.S. 488; *Engel v. Vitale*, 370 U.S. 421; *Abington School District v. Schempp*, 374 U.S. 203. Cushing Strout, *The New Heavens and New Earth: Political Religion in America* (New York: Harper and Row, 1974), 205-313.
24. *Congressional Guide to Current American Government* (Spring 1989), 115.

alone was strong enough to maintain strict sexual mores. On the contrary, in the second volume he pointed out that the "inexorable public opinion" that so stringently regulated the behavior of women in America had commercial as well as religious roots. The economic conditions Tocqueville pointed out that kept men and women separate most of the time in nineteenth-century America have vanished, and with them much of the public opprobrium of premarital sexual relations. Americans now sharply distinguish between the sexual behavior they find acceptable among unmarried "consenting adults" and that appropriate for married couples, especially the parents of children. Despite the high divorce rate, Americans still view both marriage and parenting as important responsibilities.[25]

Religious groups are as prominent and visible in American politics in the second half of the twentieth century as they were in the first half of the nineteenth. Contrary to the predictions of those sociologists who argued that modernization would inevitably be accompanied by secularization, Tocqueville appears to have been correct in arguing that religion and democracy were not necessarily incompatible. By bringing large numbers of previously apathetic, if not disenfranchised citizens into the American political mainstream, the church-led civil rights, "moral majority" and pro-life movements have all indubitably contributed to healthier, more democratic politics in the United States. Whether the political action promoted by late twentieth-century American religious organizations has served to spread or sustain faith is more debatable.

Direct involvement in the passing political concerns of the day compromises the churchman's claim to be concerned primarily, if not solely with the divine, Tocqueville warned. And in the wake of the civil rights movements, some critics have suggested, black churches may have "lost their souls" by becoming almost entirely political.[26] Reminded by Martin Luther King of the political relevance of Christian precepts, liberal ministers of "established" northern Protestant churches like William Sloane Coffin extended their political activity by protesting American military involvement in Vietnam. At the same time, the membership of mainline Protestant denominations declined substantially, while the numbers of people joining

25. According to *Public Opinion* (November/December 1986), 30-33, only 20% of the American public under 30 years of age in contrast to 57% of those over 57 believed that premarital sex was almost always wrong (the national average was 37%). However, 85-95% of those polled objected to adultery.
26. E. G., Joseph R. Washington, *Black Religion*, cited by Charles H. Long, "Civil Rights—Civil Religion," in Russell E. Richey and Donald G. Jones eds., *American Civil Religion*, 216, and Williams L. Banks, *The Black Church* (Chicago: Moody Bible Institute, 1972), 100.

fundamentalist or evangelical churches that stress the personal salvation of the individual and generally eschew comment on broader social issues have dramatically increased.[27] Like Billy Graham and Jerry Falwell, some ministers of these churches have also become politically prominent. But having led the "moral majority" for more than a decade, Falwell apparently came to a more Tocquevillian view of the relation between religion and politics, since he explicitly retired from public life on similar grounds.

Led by the Pope, the Catholic church has also taken a strong public stance against abortion. Like fundamentalist and evangelical ministers, however, American priests have found their congregations deeply divided over issues concerning birth control. The religious convictions of their membership have added strength to the "pro-life" movement, but it is not clear that the movement has strengthened the churches in like measure.

As Cushing Strout has pointed out, American religious organizations constitute some of the most important examples of the voluntary "moral" and "civil" associations Tocqueville thought were so important in effectively preserving freedom of speech as well as economic enterprise in the United States.[28] Like local institutions of government, churches serve as free schools in the techniques and importance of the art of organization. King's Southern Christian Leadership Conference trained the leaders of non-religious civil rights organizations like the Congress for Racial Equality (CORE) and the Student Non-violent Coordinating Committee (SNCC);[29] participation in these civil rights groups, in turn, taught future activists in the "Women's Liberation" movement the importance not only of consciousness-raising but also of organization.[30]

Many of the leaders of the opposition to the Equal Rights Amendment also acquired their practical training and organizational skills through previous community service as volunteers, especially in connection with their churches. As Tocqueville observed, in a democracy it is difficult for an individual to articulate and defend an unpopular "minority" position; people are much more willing "to take a stand" if they can get others to line up with them. But unlike the regular religious denominations that have historically

27. Cf. Kevin Phillips, *Post-Conservative America* (New York: Random House, 1982); Martin Marty, *Religion and Republic* (Boston: Beacon Press, 1987), 270-302.
28. "Nothing, in my view, more deserves attention than the intellectual and moral association in America.... In democratic countries knowledge of how to combine is the mother of all other forms of knowledge" (517). Cushing Strout, *Heavens*, 102-109; Catherine Zuckert, "Reagan and that Unnamed Frenchman," *Review of Politics*, 45 (1983), 422-432.
29. See Eric Lincoln, *Race, Religion and the Continuing American Dilemma* (New York: Hill and Wang, 1985), 95-122.
30. See Sara Evans, *Personal Politics* (New York: Knopf, 1979).

served as spawning grounds for the leadership and organization of intense, "single-issue" groups, these "causes" tend to have relatively brief organizational lives.

Despite the Supreme Court, it is still probably true, as Tocqueville observed, that "in the United States... there are some who profess Christian dogmas because they believe them and others who do so because they are afraid to look as though they did not believe them." But it is no longer true that "Christianity reigns without obstacles, by universal consent."[31] Most Americans still appear to adhere to the most general tenets of Scriptural religion. Today, however, not only literary authors and professed atheists, but Buddhists and Bahai also feel free to dissent. In the more restricted sense he presented in the second volume, however, religion in American still remains very much alive, if not well. As Bellah and his colleagues have shown, the religious beliefs and practices of contemporary Americans tend to be fundamentally self-regarding.[32] Whereas Bellah bemoans this state of affairs, Tocqueville thought such a marriage of faith and interest was necessary, if faith were to be preserved under democratic conditions. A devout Christian or Jew might well find the religious beliefs and practices of his American associates all-too-loosely or generally defined. Their faith does not prevent most Americans from seeking to acquire material goods. It may, indeed, even facilitate the process. Nor do American religious beliefs prevent them from exhibiting rather loose personal morality—in public as well as in private. To the faithful, American religion may generally appear to be all-too-secular, all-too-ineffective. But from an essentially political, Tocquevillian perspective, the saving minimum is still in place. Late twentieth-century American politics remain both liberal and moderate. Both religious and secular beliefs coalesce in the conviction that matters of individual conscience should be free from governmental control. There are still some things the vast majority of Americans do not think government should do, and these limits are still associated with widespread popular American belief in the sanctity of the individual spirit or soul.

---

31. *DA* [M-L], 292.
32. Robert N. Bellah et al., *Habits of the Heart* (New York: Harper and Row, 1985), 219-249.

THE VIRTUES OF FREEDOM

[3]

The People and the Great: Tocqueville and Machiavelli on the Art of Being Free

Joseph Alulis

One does not ordinarily associate Tocqueville with Machiavelli and this for good reason. While Tocqueville praises the founders of New England for their obedience to the law of God, Machiavelli praises those men of Florence who thought more of their city's liberty than their souls' salvation.[1] But this apparent difference should not obscure what the two clearly have in common. In each case the polity praised is a free one and both praise this polity for the same reason: a free polity is best because none is more powerful. For Tocqueville as much as for Machiavelli, it is because power is the proper object of politics that the proper task of the founder of the polity is to teach its members how to be free. Nowhere is Tocqueville closer to Machiavelli than in his famous tribute to freedom: "It cannot be repeated too often: nothing is more fertile in marvels than the art of being free, but nothing is harder than freedom's apprenticeship."[2] If these two thinkers are so much at one in so vital a matter, can the difference between them be significant?

What follows will be divided into two parts. In the first I will show that both thinkers teach the same lesson about the value of freedom and that both give the same content to the art of being free. In the second I will show that each conceives of freedom and power in a radically different way.

---

1. *DA* [M-L], 45-47. *Florentine Histories*, Laura Banfield and Harvey Mansfield, Jr. trans. (Princeton, N.J.: Princeton University Press, 1988), 114.
2. *DA* [M-L], 240.

On Being Free

A comment Tocqueville makes about one of his colleagues in French political life might be applied to himself: "all his ideas were so closely linked together that, when one came out, it was pretty well inevitable that all the
others would follow."[3] It is not surprising, then, that the single reference to
Machiavelli in *Democracy in America* leads the reader to one of
Tocqueville's central ideas, revealing a fundamental agreement between the
two thinkers.

Tocqueville writes:

> Machiavelli observes in *The Prince*: "It is much more difficult to subdue a people
> who have a prince and his barons to lead them, than a nation led by a prince with
> slaves."[4]

The reference is to the fourth chapter of *The Prince*. Here Machiavelli divides principalities into two kinds according to the mode in which they are
governed:

> either by one prince, and all the others servants who as ministers help govern the
> kingdom by his favor and appointment; or by a prince and by barons who hold
> that rank not by favor of the lord but by antiquity of blood.[5]

He proceeds to argue that while the former are harder for a conqueror to
take, the latter are harder to hold.[6]

This observation anticipates Tocqueville's argument as to the value of local liberty. The two modes of government of which Machiavelli speaks are
compared to the same effect by Tocqueville as systems of administrative
centralization and decentralization.

> Administrative centralization succeeds, it is true, in assembling, at a given time
> and place, all the available resources of the nation, but it militates against the in-
> crease of these resources. It brings triumph on the day of battle, but in the long
> run diminishes a nation's power.[7]

---

3.   *Recollections*, J.-P. Mayer and A. P. Kerr eds., George Lawrence trans. (New
      Brunswick, N.J.: Transaction Books, 1987), 169.
4.   *DA* [M-L], 661.
5.   *The Prince*, Harvey Mansfield, Jr. trans. (Chicago: University of Chicago Press,
      1985), 17.
6.   *Ibid.*, 17-18.
7.   *DA* [M-L], 88.

Locally elected magistrates are the democratic equivalent of independent barons: each is a form of administrative decentralization.[8] In either form, this mode of government is characterized by Tocqueville as free and as such is distinguished by the same quality Machiavelli attributes to it, in Tocqueville's words, it is "more difficult to subdue."

Tocqueville's reasoning is the same as Machiavelli's. Each locality, being independent of the center, constitutes a distinct locus of political activity and hence a separate point of resistance. Tocqueville describes the spirit of the New England system of local liberty in Machiavellian terms:

> The New England township combines two advantages which, wherever they are found, keenly excite men's interest; they are independence and power.... It is important to appreciate that, in general, men's affection are drawn only in directions where power exists. Patriotism does not long prevail in a conquered country.[9]

Both thinkers argue that it is the dispersal of power, not its concentration, that makes a polity stronger. In the immediately succeeding chapter of *The Prince*, chapter five, Machiavelli carries the argument a step farther. As a king and his nobility is "more difficult to subdue" than a despot and his slaves, so a republic is indomitable:

> And whoever becomes patron of a city used to living free and does not destroy it, should expect to be destroyed by it; for it always has as a refuge in rebellion the name of liberty and its own ancient orders which are never forgotten either through length of time or because of benefits received.[10]

This line of reasoning complements the implicit argument of chapter three of *The Prince*. Here Machiavelli explains France's failure to conquer Italy by its violation of principles drawn from consideration of the successful conquests of republican Rome.[11] In taking as well as keeping, the freer polity is

---

8. *DA* [M-L], 696-697: "The Americans, who attach less importance to words than we do, have retained the word 'county' to describe their largest administrative districts, but they have partly replaced functions of the county by those of the provincial assembly.... Election is a democratic expedient which secures the independence of officials in face of the central government even more effectively than it was secured by hereditary rank among aristocratic peoples."

9. *Ibid.*, 68. Tocqueville's comment about patriotism in a defeated country is reminiscent of Machiavelli's comment that "men forget the death of a father quicker than the loss of a patrimony," *The Prince*, 67. But in fact in his apparent realism Tocqueville is more Machiavellian than Machiavelli. The Florentine knows that memory of a polity's liberty will retain a hold on men for a hundred years after the polity's defeat, *The Prince*, 21.

10. *The Prince*, 20-21.

11. *Ibid.*, 11-13.

superior to the less free.[12] Insofar as complete prudence requires the capacity
for both as a necessary part, the free polity is wiser.[13] The central maxim,
not adequately grasped by France, but inscribed, so to speak, on Rome's
heart is that "war may not be avoided but is deferred to the advantage of
others."[14] There is no qualification to this maxim. "War may not be avoided"
by mankind because it is the necessary consequence of the human condition.
Of necessity or by nature, everyman's hand is raised against that of every
other man.[15] This condition explains the natural attraction power holds for
men, and when their appetite is exercised, it grows. Tocqueville's account of
the great activity that prevails in a free country reflects his own recognition
that possession of power fosters a life led in pursuit of greater power. He observes that were the citizen of a free country deprived of political power
"half of his existence would be snatched from him."[16] That he proceeds to
illustrate this by alluding to "the despair of certain Roman citizens" in the
wake of the republic's fall rather heightens the parallel with Machiavelli.[17]
In short, what makes freedom valuable is that in the free polity, one in which
power is dispersed by means of independent local institutions, one ever finds
"a picture of power, somewhat wild perhaps, but robust, and a life liable to
mishaps but full of striving and ambition."[18]

Just as surely as Tocqueville does in *Democracy in America*, Machiavelli
in *The Prince* leads the reader to the thought that "nothing is more fertile in
marvels" than freedom. And just as Tocqueville added that this art is not
easily learned, so Machiavelli raises the question of how a people comes to
"know how to live free."[19] One is brought to the issue of the meaning of the
art of freedom and the means of its acquisition.

The paradox of freedom is that it tends both to make the polity stronger
and to destroy it. The very avidness for power on the part of each member

---

12. The progress of the argument suggests Montesquieu's division of governments into
    republic, monarchy and despotism, *The Spirit of the Laws*, Anne Cohler, Basia
    Miller and Harold Stone trans. and eds. (Cambridge: Cambridge University Press,
    1989), 10. Machiavelli expressly makes this kind of tripartite division when subse-
    quently he speaks of one's own arms as either "subjects or citizens or your crea-
    tures," *The Prince*, 74.
13. Cf. *Republic*, 333e-334b where it is observed that the man who is good at keeping
    must also be good at taking; also, *Politics*, 1277b20-30 where Aristotle appears to
    separate these two parts of prudence.
14. *The Prince*, 12-13.
15. In this way Machiavelli anticipates Hobbes's account of the natural condition of
    mankind as a state of war of every man against every man, *Leviathan*, ch. 13.
16. *DA* [M-L], 243.
17. *Ibid.*, 243, footnote.
18. *Ibid.*, 92-93.
19. *The Prince*, 21.

that fills the whole with such "striving and ambition" makes any whole impossible unless the polity's members learn to cooperate. That capacity of each member to make a union with his fellows without loss of his own independence is the art of being free. Tocqueville describes this art as a "respect" for the "idea of rights."[20] It is the capacity to distinguish in each instance the limits of conflicting rights, to strike the just balance between them. In particular Tocqueville is concerned that "the man of the people" not abuse the political rights which he enjoys in a democratic republic.[21] The sovereign people must recognize that justice constitutes a limit to their power.[22] Here, too, Machiavelli seems to anticipate Tocqueville. A consideration of what he has to say about the art of being free enables us to grasp more clearly just what the ground and content of that limit upon a sovereign people is for Tocqueville.

If in chapter three of *The Prince* Machiavelli offers a picture of the Roman polity at the height of its power, free and wise, in chapter nineteen he offers the proper counterpart, that polity in its decline. The same symmetry is observed in his discussion of the origin of each state: while chapter six treats the founding of the free polity, chapter nine treats the founding of the empire, that is, the fall of the republic.[23] The art of being free is to be collected from an account of how a republic fails to preserve its freedom.

Chapter nine is devoted to "the civil principality" which arises "when a private citizen becomes prince of his fatherland, not through crime or other intolerable violence but with the support of his fellow citizens."[24] This support must come from either the people or the great:

> For in every city these two diverse humors are found, which arises from this: that the people desire neither to be commanded nor oppressed by the great, and the great desire to command and oppress the people.

The two humors by which alone these groups are distinguished are defined as diametrically opposed one to the other. The city then, is always marked by a tension between these two groups. Given this tension, Machiavelli observes that there are three possible outcomes. "From these two diverse ap-

---

20. *DA* [M-L], 237-240.
21. *Ibid.*, 238-240.
22. *Ibid.*, 250-251.
23. Though Machiavelli does not in chapter nine speak of the true founder of the Roman Empire, Julius Caesar, he does describe him a few chapters later as "one of those who wanted to attain the principate of Rome" and of whom some say he "attained empire with liberality," ch. 16, 64. Caesar's liberality was aimed at winning the support of the people, the path to power that is the principal object of Machiavelli's discussion in ch. 9.
24. *Ibid.*, 38-39.

petites one of three effects occurs in cities: principality or liberty or license."[25] As the civil principality by definition involves the triumph of one
group over the other, that is, the release of the tension between them, it
follows that liberty is to be distinguished from license by the form in which
the tension is preserved. The art of being free is the art of preserving this
tension in a manner that binds the members of the polity together rather than
driving them apart. The tension is preserved if both appetites are satisfied to
some degree but neither entirely. Machiavelli's statement of the two
conflicting appetites suggests how this may be done: the people agree to be
ruled by the great on the condition that they will not be oppressed and the
great agree not to oppress the people on the condition that they will be
allowed to rule. The art of being free is the capacity at each moment to
distinguish what belongs to each. When the members of a polity lose this
capacity, their liberty degenerates into license: the people reject rule as oppression and the great call oppression rule.[26] The resulting state combines
the two appetites in a destructive manner: the great oppress and the people
are not ruled. The civil principality that puts an end to this license in turn
degenerates into another form of it. In chapter nineteen Machiavelli portrays
a polity in which the people suffer at the hands of the soldiers whose whims
the prince is powerless to deny.

The object of the founder of the polity, and those who succeed the
founder, must be to institute and preserve the means by which the appetites
of each group are satisfied in a state of creative tension. Machiavelli writes,
in chapter nineteen:

> And well-ordered states and wise princes have thought out with all diligence how
> not to make the great desperate and how to satisfy the people and keep them con-
> tent, because this is one of the most important matters that concern a prince.[27]

Machiavelli offers the France of his time as an example of a well-ordered
state, a view which Tocqueville's *Old Regime* implicitly supports.[28] The institution Machiavelli cites is one which redresses an imbalance favorable to

---

25. *Ibid.*, 39.
26. Marx's account of "political power" in *The Communist Manifesto* simply equates
    rule and oppression.
27. *The Prince*, 74.
28. In *L'Ancien Régime et la Révolution* (*OC*, II:1, 96.) Tocqueville depicts France in
    1789 as a nation unable to regain its freedom because its capacity to be free had
    been weakened by a process that stretched over "ten generations." In Machiavelli's
    time this process had only just begun.

the great, precisely the imbalance to which an aristocratic society would be most liable.[29]

In *Democracy* Tocqueville offers the same idea of the art of being free. There are, he writes, two great parties that are "found under different forms and with various names in all free countries. One party [wants] to restrict popular power and the other to extend it indefinitely."[30]

Clearly, liberty for Tocqueville, as for Machiavelli, involves a tension between two contending groups. And just as clearly, Tocqueville's two parties are composed of those Machiavelli describes as the people and the great. For as it is the great who suffer when the popular power is extended indefinitely, it is they who will oppose that extension.

Thus Tocqueville goes on to comment, however much petty aims appear to dominate the political contests of a free polity, "aristocratic or democratic passions can easily be found at the bottom of all parties... [they are] the nerve and soul of the matter."[31] Tocqueville defines an aristocracy as "the principal persons in the nation" of which group "the proper character" is "to be a body of citizens who govern."[32] The great party that opposes the extension of popular power is to be characterized as Machiavelli characterized the great, by the desire to rule.

This is not to say that every party opposed to the extension of popular power is aristocratic. By hypothesis, we are speaking of a free country. In a country that had lost the capacity to be free, the wealthy might oppose popular power without thereby seeking to rule themselves.

This is the burden of Tocqueville's account of the middle class of the July Monarchy.[33] But not every middle class is like that of France's July Monarchy.[34] Clearly, for Tocqueville, the American middle class is aristo-

---

29. *The Prince*, 74-75. Mansfield identifies Louis IX as "perhaps" the one to whom Machiavelli attributes the superior order of France. This is noteworthy in view of the favorable attention Montesquieu also gives to St. Louis in *The Spirit of the Laws*, bk. 28, passim. Anne Cohler thought that, for Montesquieu, Louis IX was France's greatest king, the hero, so to speak, of the account of France's history that he gives in *The Spirit of the Laws*.
30. *DA* [M-L], 175.
31. *Ibid.*, 178.
32. *L'Ancien Régime*, 147.
33. *Recollections*, 5.
34. In fact, the French middle class of the nineteenth century is treated by Tocqueville as something of an anomaly: "I doubt if one can find a single example of any people engaged in both manufacture and trade, from the men of Tyre to the Florentines and the English, who were not a free people. There must therefore be a close link and necessary relationship between these two things, that is, freedom and industry." *DA* [M-L], 539.
Though Tocqueville might appear, at least implicitly, to compare the *bourgeoisie* unfavorably with his own ancestral class, in his last work he traces the political

cratic. The economic character of a class does not determine its political character. In a free capitalist country like the United States, the party of the great is "middle class."

Because the art of being free involves a respect for the claims of the great, this issue figures prominently in Tocqueville's discussion of tyranny in *Democracy*. As Marshall and Drescher observe, while "Tocqueville paid particular attention to the role of leadership" throughout *Democracy*, nowhere is this concern more evident than in that most important section of his first volume devoted to the "tyranny of the majority." Repeatedly throughout this section, the problem of leadership crops up, but most forcefully at its very climax, in many respects the focus of the entire volume.[35]

The whole of *Democracy* up to this point is, in a way, directed to these chapters as its conclusion. For in the chapters devoted to the danger of majority tyranny and the means to combat it, Tocqueville considers tyranny, liberty and license, the possible outcomes, by Machiavelli's account, of the struggle between the people and the great. And that struggle runs like a thread through the entire first volume of *Democracy*.

The end is in the beginning. The trial and acquittal of John Winthrop in the "Point of Departure" chapter foreshadows the successful resolution of a struggle between the two parties. The struggle as carried on in Jacksonian America is first suggested in the succeeding chapter where Tocqueville describes the western states as a place where "the population escapes the influence not only of great names and great wealth but also the natural aristocracy of education and probity."[36]

Tocqueville concludes this chapter by contrasting a liberal with an illiberal democratic impulse: the desire to rise "to the rank of the great" and the desire "to drag the strong down."[37] In the chapter on local government the specter of civil war appears. The American republics, where the people's sovereignty is unquestioned, have no standing armies, Tocqueville observes, because "so far no minority has been reduced to an appeal to arms." Then,

poverty of France and hence of the French middle class to the "cowardice" of the French nobility: *L'Ancien Régime*, 160. On this question, see my "Freedom, Power, and the Common Good: Tocqueville's *Old Regime*," a paper presented at the 1989 annual meeting of the American Political Science Association.

35. Lynn Marshall and Seymour Drescher, "American Historians and Tocqueville's *Democracy*," *Journal of American History*, 55 (1968), 512-532, 529. The comparison with Machiavelli helps us understand that the treatment of the claim of some "to play a privileged leadership role" (530) so far from being "forced... into a discussion of another only distantly related matter" (529) is central to the discussion of majority tyranny.

36. *DA* [M-L], 55.

37. *Ibid.*, 57.

without elaborating upon this possibility, Tocqueville highlights it in a manner that no French reader could fail to understand. He compares the legislatures of the American Republics to "the Convention."[38]

In the second part of the first volume, once he has introduced the idea of the two great parties that divide a free society, Tocqueville considers the consequences of an imbalance between them.

> It sometimes happens in a nation where opinions are divided that the balance between the parties breaks down and one of them acquires an irresistible preponderance. It breaks all obstacles, crushes its adversary, and exploits the whole of society for its own benefit.[39]

The great, "being unable to assume a rank in public life analogous to that which they occupy in private life, they abandon the former and concentrate upon the latter."[40] Tocqueville portrays a government in which "natural instincts lead the people to keep men of distinction from power."[41] At the same time, the broad discretion it gives to the magistrates it chooses expresses its desire not to be ruled. The people prefer "to let [its magistrates] follow their own devices rather than to bind them with invariable rules which, in restraining them, would also in a sense control itself."[42] Under such a government the great but await a crisis that will offer an opportunity to overturn the republic.[43] For the most part, Tocqueville notes, they bear with the evil in silence since "among civilized nations it is generally only those with nothing to lose who revolt."[44] But the imbalance between the two parties inevitably has the result of driving the great "to desperation and forcing them to appeal to physical force."[45] In this way a free democratic society loses its liberty. Here, at the end of the chapter on the omnipotence of the majority, Tocqueville quotes Madison's description of how the "misrule" of the stronger faction in the democratic republic eventually leads even the more powerful to appeal "to some power altogether independent of the people."[46] This is nothing else than Machiavelli's account of the rise of the civil principality.

---

38. *Ibid.*, 89-90. The association with the Terror is strengthened by the treatment in the two succeeding chapters of judicial checks on popular power and trial for political crimes.
39. *DA* [M-L], 178.
40. *Ibid.*, 179.
41. *Ibid.*, 198-199.
42. *Ibid.*, 205.
43. *Ibid.*, 179.
44. *Ibid.*, 241.
45. *Ibid.*, 260.
46. *Ibid.*, 260.

The liberal alternative to this is portrayed in the succeeding chapter where Tocqueville praises institutions that check the popular power in a democratic society.[47] He offers the use of the jury in civil cases as an institution where, in the person of the judge, the man of the people encounters "the best educated and most enlightened members of the upper classes" in such a way as to "feel confidence in him and listen to him with respect."[48] The judge's rule in this case is complete: "The jurors pronounce the decision made by the judge. They give that judgment the authority of the society they represent, as he gives it that of reason and of law."[49]

Tocqueville expressly praises this institution as "the very best way of preparing people to be free."[50] It serves this function by instilling in the man of the people judicial habits which include a "respect for the thing judged and for the idea of right."[51] Possessed of such habits the citizen takes it as a responsibility to accord rule to those who have the greatest right to it, to the principal persons of the nation, the aristocratic party of society. Thus, the judge's "influence extends far beyond the precincts of the courts" even to "the turmoil of politics."[52]

We have come full circle to the model of a free society Tocqueville offers us in the case of John Winthrop. The "influence" of the great is not unchallenged; a free politics always involves "turmoil" as the two parties endeavor to discover the proper limits of their respective rights. What distinguishes a free society is the capacity both to grasp the need to strike a balance between the two parties and to find the means to do so.[53] Lacking this art, a society is condemned to either license or tyranny or, more likely, to "spend a wretched life between alternate swings to license and to oppression."[54]

47. Cf. *DA* [M-L], 543.
48. *Ibid.*, 275.
49. *Idem.*
50. *Ibid.*, 274 .
51. *Idem.* Lawrence's translation amended.
52. *Ibid.*, 276.
53. *Ibid.*, 46 and footnote. Perry Miller gives an account of the events surrounding this speech in *Orthodoxy in Massachusetts, 1630-1650* (Gloucester, Mass.: Peter Smith, 1965), 287-294. His interpretation of Winthrop's speech is contrary to that of Tocqueville. Where Tocqueville sees the people's respect for Winthrop as the necessary underpinning of a free polity, Miller sees it as symptomatic of an oligarchical and authoritarian state. In the context of the trial, which he describes as a "trick" played by the magistrates upon the people, he calls it "the final twist of an inquisitorial thumb-screw" (291, 292). Such a reading, offered in defense of democratic liberty, suggests the continuing importance of what Tocqueville has to say about the art of being free.
54. *Recollections*, 65; cf. *DA* [M-L], 94.

The Idea of Power

> For in every city these two diverse humors are found, which arises from this: that the people desire neither to be commanded nor oppressed by the great, and the great desire to command and oppress the people.

For Machiavelli, political liberty appears to consist in this, that the people are not oppressed and the great command. On a deeper level, however, human liberty as such is understood by Machiavelli in terms of the opposite set of alternatives: the people are not commanded and the great oppress the people.

Clearly freedom means not being commanded or ruled, at least in the sense of not being ruled by another. For mankind as such it means that there is nothing higher than man that rules him, neither God nor nature. Surely natural necessity constrains man. But nature, in this respect, as blind and stupid constraint, is not higher than man and, in any case, such constraint is not the same as rule. Yet if man is to be free in the sense of ruling himself, as well as not being ruled by another, this natural constraint must be overcome so far as it can be. Given that nature constrains human beings by means of the body, by means of pleasure, the overcoming of this constraint is a kind of cruelty. The desire to oppress is the agency by which freedom as not being ruled is won. While political freedom involves putting a check to this desire, it remains that this desire is itself the source of human freedom. Insofar as human dignity consists in human freedom, this appetite to oppress not only characterizes the great but is the ground of their title. What makes man great is his glorying in the imposition of his will, an expression of will in the face of opposition for the sake of that expression.

Machiavelli is not alone in noting in the great a desire to hurt seemingly for its own sake. In his account of the origins of inequality Rousseau compares those who first taste "the pleasure of domination," to "wolves which, having once tasted human flesh, refuse all other food and thenceforth want only to devour men."[55]

> In all times—he writes—powerful and rich men prize things they enjoy only insofar as the others are deprived of them; and because, without changing their status, they would cease to be happy if the people ceased to be miserable.[56]

---

55. Rousseau, *The First and Second Discourses*, Roger Masters ed., Roger and Judith Masters trans. (New York: St. Martin's Press, 1964), 157.
56. *Ibid.*, 175.

Hobbes makes clear the ground of this pleasure even if he condemns it. The laws of nature in his eyes prohibit "cruelty" which he defined as "glorying in the hurt of another, tending to no end," that is, a kind of "vain glory and contrary to reason."[57] But for the great the glorying is itself the end. Hobbes defines glorying as "joy arising from imagination of a man's own power and ability."[58] The hurt inflicted on others is a testimony to that power, the desire for which, by Hobbes's own account, is central to man.[59]

Tocqueville, too, speaks of the cruelty of the aristocracy. "The Chroniclers of the Middle Ages," he observes, aristocratic "by birth or assimilation," narrate "without wincing massacres and tortures of the common people."[60] Nor is this a matter of the barbarism of the age. In a later, more civilized age, a noble woman like Mme de Sévigné in her letters to her daughter can indulge in "cruel jokes" at the people's expense.[61] Indeed, this cruelty is a sign of her nobility. "Real sympathy," Tocqueville argues, "can exist only between people of like sort," who are on a common footing.[62] But it is the distance between themselves and the people that is the measure of the greatness of the nobility and they strive to preserve it.[63] The stronger the sense an aristocracy has of the height it occupies, the more difficult it is for it to stoop to put itself on any kind of equal footing with the people.[64] The reduction of that sense of distance Tocqueville describes as a "softening of mores" and in his letters he regrets this phenomenon as "the greatest malady that threatens" democratic society.[65] By the same token, Tocqueville writes of nineteenth-century European imperialism "it is the enslavement of four parts of the world by the fifth," grounds, he argues, for not thinking poorly

57. *Leviathan*, C. B. MacPherson ed. (Baltimore: Penguin Books, 1968), 210 (ch. 15); cf. 126 (ch. 6).
58. *Ibid.*, 124-125 (ch. 6).
59. *Ibid.*, 161 (ch. 11). Cf. Nietzsche, *On the Genealogy of Morals*, Walter Kaufmann ed., Walter Kaufmann and R. J. Hollingdale trans. (New York: Random House, 1967), 65 ("Second Essay," sec. 5). Punishment affords "a kind of *pleasure*—the pleasure of being allowed to vent his power freely upon one who is powerless" and of taking joy in the contemplation of that act. In punishing one "participates in a *right of the masters*." (In this and all succeeding passages from Nietzsche, the italics are in the original.)
60. *DA* [M-L], 562.
61. *Ibid.*, 562-564.
62. *Ibid.*, 562.
63. Cf. Nietzsche on the "pathos of distance" in aristocratic morality, *Genealogy of Morals*, 26 ("First Essay," sec. 2).
64. *L'Ancien Régime*, 159-160.
65. *DA* [M-L], 561, chapter title; letter to John Stuart Mill, March 18, 1841, in Alexis de Tocqueville, *Selected Letters on Politics and Society*, Roger Boesche ed., James Toupin and Roger Boesche trans. (Berkeley, Cal.: University of California Press, 1985), 150.

of the age.[66] Yet, ultimately, for Tocqueville this quality of the great is as much the cause of freedom's destruction as its source. However much Tocqueville assents to Machiavelli's account of political freedom, he differs from him as to the meaning of human freedom as such.

Machiavelli devotes a chapter to cruelty and mercy in *The Prince.* Here he blames the Republic of Florence for showing "too much mercy" in its dealings with Pistoia and praises Hannibal for "his inhuman cruelty" in ruling his army.[67] In both instances the effect of cruelty is the same: to impose unity upon a divided community. This is the same task performed by the greatest of those who have "founded kingdoms." "All the armed prophets conquered and the unarmed ones were ruined." For "the nature of peoples is variable"; to hold them to the "new orders" he introduces, the founder must be "able to use force."[68] In the interests of the collective power, to render faithful to an order that binds them together a multitude of changeable individuals each striving for power and independence: this is the task of the founder and is nothing else than to teach men the art or habit of freedom. Insofar as possession of this art is of benefit to men and cruelty is the necessary means by which it is taught, cruelty is ultimately more merciful than mercy.[69]

It is Nietzsche who makes vivid the full import of Machiavelli's meaning, the more vivid as in the intervening centuries Europe had lost sight of it and acquired a distaste for it.[70] Insofar as freedom depends upon the acknowledgment of right, Nietzsche makes clear how punishment is the necessary means by which men become free. What Hobbes seems to assume, Nietzsche takes as a problem: "to breed an animal *with the right to make promises*—is not this the paradoxical task that nature has set itself in the case of man?"[71] The covenant that men make to constitute that great power that is a free polity, a union of sovereign individuals, that covenant depends upon "a real memory of the will" that Hobbes himself acknowledges is foreign to so changeable a being as man.[72] The work of inculcating this capac-

---

66. Letter to Henry Reeve, April 12, 1840, in *Selected Letters*, 141-142.
67. *The Prince*, 65, 67.
68. *Ibid.*, 22-24.
69. *Ibid.*, 65.
70. "To see others suffer does one good, to make others suffer even more: this is a hard saying but an ancient, mighty, human, all-too-human principle to which even the apes might subscribe." *Genealogy of Morals*, 67 ("Second Essay," sec. 6).
71. *Ibid.*, 57 ("Second Essay," sec. 1).
72. *Ibid.* Hobbes: "And because the constitution of a mans Body, is in continuall mutation; it is impossible that all the same things should always cause in him the same Appetites, and Aversions; much lesse can all men consent, in the Desire of almost any one and the same Object." *Leviathan*, 120 (ch. 6).

ity to make promises is "the labor performed by man upon himself during the greater part of the existence of the human race." "The emancipated individual,... this master of a *free* will" is the product of this long labor.[73] That labor of creating a memory of the will must have been "fearful and uncanny," its principle: "If something is to stay in the memory it must be burned in: only that which never ceases to *hurt* stays in the memory."[74] This is the meaning of Machiavelli's maxim: "Things must be ordered in such a mode that when [the people] no longer believe, one can make them believe by force."[75] Man is punished not because he is responsible; he becomes responsible because he is punished.[76] There is nothing to which he owes allegiance, an allegiance that is alive and compelling to him, so that he may be held responsible for failing to act on this allegiance. Rather, it is the punishment itself that creates from nothing the only allegiance man knows. Insofar as we are defined by that to which we pay allegiance, man is the creator of himself.[77] In Machiavelli's words, into the formless but malleable "matter" that constitutes the human animal the great "introduce any form they pleased."[78] Man's freedom consists in this, that he possesses a sovereign will, that is, he is not ruled; and he has come to possess that sovereignty by his own act, that is, by means of cruelty.

For Tocqueville such an idea contains the germ of tyranny. He cites with approval the fourteenth-century maxim: "By requiring too great a freedom and liberty men fall into too great slavery."[79]

This is implicit in Tocqueville's discussion of majority tyranny. Here though he argues for a limit to what a nation may rightfully do, he seems to describe mankind as author of the only law that binds it.

> A nation is like a jury entrusted to represent universal society and to apply the justice which is its law.... Consequently, when I refuse to obey an unjust law, I by no means deny the majority's right to give orders; I only appeal from the sovereignty of the people to the sovereignty of the human race.[80]

---

73. *Genealogy of Morals*, 59 ("Second Essay," sec. 2).
74. *Ibid.*, 61 ("Second Essay," sec. 3).
75. *The Prince*, 24. Cf. Nietzsche: "the welding of a hitherto unchecked and shapeless populace into a firm form was not only instituted by an act of violence but also carried to its conclusion by nothing but acts of violence." *Genealogy of Morals*, 86 ("Second Essay," sec. 17).
76. *Genealogy of Morals*, 63 ("Second Essay," sec. 4).
77. Cf. *Republic*, 505e.
78. *The Prince*, 23.
79. *L'Ancien Régime*, 198. Cf. *Republic*, 562b-c.
80. *DA* [M-L], 250-251.

But Tocqueville does deny or at least qualifies the sovereignty of the human race only two pages later:

> Omnipotence in itself seems a bad and dangerous thing. I think that its exercise is beyond man's strength, whoever he be, and that only God can be omnipotent without danger because His wisdom and justice are always equal to His power.[81]

In fact, this qualification is present in Tocqueville's first statement of the sovereignty of mankind:

> There is one law which has been made, *or at least adopted*, not by the majority of this or that people, but by the majority of all men. That law is justice.[82]

The sovereignty of the human race extends only this far; the law of justice that Tocqueville attributes to the majority of all men is not made but "adopted" by mankind. Ultimately that law is authored by God. Liberty is obedience to a law adopted by mankind, but obedience nonetheless to something higher than man.

It is our natural allegiance to something higher which defines us as human. This is the content of that "beautiful definition of liberty" found in the speech of John Winthrop that Tocqueville places at the start of *Democracy*:

> Let us not deceive ourselves about what we ought to understand by independence. There is, in fact, a kind of corrupt liberty, the usage of which is common to animals as well as to man, and which consists in doing whatever one pleases. This liberty is the enemy of all authority; it suffers all rules with impatience; by it, we become inferior to ourselves; it is the enemy of truth and of peace; and God thought he must set Himself against it. But there is a civil and moral liberty which finds its strength in union, and which it is the purpose of power itself to protect: this is the liberty to do without fear all that is just and good. This holy liberty we must defend at all hazards, even, if necessary, at the risk of our life.[83]

The very fact that Tocqueville takes the Puritan experience as the true founding of the American democratic republic is indicative of his understanding of liberty as obedience to a divine law.

81. *Ibid.*, 252 .
82. *Ibid.*, 250. Emphasis added.
83. This is my translation of Tocqueville's paraphrase of Winthrop's speech, *DA* [N], I, 35. The Mayer edition of *Democracy* does not give a translation of Tocqueville's text but reprints from Cotton Mather's *Magnalia Christi Americana* roughly, but not exactly, that portion of Winthrop's speech that corresponds to Tocqueville's paraphrase, 46.

Nietzsche has no difficulty in recognizing in the Puritans the telltale sign of the great: "all religions are at the deepest level systems of cruelty."[84] But the question is how to interpret this phenomenon.

When Nietzsche looks for greatness in the modern age he finds it in the aristocracy of the *Ancien Régime*.[85] Tocqueville too praises this aristocracy as retaining "the spirit of independence" despite the loss of "public liberty."[86] He finds evidence of it in all the higher classes. Both the old nobility and the leaders of the clergy displayed "pride," "a natural confidence in their own strength," an "indocility"; the bourgeoisie often showed the same "pride and spirit of resistance"; the courts defended their rights with "courage."[87] Tocqueville wishes his contemporaries would show something of this "grandeur."[88] Essential to liberty is a certain spiritedness, a determination to have one's will done for no other reason than that it is one's will. Tocqueville comments ironically on the way in which the leaders of an eighteenth-century city obsequiously expressed their submission to "the wishes" of an intendant: "Thus did the bourgeois class prepare itself for government and the people for liberty."[89]

"The French who made the Revolution," on the other hand, had a "proud confidence" in their own strength.[90] This confidence was "a kind of new religion," their will taking the place of God's fiat, and it produced some of the great effects of religion such as heroic self-sacrifice.[91] Here is that power of human will so much admired by Nietzsche in Periclean Athens, in Rome, and among the Germanic tribes who conquered Rome.[92] But such strength of will alone constitutes a "kind of singular liberty," not liberty itself.[93] Without it a nation is capable only of serving; but alone it produces an immense public evil. The revolutionaries inspired by this new religion

---

84. *Genealogy of Morals*, 61; see also 69 as regards Luther and Calvin ("Second Essay," secs. 3 and 7).

85. *Ibid.*, 39 ("First Essay," sec. 10), for example.

86. *L'Ancien Régime*, 168.

87. *Ibid.*, 169, 170, 171, 173, 174.

88. *Ibid.*, 176. See also: *DA* [M-L], 632; letters to Royer-Collard, August 20, 1837 and Arthur Gobineau, December 20, 1853, in *Selected Letters*, 118, 303.

89. *L'Ancien Régime*, 119.

90. *Ibid.*, 207.

91. *Ibid.*, 208.

92. *Genealogy of Morals*, 40-42, 52-53 ("First Essay," sec. 11 and 16). Cf. Tocqueville on this singular spirit of liberty among the Romans, "France before the Revolution," in *Memoir, Letters, and Remains of Alexis de Tocqueville* (Boston: Ticknor and Fields, 1862), I, 246-247.

93. *L'Ancien Régime*, 168.

"carried audacity to madness" and hesitated at nothing; they were "slowed by no scruples" and "surprised by no novelty."[94]

True liberty is as distant from this as the peaceful progress of society is from the rule of the Convention. This spiritedness is an "irregular," "deformed," "unhealthy" kind of liberty; by itself it is an obstacle to a regular and beneficial liberty.[95] The determination to be bound by one's own will is a part of liberty but not all. It is equally essential that one's will be in conformity to the divine order. True liberty requires that the great bend under the "empire of law."[96] In the last analysis, law means not merely the law of the sovereign nation but the "laws of God for the conduct of societies."[97]

A society, a union of free and equal human beings, must if it is to be free, conform to the law of God. It is not, as some of the Enlightenment thinkers conceived, something one makes as one likes. Tocqueville emphatically rejects the idea that the state "was not only to command the nation but to fashion it in a certain manner," that "it not only reforms men, it transforms them," that as of right "it belongs to it perhaps to make them something other [than men]!"[98] Tocqueville would see in Machiavelli the same idea, what he criticizes as an "adoration of human reason, an unlimited confidence in its omnipotence."[99]

For Tocqueville what is decisive in the great is the habit of the judge, not the "splendid blond beast"; "the thing judged," not the thing willed.[100] The desire to command expresses a desire to conform to the laws of God which alone makes lasting rule possible; the desire to oppress is a desire to suppress all that would distract from this obedience.

For Machiavelli no less than Tocqueville, nothing is more fertile in marvels than the art of being free. Moreover, the two thinkers agree that this art involves a respect for the right of the great or the noble. For both, it is the great who are the authors of a nation's freedom. But the right of the great and thus freedom has for Tocqueville a significance very different from that it has for Machiavelli. The great do not, by right, shape men as they please; man is not free by reason of not being ruled by something higher than him-

---

94. *Ibid.*, 207-208.
95. *Ibid.*, 176, 177, 169.
96. *Ibid.*, 170, 177.
97. *Ibid.*, 189. As I have already suggested above, the same idea is implicit in *Democracy*: in Winthrop's speech and in Tocqueville's discussion of the law that limits the right of the sovereign people, a law "adopted" by mankind but authored by an omnipotent God. *DA* [M-L], 37, 250-252 .
98. *L'Ancien Régime*, 212.
99. *Ibid.*, 306, note to 195.
100. *Genealogy of Morals*, 40 ("First Essay," sec. 11). *DA* [M-L], 274 .

it has for Machiavelli. The great do not, by right, shape men as they please; man is not free by reason of not being ruled by something higher than himself. Rather, greatness consists in the determination to conform to the higher law that rules man; freedom consists in conformity to this law.

Despite the way in which Machiavelli anticipates Tocqueville in *The Prince*, Tocqueville in one of his letters refers to that work as "superficial" because it neglects "a vague, but powerful, sentiment of justice" that exists "at the core of the human heart."[101] That sentiment was given to man by his creator. Tocqueville's criticism of Machiavelli finally comes to this: "for him, the world is a great arena, from which God is absent."[102]

In *Otello*, Verdi gives this profession of faith to Iago: "I believe in a cruel God." For Machiavelli as for Nietzsche, God is cruel; and man is God. Tocqueville dissents from both propositions.

101. Letter to Royer-Collard, August 25, 1836, in *Selected Letters*, 110.
102. Letter to Kergorlay, August 5, 1836, in *Memoir*, I, 319.

[4]

Virtue and Politics in Tocqueville

In 1934, in a *Report on the Prizes of Virtue* at the French Academy, Paul Valéry was heard to exclaim:

> Virtue, my dear sirs, the word virtue is dead, or, at the very least, dying.... It is not present to today's intellects as an expression with an imaginable reality. We have arrived at a point where the words virtue and virtuous can only be found in catechism, in farce, in the Academy and in light opera.

Recently Alasdair MacIntyre showed the extent to which we have lost—that is, if it has not been completely lost—the theoretical as well as the practical understanding of morality.[1] Since the Enlightenment, our moral judgments rest on affect. They express attitudes or sentiments: they are neither true nor false, and agreement is not assured by any rational method for there is none.[2] This explains the contemporary confusion—the main cause of despotism, according to Jouvenal—that begins with the loss of the very idea of virtue, which has become indifferent as societies have become more and more atomized.

In truth, social integration depends far more on virtue than it does on rationality; it depends on customs (Aristotle) more than it does on knowledge or regulations. The morality of public duty that one opposes to private

1. *After Virtue. A Study in Moral Theory*, 2nd. ed. (London: Duckworth, 1985), 2.
2. *Ibid.*, 12. Perhaps visions predominate. "Reality is far too complex to be comprehended by any given mind. Visions are like maps that guide us through a tangle of bewildering complexities. Like maps, visions have to leave out many concrete features in order to enable us to focus on a few key paths to our goals." Thomas Sowell, *A Conflict of Visions. Ideological Origins of Political Struggles* (New York: William Morrow and Co., 1987), 7.

55

morality (Comte) remains too abstract and inefficacious without the latter, and democratic regimes may, as a result, become "impolitic" (Julien Freund).

The concept of a virtuous man, as Joseph Pieper reminds us, designates a man who is true, authentic, and implies, for man, elevation in his being, the *ultima potentiae*, according to Thomas Aquinas, the highest good to which he can aspire. The virtuous man realizes the good by following his most intimate inclinations, which happen to correspond to an idea of order.

There is without a doubt nothing in Tocqueville that resembles a doctrine of political virtue, yet the question of how a democratic man can be politically virtuous is posed in his work. Tocqueville did not believe in the goodness of man, nor did he believe in his absolute evil. Rather he believed, in accordance with a Christian and liberal tradition, that man is a weak and fallible being. The famous saying of Pascal, one of Tocqueville's strongest influences, that "man is neither angel nor beast, and the misfortune is that he who would be the angel becomes the beast" reflects the anthropological conception of Tocqueville.

His purpose is not to moralize but to expose, in his capacity as pure political thinker, the circumstances of the best possible regime that could be put into practice. In democracy he saw the ideal state, on the condition that it not deprive man of the feeling of personal responsibility that is, for Tocqueville, inseparable from freedom. He believes that this sentiment depends in large part on the institutional order, but also on mores and religion. On *virtue*, in the end, which combines all of the above elements. He believes that while democracy in the United States is relatively free from danger, thanks to its political and social institutions, to the power of its *mores* and to the firmness of its religious dogmas, such is not the case in Europe. He explains the situation by invoking history: "for the Americans, freedom is very old," whereas in Europe "equality, introduced by the absolute power and under the eyes of kings, had already entered into the customs of the people long before freedom came into their ideas."[3] Public virtue could not easily accompany democracy in Europe, as there was no history of freedom; there was a lack of feeling of political responsibility.[4] Virtue makes men socially responsible and predisposes them toward freedom.[5]

---

3.   *DA* [N], II, 246.
4.   Recently Peter V. Saladin has pointed out that responsibility and freedom "are the two elements constitutive of personal being" in relation to the political. *Verantwortung als Staatsprinzip* (Bern and Stuttgart: Paul Haupt, 1984), III, 82.
5.   For Hans Jonas, in the "ethical vacuum" that characterizes the period, anguish is very often "the best *Ersatz* for practical virtue and wisdom (wirkliche)." *Das Prinzip Verantwortung* (Frankfurt am Main: Insel Verlag, 1979), 57.

It is surprising, furthermore, to see how few references there are to political virtue in Tocqueville, the alleged disciple of Montesquieu. The word virtue appears very little, and instead of political virtue Tocqueville often uses public virtue. He always defines what he means by this expression, except when he compares it rhetorically to freedom or when he says:

> with the general notion of virtue, I cannot think of any notion more glorious than that of rights, or rather, these two notions are the same. The idea of rights is nothing else but the idea of virtue introduced into the world of politics.[6]

This leads one to inquire as to the meaning of political virtue for Tocqueville and to the role that he attributes to it in a democratic society; the subject of virtue works through all of Tocqueville's work as an afterthought. This question becomes a contemporary one when we consider democracy today.

We will mention here the three most essential points concerning the relation between virtue and politics in Tocqueville: the relative opposition of Tocqueville to Montesquieu and the classical tradition of political virtue, virtue as social mediation between independence and political freedom in a democracy, and the importance of the social acceptance of the idea of the existence of a universal order of extra-human origin for the practice of virtue.

Montesquieu's Virtue

The concept of virtue is fundamental in the work of Montesquieu. It is the driving force of a republic, and has no part in a monarchy. Leaving aside the latter, Tocqueville converts what for Montesquieu were simply types of governments—republican, aristocratic or democratic—into the basic forms of social life.

One cannot help but have the impression that Montesquieu uses the idea of political virtue (a little forced, perhaps), in part out of loyalty to the republican tradition, to explain the principle of regimes, "that which makes them act," in contrast to their nature, "that which makes them as they are." First there are the "human passions that move [them];" then "[their] particular structure."[7] With virtue he is able to combine methodological individualism with a holistic perspective.

Individualism appears behind the affirmation according to which "in a people's republic one needs an additional motivating factor—apart from

6.   *DA* [N], I, 186.
7.   *L'esprit des lois*, bk. III, ch. I.

laws—which is virtue."[8] In addition, virtue is an antidote to political vice: "when, in a people's government, the laws have ceased to be executed, as this can only come from the corruption of the republics, the state is already lost."[9]

In a republic the opposite takes place from in a monarchy where "politics make great things happen with the least amount of virtue possible." In a monarchy "the state subsists independently from the love for the nation, from the desire for true glory, from self-abnegation, from the sacrifice of the interests one holds most dear and from the heroic virtues that we find in the Ancients and of which we have only heard spoken."[10] This is what Montesquieu concludes with a certain sarcasm.

He explains in a footnote in the same chapter that there is a difference between political virtue and moral virtue: "here I am speaking of political virtue which is moral virtue in the sense that it is directed toward the general good; I am speaking less of particular moral virtues and not at all of that virtue which has a relation to revealed truths." In chapter II of book V, to which he is referring, he explains what virtue is in a republic: "it is a very simple thing; it is love for the republic; it is a feeling and not a series of thoughts; the last man of the state can have this feeling just the same as the first."

Montesquieu makes a vicious circle in his effort to describe political virtue: "love for one's nation leads to the goodness of mores, and the goodness of mores leads to the love of nation." If the republic is democratic, "the love of democracy is one of equality" and "the love of democracy," he continues to explain in chapter III of the same book, "is, furthermore, the love of frugality." We know that in the aristocratic republic, political virtue—here he says "the soul of these governments"—is moderation.[11] In the end, as Newtonian as his era, Montesquieu found it crucial to determine which concrete virtue served as the law of gravitation in each regime.

From Montesquieu Tocqueville retains the idea of an organizational principle, but not the idea of political virtue. (There is room for discussion of the assertion that the baron de la Brède was the great influence of Tocqueville.)[12]

On the one hand, the static, structural perspective predominates in the thinking of Montesquieu. On the other hand, it is pure convention that virtue

8.   *Ibid.*, bk. III, ch. III.
9.   *Idem.*
10. *L'esprit des lois*, bk. III, ch. V.
11. *Ibid.*, bk. III, ch. IV.
12. Cf. Luis Díez del Corral, *El pensamiento político de Tocqueville* (Madrid: Alianza Editorial, 1988), ch. VI.

should be the driving force which Montesquieu was looking for, more a mechanical *Triebfeder* than a *soul*. An essential trait that helps one to understand the difference between Tocqueville and Montesquieu is that Tocqueville, as a methodological individualist, accentuates the intrinsic dynamism of social formations.

The author of *Democracy in America* does not see types of government in aristocratic and democratic regimes but forms of social and political life, regimes in which the structure is not independent from its *dynamis* or power of being.

Virtue is essential in a good regime. The perversion of regimes arises with the lack of virtue, especially in the case of a democratic regime. This does not mean, however, that Tocqueville concedes a special *status* to the virtue called *political virtue* as the concrete element of certain regimes.

If the formal difference between Montesquieu's and Tocqueville's virtue is evident, the difference in content is no less evident. For Tocqueville, love of democracy does not necessarily correspond to love for the nation nor does it concern love of frugality. On the contrary, it is in opposition to the latter, as the love of democracy is put in relation to "the spirit of well-being." Raymond Aron says, perhaps a bit equivocally, that "the principle of modern democracy [in Montesquieu's sense], according to Tocqueville is thus interest and not virtue at all." Aron points out that in both cases citizens must submit to a moral discipline, as the stability of the state depends on the dominant influence that *mores* and beliefs exert upon individual behavior.[13]

For Tocqueville, according to a draft of the second part of *Democracy in America* that is often quoted as evidence, the idea of virtue in Montesquieu cannot be strictly interpreted. "What this great man wished to say was that a republic cannot subsist through the action of the society upon itself. What he means by virtue is the moral power exerted by each individual upon himself and that prevents him from violating the rights of others." Following this strong nuancing of the concept of political virtue, Tocqueville continues:

> when the triumph of man over temptation is due to the weakness of the temptation or to the calculation of personal interest, then it does not constitute virtue in the eyes of the moralist, yet it is included in the idea of Montesquieu who was speaking of the effect of virtue far more than its cause.[14]

13. *Les étapes de la pensée sociologique* (Paris: Gallimard, 1967), 237.
14. *DA* [N], I, 243. But Eduardo Nolla points out how in another place Tocqueville seems to doubt whether it is possible for a historical society to be free without being virtuous (*idem*).

Political virtue is not autonomous, but rather an effect of a social system that results from the virtues of individuals, as it is said in a reference of Tocqueville's to North America. Here,

> it is not virtue that is great, it is temptation that is small, which is the same. It is not disinterest which is great, but interest which is well assessed, which is almost the same again. Therefore, Montesquieu was correct although he spoke of ancient virtue, and what he said about the Greeks of the Romans still applies to the Americans.

However, virtue is a very different concept in the United States; the history of the Greeks and the Romans is simply inadequate to it.[15] However, from the ancient tradition he preserves, over and against the Enlightenment and its posterity (Rousseau, Comte, Marx,...), the idea that the individual, not society or the "system," is entirely responsible for his acts.

Tocqueville had three good reasons for abandoning virtue as the main political specificity in a traditional democracy.

Morphology put into question all of Montesquieu's doctrine. For Montesquieu the form of a republic, although he also discusses other political forms, is only possible in nations of small dimensions, like the cities of antiquity, or in modern times, Venice, etc. He would have been surprised to see democracy in a country as large as North America. This new fact was destined to overthrow many of the accepted ideas of the political tradition.

First of all, the principle could not operate in the same way in a country that was more extensive and had a much more significant population than the small republics—where only some were citizens—in which one could speak of "face to face" relations. This could only work in small, local communities but not for the nation as a whole.

The second reason consisted in the direct perception of what democracy in the United States was—neither frugal, nor belligerent, as were the ancient democracies in which equality depended on the absence of business relations. On the contrary, in modern democracy as Tocqueville sees it across the Atlantic, commerce and industry not only do not interfere with equality but *social mobility* itself guarantees it:

---

15. "When I compare the Greek and Roman republics to these American republics, the manuscript libraries of the former and their vulgar populace, to the thousand magazines that criss-cross the latter and the enlightened people that inhabit its republics; when finally I think of all of the effort that is spent judging the ones with the help of the others and predicting, by way of what happened two thousand years ago, what will happen in our days, I am tempted to burn all of my books in order to apply only new ideas to a social order that is new." *DA* [N], I, 235.

> Among a democratic people new families are always arising out of nothingness, others are always falling into it, and all those families that remain change face; time leaves nothing unchanged, and the vestiges of generations are erased. One easily forgets those who preceded one, and one has no idea as to those who will follow. Only those who are close are of interest to us.[16]

The third reason for contesting virtue as the direct source of political action is the perception of the equality of conditions as a presupposition for democracy: "the century of blind devotions and instinctive virtues already escapes us, and I see approaching a time in which freedom, public peace and social order even, will not be able to do without enlightenment."[17] Thus the enlightenment is the democratic counterpoint to virtues such as fidelity and loyalty on which political obedience depended in other eras—although they operate in every regime, according to David Hume. However, for Tocqueville, since authority can be questioned in democracies, opinion is forced to justify itself and almost nothing stable unifies men. Apparently, there remains no other form of legitimacy save Weberian rationality in relation to ends (*zweckrational*) or in relation to a value (*wertrational*) as a principle of cohesion for social action. In any case, Tocqueville is very far from Weber in the theodicy of values; he is also very far from the Enlightenment.[18] *Equality of conditions* is for Tocqueville the *principle of democracy*.[19]

For these three reasons, Tocqueville could neither follow his alleged mentor in determining the type of political virtue that corresponds to the social democratic state, nor could he even accept the idea of political virtue. "We need a new political science for a world so completely new."

Demystification of the Classical Tradition

The tradition, according to the literary examples of antiquity—exaggerated by the French Revolution—sees political virtue as the *conditio sine qua non* of free or republican regimes. The majority of liberal political thinkers, without rejecting the classical tradition are still very critical of it.[20] Benjamin

---

16. *DA* [N], II, 98.
17. *DA* [N], II, 115.
18. "I am even further from thinking, as a good number of people in Europe do, that it would suffice to teach men to read and to write in order to make citizens of them outright. True enlightenment begins with experience for the most part." *Ibid.*, I, 236.
19. Díez del Corral, *El pensamiento político de Tocqueville*, 57.
20. See Luis Díez del Corral, *La desmitificación de la antigüedad clásica por los pensadores liberales, con especial referencia a Tocqueville* (Madrid: Fundación Pastor, 1969).

Constant's famous comparison of ancient freedom to modern freedom is one
of the best known examples.

With due courtesy to Montesquieu, Tocqueville does away with political
virtue as a particular type of virtue. He dismantles it:

> I doubt that men were more virtuous in aristocratic centuries than in other cen-
> turies, but it is certain that they spoke incessantly about the beauty of virtue; only
> in secret did they let it be understood in which way it was useful.

When they discovered an instance in which "an individual interest encountered the general interest and came together with it, they hastened to bring it
to light." There are no "political" virtues. In the last analysis, political
virtues are what one calls the coincidence between individual and common
interest: "in the United States, one almost never says that virtue is glorious.
One maintains that it is useful, and this is proved every day." The American
moralists:

> do not claim that one needs to sacrifice oneself to one's fellow-men, because it is
> noble to do so; but they say boldly that such sacrifices are as necessary to him
> who imposes them on himself as to him who profits by them.[21]

The foundation of the democratic version of the so-called political virtue is
thus, as Aron suggested, personal interest that:

> does not produce great devotion, but suggests small sacrifices every day; by itself
> it could not make a man virtuous, but it forms a multitude of well-ordered citizens
> who are temperate, restrained, provident, masters of themselves. And if it does not
> lead directly unto virtue through will, it nevertheless draws it closer imperceptibly
> through habituation.[22]

The assessment of one's interest encourages a certain behavior, the effect of
which is a kind of public virtue; but a public space is not exclusively a political one. Human action is directly social and only indirectly political.[23] And
virtue belongs to the social space. For Tocqueville, virtue, as habit, according to the Aristotelian tradition of middle grounds, is consubstantial with the
social democratic state. Combined with modern conditions of enlightenment,
and understood in this particular sense, private virtue is at the origin of virtue
said to be political.

The essential becomes the coincidence of individual interest, ruled by
private virtue, with the general interest. The results are the public customs

21. *DA* [N], II, 114.
22. *Ibid.* 115.
23. On the social and unpolitical nature of the public, see Julien Freund, *L'essence du
     politique* (Paris: Sirey, 1965).

that shape the particular *ethos* of political society. The question of political, democratic morality thus consists in controlling the type of individualism that arises from independence, through habituation.[24]

Individualism is recent—"our thoughts know only egoism."[25] Its origir. is democratic:

> a feeling reflected upon and peaceful that inclines every citizen to isolate himself from the mass of his fellow-creatures and to withdraw with his family and friends in such a way that, after having thus created a little society to his purposes, he voluntarily abandons the larger society to itself.[26]

The following passage contains the essential of Tocqueville's thought on the subject of virtue:

> Egoism desiccates the germ of all virtues; at first individualism only dries up the source of public virtues, but, in the end, it attacks and destroys all of the others and finally it becomes absorbed in egoism.[27]

Egoism is consubstantial with human nature. Individualism is an historical product of social life. Given certain circumstances—in particular, materialism combined with egalitarian desire[28]—in a society that has become individualistic egoism and individualism coincide: egoism thus characterizes the entirety of social life, and social life becomes debased.[29]

However, democratic individualism is the consequence of independence: "the equality that makes men independent of each other gives them a taste for and causes them to grow accustomed to the pursuit of their own desires in their individual actions."[30] In part, it is true that

> this complete independence which they enjoy continually vis-à-vis their equals and in the expression of their private lives inclines them to look discontentedly upon all authority and soon suggests to them the idea and the love for political freedom.[31]

24. On the two types of individualism, see Friedrich A. Hayek, *Individualism and Economic Order* (London: Routeledge and Kegan Paul, 1976), "Individualism: True and False," 1-32.
25. *DA* [N], I, 97.
26. *Idem.*
27. *Idem.*
28. Helmut Schoeck, *Der Neid. Eine Theorie der Gesellschaft* (Freiburg and Munich: Karl Alber, 1966), and Gonzalo Fernández de la Mora, *La envidia igualitaria* (Barcelona: Planeta, 1984).
29. On the degeneration of democracy and the corruption stemming from its moral sentiments when they are regarded as sacred, see Stan M. Popescu, *Autopsia de la democracia. Un estudio de la anti-religión* (Buenos Aires: Euthymia, 1984).
30. *DA* [N], II, 239.
31. *Idem.*

However, democracy does not only cause man to abandon his ancestors, but, according to Tocqueville, it "always brings him back to himself and threatens finally to enclose him entirely within the solitude of his own desire."[32] The problem is thus that independent men in democratic societies, withdrawn into themselves, "develop a presumptuous confidence in their powers and cannot imagine that they might ever have to ask their fellow-man for anything; they have no trouble in showing that they are only thinking of themselves."[33] The most perilous consequence of this Kantian *Mündigkeit* in conjunction with egoism is that the newcomers to democracy, without the experience of freedom, will be content with being independent.[34]

Once they are equal in their conditions, democratic citizens "do not owe anyone anything. They do not expect anything from anyone, and they are accustomed to considering themselves in isolation. They readily figure that their entire destiny is in their own hands."[35] Preoccupied only with themselves, they give in to the enjoyment of material things little by little, without noticing the change in themselves: in confusing independence with freedom they make their way toward servitude.

Independence is the condition of individual freedom, but freedom without virtue can come to oppose itself in passing for the latter while remaining an individualism without freedom. Thus, *public* virtue, if we can call it this, is, in dialectical terms only the necessary intermediary in a liberal society between independence and freedom: virtue is not "political."

When democracy is on the way to despotism, the latter encourages independence, for its vices are "precisely those which equality furthers."[36] It finds "good citizens [in] those who withdraw completely into themselves," and turns "an indifference into a kind of public virtue."[37] Indifference toward general affairs, following an independence without virtue is the characteristic of despotism, not of freedom. Freedom "creates individual hatreds," while "despotism creates general indifference,"[38] remarks Tocqueville. Thus

32. *DA* [N], II, 98.
33. *Idem.*
34. *DA* [N], I, 224, Tocqueville explains that because Catholicism encourages equality, it is more favorable to liberal democracy than Protestantism, which encourages independence.
35. In commenting on Hayek, François Bourricaud writes: "'true' individualism can be distinguished from false individualism in that, unlike the latter, it nourishes neither angelic nor Promethean ambition. It believes neither in the omnipotence of will, nor in the omnipotence of reason." *Le retour de la droite* (Paris: Calmann-Lévy, 1986), 250. This is, in the end, the distinction between an *amor sui* and an *amor Dei.*
36. *DA* [N], II, 100.
37. *Idem.*
38. *Idem.*

there is always the danger that the democratic individual—even in the spirit of well-being—might become complacent in the narcissism of independence and disinterested in freedom,[39] that he might lose the feeling of his responsibility and reject virtue, the condition of free, social life which seeks the common good indirectly.[40]

The Tocquevillian aporia consists then in fighting the tendency of the spirit of independence from withdrawing into itself, while at the same time bringing together the democratic taste for well-being with the enjoyment of material goods. This is also the problem of materialism in democracy.

With independence and egoism, democratic materialism is an enemy to the common good and the surest way to despotism and to the servitude of the spirit. Materialism, spurred by the passion for equality not yet moderated by virtue, carries with it political corruption and the decadence of freedom. Even if one does not find a concrete doctrine of public virtue in *Democracy in America*, the corruption that results from its absence is the cause of a specifically democratic tyranny. In democracies, according to Tocqueville, politicians are poor and have to make their fortunes.[41] Yet one knows that corruption is not inherent to democracy. In any regime, it is the result of a lack of virtue.

Tocqueville thus explains the corruption specific to democracies. Egalitarianism reduced to independence can give rise to opposed tendencies:

> The first leads men directly to independence, and can push them suddenly all the way to anarchy; the second leads them, on a longer and more secret yet more certain route to servitude.[42]

In truth, corruption can be circumstantial in a democracy just as in any other regime. But in democratic societies, if the materialist tendency wins out, it can become structural and the state of the spirit is without freedom, merely

39. See Gilles Lipovetsky, *L'ère du vide. Essais sur l'individualisme contemporain* (Paris: Gallimard, 1983).
40. Michael Novak has recently opposed the "Common good as Practical Intelligence" in Tocqueville's sense, whom he quotes explicitly, to the "Common Good of the Tribe": "the particular philosophy of man embodied in the U.S. Constitution, for example, is not devoid of practical effect. The U.S. Constitution would work neither for angels nor for the morally unscrupulous. Its very design presupposes citizens committed to the virtues that nourish reflection and choice; citizens who are not saints, but quite capable of self-government." *Free Persons and the Common Good* (New York and London: Madison Books, 1989), 76.
41. "In aristocratic States, governments are less susceptible to corruption and have only a moderate desire for money, whereas the contrary is true in democratic peoples. Where the men who lead aristocracies seek to become corrupt, the leaders of democracies reveal themselves to be corrupt." *DA* [N], I, 172.
42. *DA* [N], II, 239.

content with enjoyment: whence anarchy or servitude, but also the anarchic servitude which characterizes all too often modern societies.

These societies appear to be anarchical. But there are reasons—in accordance with the analysis of Tocqueville—to suspect that a certain anarchy in customs and habits, even in vices, is the alibi of a new despotism that passes off servitude as independence. In the name of total liberation or complete independence used as a political weapon, the centralized state power degrades mores; it compensates the diminishing economic, social, religious and even political freedoms essential to the free person with certain forms of independence. Thus only the appearance of political freedom remains:

> Men who live in centuries of equality naturally like the central power and willingly extend its privileges; but when it happens that this same power faithfully represents their interests and reproduces their own instincts then the confidence which these men lend it is almost without boundary, and these men think that they grant themselves everything that they give it.[43]

For whoever controls the sentiment of well-being it is easy to pass from the *government by consent* to the *government by corruption*, proper to tyranny. The greatest risk to democracy is that the men dedicated to the "honest and legitimate search for well-being" come to lose the use of their most sublime faculties and in an attempt to make things better, degrade themselves. Finally materialism, which arises from egalitarian independence, "fits marvelously with the most familiar vice of the heart" of a democratic people.[44]

It is debatable whether many democratic societies are not, in fact, heading straight for servitude, straight for the type of "liberal" totalitarianism perceived by Tocqueville to emerge from the corruption at the heart of the government, a totalitarianism that tempts with the promise of equality and independence.[45] The *Welfare State*, in mixing independence and freedom, becomes more and more bureaucratically restrictive: it conditions opinion, individual and social freedoms in substantive spaces.[46] At the same time it stimulates materialism, which destroys the structuring customs of

43. *DA* [N], II, 250.
44. *Ibid.*, 128-132.
45. See in particular Horst-Eberhard Richter, *Die hohe Kunst der Korruption. Erkenntnisse eines Politik-Beraters* (Hamburg: Hoffmann und Campe, 1989), and Guy Hermet, *Le peuple contre la démocratie* (Paris: Fayard, 1989).
46. Robert Nisbet has lodged a complaint in his book *The Present Age. Progress and Anarchy in Modern America* (New York: Harper and Row, 1989) against "the Leviathan-like presence of the national government in the affairs of states, towns, and cities, and the lives, cradle to grave, of individuals," in the United States.

freedom—including political obedience—and replaces them surreptitiously with customs of servitude. In 1913 Hilaire Belloc announced that one was moving to *The Servile State*.[47] In spite of the two world wars, *perestroika*, etc., it is not certain that the process is finished. On the contrary. For example, as Montesquieu said "a poll tax is more natural to servitude, a tax on merchandise is more natural to freedom, because its relation to the person is less direct."[48]

Jakob Burckhardt, a reader of Tocqueville, saw taxes on revenue as the surest sign of impending tyranny. However, in the name of equality and social justice, one makes of poll taxes—the tax of servitude—a more subtle means than a policy of regulating the masses from a center. Today this is the key fiscal reality said to be democratic. Through the ministry of finance, governments can control everything in good and fine form. Without appealing directly to force against all at once, they transform and make immaterial the physical violence of classical tyrannies by adapting the principle of *divide* and *impera* which operates against all citizens one by one. Nevertheless, no one contests the political perils and the moral effects of poll taxes.

Today there is a greater political freedom centered around the citizen, but this freedom is an illusion for as long as the individual and social freedoms that belong to a free man, and without which freedom becomes irrelevant, diminish. There is a deceptive tendency to oppose the citizen to the free man.[49] One should remember in this context a classical example: in the year 212, Caracalla accorded the right of citizenship to all of the inhabitants of the Empire in exchange for a poll tax, that is in exchange for freedom. But it must be noted that, before this event, the citizens did not cultivate virtue. Virtue spurs the intellect and protects the individual against the deceptive tactics of despotism and pushes the will to confront tyranny.

Institutional Remedies

In a democracy it is difficult to make the classical distinction, revealed by Aristotle, between the good man and the good citizen. Today freedom does

47. *The Servile State* (Indianapolis: Liberty Classics, 1977). Introduction by Robert Nisbet.
48. *L'esprit des lois*, bk. XIII, ch. XIV.
49. "Montesquieu, it seems to me"—writes Raymond Aron—"is perfectly correct in maintaining the radical distinction between the power of the people and the freedom of its citizens. It may happen that with a sovereign people, the safety of its citizens and the moderation in the exercise of power disappear."

not only affect free men who, in addition to being free, are also citizens as in antiquity: today the quality of being a citizen belongs to all men. This is why such a distinction also suggested by a double morality is impossible in a modern democracy.

Tocqueville noted that "with freedom the Americans fought individualism that equality gave rise to, and they defeated it."[50] This is to say: in a social democratic state, "public" virtue is neither a device nor an individual quality that makes the institutional system work. On the contrary, it must be the result of prior individual and social freedoms, of private virtues.

Tocqueville knows how difficult it is to interest a man in "the destiny of the entire State, because he does not understand how the destiny of the State can influence his condition." Tocqueville proposes remedies concerning political and social institutions in the hope of encouraging the custom of public virtue and freedom. In the end, freedom can lead to the common good both indirectly by means of individual and social freedoms, and directly by means of political freedoms.

In modern democracy, the representative regime is, in general, the ideal way.[51] As the problem is always the independence of the individual, Tocqueville thinks that "every man perceives that he is not as independent from his fellow fellow man as he previously thought, and that in order to rally their support he often must lend his support." In respect to the government, the principle means consists in not being contented with

> giving to the nation as a whole a representation of itself; they [the Americans] also thought to give a political life to each portion of the territory in order to multiply indefinitely the opportunities of the citizens of working together, and to make them feel that they depend upon each other every day.[52]

Local freedoms, in particular, bring men together in spite of the instincts that pull them apart by forcing them to help one another.[53] It is

> by charging the citizens with the administration of small affairs much more than by giving them the government of large ones, that one interests them in the public

---

50. *DA* [N], II, 101.
51. "I am firmly convinced that the fate of modern nations depends on its solution. But how few people even perceive this and in perceiving it how few point it out!" Letter to Stuart Mill, October 3, 1835. Mill (December 11, 1835) answers: "As you do, I consider the distinction between delegation and representation as crucial." *Correspondance anglaise*, *OC*, VI:1, 303-305.
52. *DA* [N], II, 101.
53. "Without communal institutions a nation can give itself a free government, but it does not have the spirit of freedom." *DA* [N], I, 50.

good, and that one makes them see the need they have for each other in order to bring it about.[54]

This is an example, the practical effect of which is individual political freedom, not as a mechanical or artificial device, but rather as the result of habituation proper to "public" virtue. Such is, without a doubt, the meaning of Tocqueville's famous formula: "to fight the evils that equality produces, there is only one effective remedy: and that is political freedom."

The same pedagogical lesson must extend to the strictly civilian space. Here Tocqueville emphasizes the extreme importance of associations: "in democratic countries, the science of association is the mother science; the progress of all other sciences depends upon the progress of this one."[55] This presupposes that the state is scaled-down and that its limits are well defined, that the government is exclusively political and not administrative as in Europe, which Tocqueville always compares to North America saying: "the political associations that exist in the United States represent but a small detail in the center of the immense picture that the whole of associations represent."[56] Association is necessary when all of the citizens in a democratic state are both independent and weak. Tocqueville describes the scene to draw out the contrast:

> Americans of all ages, in every condition, of all minds are always uniting themselves.... At the head of a new enterprise, where in France you would see the government and in England a powerful lord, be assured that you will see an association in the United States.

In Europe, on the other hand, the tradition of centralization—the institutional counterpoint to the freedom that arises from self-government—has firmly introduced the belief that "as citizens become weaker and more incompetent, one must make the government more cunning and more active, in order that society be able to execute that which individuals cannot."[57]

Tocqueville thought association so important as a means of forming public virtue that he saw in it the law—"more precise and more clear"—of human societies, because "for men to remain or to become civilized the act of association must be developed and perfected between them as the equality of conditions increases."[58]

In reaction to the confusion between independence and freedom where the vices of democracy originate, Tocqueville proposes to encourage the

54. *Ibid.*, 100.
55. *Ibid.*, 106.
56. *Ibid.*, 103.
57. *Ibid.*, 105.
58. *DA* [N], II, 106.

science of public habituation through a greater social and political freedom. To this greater freedom belongs, according to tradition, the virtue of value, the civilian version of force. However, the most characteristic customs of the social democratic state correspond to the virtue of temperance *(temperentia)*, in the sense of *temperare*, to make a harmonious whole out of a series of disparate elements. Temperance, as a private individual virtue, balances the interests of all and the public space by allowing democratic societies where there is not, by definition, great vice nor great virtue, to be moderate. This coincides, not without a certain paradox, with the kind of virtue that Montesquieu attributed to aristocrats. By nature, temperance is the most social of all virtues, and it accords with the tradition of middle grounds. It moderates individualism and teaches the individual "measure" and "education," manners and forms that allow him to coexist with others.

The Problem of Order

The background of Tocquevillian "public" virtue is "private" virtue or the ethical mores on which "public" virtue rests. Tocqueville reasons against the tendencies of the Enlightenment and against his century and in accordance with the tradition of a limited government; he thinks that the public realm is derived from the private realm and common interest from personal interest, and that, consequently, public virtue is simply the extension or the effect of the private virtue of temperance.

As a liberal political regime, democracy corresponds to a society in which mores, social and religious customs, the *ethos*, are well established, and rules of conduct are fixed.[59] In comparison with France, his European model where "public virtue has become uncertain, and private morality wavers,"[60] Tocqueville asserts that Americans show, in practice, that it is necessary "to make democracy moral through religion: thus what they think about themselves is a truth which must affect the notion of democracy."[61] In the final analysis, mores, to which Tocqueville dedicates several chapters, depend on religion which is an essential component of democracy where all becomes uncertain.

---

59. "Despotism can do without faith, but freedom cannot. Religion is far more necessary in a republic... than in a monarchy... and in democratic republics most of all." *DA* [N], I, 229. See Popescu, *Autopsia de la democracia*, who is very inspired by Tocqueville, on the anti-religious turn proper to democracy.
60. *DA* [N], II, 177.
61. *Ibid.*, 129.

By nature religion always gives a firm direction to individual will,[62] that is, to customs and to the interest well understood that is proper to democracy. For Tocqueville also believes that "interest is the principal means used by religions themselves to lead men, and I have no doubt that it is through this aspect that they attract the masses and become popular."[63] Yet, at the same time, Tocqueville does not think "that the only incentive of the religious man is interest." In fact, says Tocqueville, "I refuse to believe that all who practice virtue in the spirit of religion act only with a reward in mind."[64] He rejects the polemical idea according to which the doctrine of interest "moves men away from religious beliefs." On the contrary, he believes that such a doctrine brings them together. He rejects the ideological conception of religion—before its time—as the opium of the people.[65]

Like Comte, Tocqueville understands that the fundamental problem is always the existence of solid social beliefs and consequently, of the idea of order: "without communal ideas, there is no communal action, and without communal action, man still exists, but the social body does not."[66] Using Carl Schmitt's typology of orders,[67] one can say that Tocqueville excludes, by definition, the decisionist order that corresponds to despotism. Furthermore, the normative order is no better. Not only because beliefs and customs are more important, and mores more important than laws, but because, in the end, a normative order is a sort of Procrustes bed: by means of laws, the spirit of well-being, left to itself, can push democracy toward tyranny, as it happens when mores, the direct source of virtue, diminish.

---

62. Aside from the freely given support of citizens "in the world there is only patriotism or religion that can make the universality of citizens move toward a common goal for an extended period of time." *DA* [N], I, 77.
63. *DA* [N], II, 117.
64. *Idem.*
65. "It may help a man as an individual to know that his religion is true, but such is not the case for society. Society has nothing to fear nor to gain from the other life, and what matters most for society is not that all citizens profess the true religion, but that they profess a religion." *DA* [N], I, 226.
66. *DA* [N], II, 20.
67. *Über die drei Arten des rechtswissenschaftlichen Denkens* (Hamburg: Hanseatische Verlagsanstalt, 1934). "The type of juridical thought that predominates in a concrete time and in a concrete people is of the utmost importance... the spiritual and political domination over a people may have to do with the predominance of a determinate type of thought," 9. As Eric Voegelin says in the preface of his great work *Order and History*, "every society is burdened with the task, under its concrete conditions of creating an order that will endow the fact of its existence with meaning in terms of ends divine and human." As it is not possible to live in a vacuum, ideology often replaces the idea of order in contemporary regimes by regarding democracy as sacred. The fact is that there are always at least visions of reality... but the problem of order remains.

Tyranny can be exercised by the law itself, and, when this happens it is no longer arbitrary, as Tocqueville says in the first part of the *Democracy*.[68] In truth, the totalitarianism or the pseudo-liberal collectivism of our times is absolutely legal.[69]

Only the belief in a fundamental order, natural or transcendent, of a non-human origin—to which concrete orders appeal for their authority—can consolidate opinion, create an insurmountable barrier around itself and give concrete meaning to the category of causality. This conception of order, *a priori* so to speak, is essential in making human action independent from the spirit of abstraction that predominates in democracy[70] and from opinion. Religious faith can moderate the faith in opinion which is the characteristic of democracy[71] by introducing skepticism. Skepticism is necessary to counterbalance democracy's tendency toward a dogmatism about human affairs and to oppose the tyranny of opinion. It encloses behavior within a circle and determines practical thought. Thus the idea of right depends on the idea of order.[72]

However, all religion and only religion presupposes by definition an order that is inaccessible to human decision making and, consequently, asserts Tocqueville "I am inclined to think that if man has no faith he must serve, and if he is free, he believes."[73] About Christianity, to which he attributes the irresistible tendency toward democracy, Tocqueville explains that religion "tells us that one must do good for one's fellow man for the love of God." Thanks to religion,

68. *DA* [N], I, 198.
69. See in particular Bruno Leoni, *Freedom and the Law* (Los Angeles, Cal.: New Publishing, 1961) and the works of Hayek.
70. "Let us recognize that equality has to do with the abstract. It is not men who are equal, for men are neither triangles nor quadrilaterals. Those things that must be posited as equal are not beings at all but rights and duties that these beings must respect in regard to each other without which there is chaos, there is tyranny with all of its horrible consequences—the power of the most base over the most noble," says Gabriel Marcel, *Les hommes contre l'humain* (Paris: Fayard, 1968), 119-120. See also José Ortega y Gasset, in particular, *La rebelión de las masas*.
71. See *DA* [N], II, 23-24, Nolla's footnote.
72. Hans Barth reminds us that "the problem of consensus and loyalty, the problem of sanctions in the most general sense of the term and the problem of ranks [*Instanzen*] and their hierarchy belong to a theory of the formations of communities and societies [*der gemeinschaftliche und gesellschaftliche Gebilde*]." *Die Idee der Ordnung* (Erlenbach and Zurich: Eugen Rentsch Verlag, 1958), 7. Even "individualism is ambiguous for as long as relations between individuals, the law and nature are not specified," writes François Bourricaud about Hayek and Tocqueville.
73. *DA* [N], II, 34. "The man who does not believe in anything, the man who holds to nothing: this is, to the letter, the man without ties. But this man cannot exist. An existence without ties is not thinkable, it is impossible." Marcel, *op. cit.*, 51. Perhaps nihilism is the spirit of a democracy without virtue.

man enters into divine thought with his intelligence; he sees that the goal of God is *order* [my emphasis]; he associates himself freely with this great design, and when he sacrifices his personal interests to the admirable order of all things, he expects no other reward than the pleasure of contemplating it.[74]

To support his thesis, he refers to Pascal's utilitarian *wager* which constitutes the *leitmotif* through which he establishes a link between democratic interest and Christianity.[75]

Whether democracy leads to servitude or to freedom and resistance to tyranny depends, according to Tocqueville, on whether virtue prevails—this being the condition of any free regime.

But he does not believe that a secular morality—the alleged public morality—can regulate conduct:

There is almost no human action, however unique one might suppose it to be, that does not originate in a very general idea that men have conceived of God, of his relations to the human race, of the nature of their souls and of their duties regarding their fellow creatures. It could not be that these ideas are not the common source from which the rest flow.[76]

For Tocqueville there are no "public" virtues in a democratic social state that are independent from private virtues and from religion.[77] He advises against destabilizing "any given religion that has sprouted deep roots at the heart of a democracy."[78]

From the meditation of Tocqueville it follows that, in the long run, interest is insufficient to insure free government in a democracy. Virtue alone can counterbalance the resentment and the envy that unleashes the democratic passion for equality. Only virtue can make the right of inequality that emerges with freedom[79] compatible with the egalitarianism of democracy.

---

74. *DA* [N], II, 117. Tocqueville has also said (*DA* [N], I, 223): "Beside every religion is to be found a political opinion which is joined to it by affinity. Let the human spirit follow its tendency, and it will regulate political society and the divine city in a uniform manner; it will seek, if I can venture to say this, to harmonize the earth with the heavens."
    See Nolla's footnote (*idem*).
75. "To be mistaken in believing the Christian religion to be true, does not cause great harm, but what a misfortune it is to mistakenly think that it is false!" *DA* [N], II, 117.
    But compare this to the new text published by Eduardo Nolla in footnote "d" (*idem*).
76. *DA* [N], II, 33.
77. He points out in *DA* [N], I, 232, that one "of the two great dangers that threaten the existence of religions" is, precisely, "indifference." The other is schisms.
78. *DA*, [N], II, 130.
79. See Helmut Schoeck, *Das Recht auf Ungleichheit* 2nd. ed. (Munich and Berlin: Herbig, 1980).

This is to say that without virtue it is all but impossible to establish and to preserve the harmony that is indispensable—but also precarious because of human nature—between the principle of democracy and the universal principle of freedom.

(Translated by Elisabeth Rottenberg)

[5]

Tocqueville Reconsidered: Foreign Policy and the American Democracy

Herbert Dittgen

Up to the present day foreign observers are puzzled by the strange character of American foreign policy. The peculiar make-up of American foreign policy is caused by frequent changes in approach, the constrained authority of the president provided for by the constitutional separation of powers, the plurality of actors and the changing mood of the American people as to the proper role the United States should play in world affairs. Europeans searching for a theme usually find only a cacophony of voices.

Tocqueville's curiosity about American democracy includes also its foreign policy. He devotes an entire chapter of his *Democracy in America* to the conduct of foreign relations. Moreover, he was the first European observer to question the ability of the American democracy to conduct prudent and long-sighted foreign policy. That is surprising, since he made his observations at a time when geography and the configuration of international power still shielded the United States from the harsh foreign policy realities confronting most other countries. A standing army was unnecessary and, because of British naval power, a navy of the first order was not essential. The American republic still followed the maxim proclaimed by George Washington in his Farewell Address: to extend commercial relations with foreign nations, but with as little political connection as possible. In Tocqueville's own words: "The Union takes no part in the affairs of Europe, it has, properly speaking, no foreign interest to discuss."[1]

---

1.   *DA* [B], I, 242.

His remarks are even more surprising in light of the success of the few episodes when the young republic had to deal with the internal impact of foreign crises. Tocqueville praises the conduct of foreign affairs under George Washington and Thomas Jefferson.[2]

One of the lifesaving accomplishments of the first president was keeping the American republic out of British-French hostilities by issuing a proclamation of American neutrality. President Jefferson succeeded in keeping the United States out of the European hostilities sparked by Napoleon's rise. Though Tocqueville approvingly quotes their foreign policy maxims at length, he voices his doubts about the qualities of democratic foreign policy:

> Foreign politics demand scarcely any of those qualities which are peculiar to a democracy; they require, on the contrary, the perfect use of almost all those in which it is deficient.... A democracy can only with great difficulty regulate the details of an important undertaking, preserve in a fixed design, and work out its execution in spite of serious obstacles. It cannot combine its measures with secrecy or await their consequences with patience. These are qualities which more especially belong to an individual or an aristocracy; and they are precisely the qualities by which a nation, like an individual, attains a dominant position.[3]

In the following pages I will discuss Tocqueville's aristocratic and European view of foreign policy, particularly regarding the compatibility of democracy with foreign affairs. I will distinguish two possible reasons for Tocqueville's skepticism: first, the special constitutional provisions for the conduct of American foreign policy; second, the suitability of the democratic instinct of American society for the conduct of foreign affairs. I will then discuss the influence of the "reflecting patriotism," as Tocqueville called it, on American foreign policy.

Separation of Powers and Foreign Relations

Tocqueville's intimate knowledge of modern political writings is well known. It can be assumed that he was familiar with the reflections of Locke, Montesquieu and Rousseau on the executive character in the conduct of foreign relations. The classical doctrine of the separation of powers considers the conduct of relations with other nations as a prerogative of the executive. John Locke was the first to write in detail on the power to transact with foreign countries. He speaks of a federative power concerning intercourse with

2.   *Ibid.*, 241-242.
3.   *Ibid.*, 243-244.

other nations, distinct from the legislative and executive power. To him the executive and federative power are only distinct in substance; usually their execution occurs through the same person:

> It is almost impracticable to place the Force of the Commonwealth in distinct, and not subordinate hands; or that the Executive and Federative Power should be placed in Persons, that might act separately, whereby the Force of the Publick would be under different Commands: which would be apt sometime or other to cause disorder and ruin.[4]

Montesquieu saw the conduct of foreign relations, including war and treaty powers, as entirely executive. By virtue of executive power (*puissance exécutrice*), he writes, the prince or magistrate makes peace or war, sends or receives ambassadors, establishes the public security, and guards against invasions.[5]

Jean-Jacques Rousseau, who established the doctrine of popular sovereignty, also distinguishes between internal laws and external affairs. What matters principally to every citizen, he writes in the *Lettres écrites de la Montagne*, is the internal observance of the law, the maintenance of private property, and the security of the individual. When all goes well regarding these three points, the government may negotiate and make treaties with foreign powers. These actions do not pose dangers to the republic. The formation of alliances, peace treaties and the declaration of war are not acts of sovereignty (*actes de souveraineté*), but acts of the government (*actes de gouvernement*); the execution of state power in foreign affairs is not placed in the people. The people have no taste for the grand maxims of statesmanship, adds Rousseau, and they can trust the rule of government, which will have no inclination to conclude treaties harmful to the interest of the fatherland.[6]

Tocqueville shares the opinion that "in foreign politics it is rare for the interest of the aristocracy to be distinct from that of the people".[7] As we will see later he also considers the people unable to comprehend the maxims for

---

4. John Locke, *Two Treatises of Government*, Peter Laslett ed. (Cambridge: Cambridge University Press 1967), bk. II, §§ 148, 384.
5. Montesquieu, *De l'Esprit des Lois*, (Paris: Garnier, 1949), I, 13-14.
6. Jean-Jacques Rousseau, *Lettres écrites de la Montagne*, in *The Political Writings of Jean Jacques Rousseau*, C. E. Vaughan ed. (Cambridge: Cambridge University Press, 1915), II, 220. In his *Contrat social* he writes: "On a regardé l'acte de déclarer la guerre et celui de faire la paix comme des actes de souveraineté: ce qui n'est pas; puisque chacun de ces actes n'est point une loi, mais seulement une application de la loi, un acte particulier qui détermine le cas de la loi, comme on le verra clairement quand l'idée attachée au mot *loi* sera fixée." *Contrat social*, (bk. II, ch. II), *ibid.*, 41.
7. *DA* [B], I, 136.

the conduct of foreign affairs. He considers a strong executive to be a pre-requisite for the intercourse with other countries. "However the functions of the executive power may be restricted, it must always exercise a great influence upon the foreign policy of the country."[8]

Tocqueville, however, does not appreciate the fact that the American Constitution denies the executive the prerogative in the conduct of foreign relations, as formulated by Locke and Montesquieu.[9] The founding fathers were profoundly suspicious of the executive power, not least due to their colonial experience. Their fear for excessive power and abuse of power extended to the authority for the conduct of foreign relations. This difference from European constitutional thought is best expressed in the *Federalist Papers* by Alexander Hamilton:

> The history of human conduct does not warrant that exalted opinion of human virtue which would make it wise in a nation to commit interest of so delicate and momentous a kind, as those which concern its intercourse with the rest of the world, to the sole disposal of a magistrate created and circumstanced as would be a president of the United States.[10]

Hamilton calls the American Constitution a "novel and absurd experiment in politics of tying up the hands of government from offensive war founded upon reasons of state," without losing the capacity to guard against the ambitions or enmity of other countries.[11] The power to declare war was therefore assigned to Congress. The founding fathers intended to form a strong national government, but one with a strong system of accountability.[12] The president was to be commander in chief and manage diplomatic intercourse and negotiations. Congress, especially the Senate, would be able to approve or reject foreign policy, exercising its power over treaties, appointments and appropriations.[13] The reliance on overlapping and shared foreign policy powers in the Constitution was in fact an "invitation to struggle for the privilege of directing American foreign policy."[14]

Tocqueville's observations on presidential power differ from those stated above; he sees that "the President of the United States possesses almost royal

---

8. *Ibid.*, 136.
9. See *DA* [B], I, 124-127.
10. *The Federalist Papers*, C. Rossiter ed. (New York: New American Library, 1961), no. 75; 451.
11. *Ibid.*, 208.
12. Arthur M. Schlesinger, Jr., *The Cycles of American History* (Boston: Houghton Mifflin, 1986), 330.
13. Abraham D. Sofaer, *War, Foreign Affairs and Constitutional Power: The Origins* (Cambridge, Mass.: Ballinger, 1976), 56.
14. Edward S. Corwin, *The President. Office and Powers, 1787-1984* (New York and London: New York University Press, 1984), 201.

prerogatives which he has no opportunity of exercising."[15] Only the fortunate circumstances of having no enemies, and therefore having only a small army and navy, would keep the presidency weak. He argues that "the practical operations of the government must not be judged by the theory of its Constitution."[16] The powers of the president are defined in the Constitution, but their actual potentials are molded by external challenges:

> It is chiefly in its foreign relations that the executive power of a nation finds occasion to exert its skill and its strength. If the existence of the Union were perpetually threatened, if its chief interest were in daily connection with those of other powerful nations, the executive government would assume an increased importance in proportion to the measures expected of it and to those which it would execute.[17]

External threat and the conduct of war have proved to be the main factors for the enormous aggrandizement of presidential power in our century. Presidential power has been nourished primarily by war, which eventually led to what Arthur M. Schlesinger termed the "imperial presidency."[18]

The balance between the president and Congress in the conduct of foreign affairs is the dominant issue of current constitutional and political debate.[19] In the early years of the republic, Congress followed the lead of the president in most cases.

In examining the conduct of foreign relations, Tocqueville's main attention thus focused upon the predominant authority of public opinion.[20] Since it is essential for the government of a republic to be responsible for its actions to the people, "the political maxims of the country," writes Tocqueville, "depend on the mass of the people, not on the President alone."[21] Representative government should comply with the "permanent determination" of the majority but at the same time have sufficient authority to resist popular "caprices and refuse its most dangerous demands." The danger of preponderant public opinion is, in Tocqueville's view, reinforced by the provision of presidential re-eligibility, by which the president would become an easy tool in the hand of the majority. "He adopts its likings and its animosities, he anticipates its wishes, he forestalls its complaints, he

---

15. *DA* [B], I, 131.
16. *Idem.*
17. *Ibid.*, 130.
18. Arthur M. Schlesinger, Jr., *The Imperial Presidency* (Boston: Houghton Mifflin, 1973).
19. Thomas E. Mann ed., *A Question of Balance: The President, the Congress, and Foreign Policy* (Washington, D.C.: The Brookings Institution, 1990).
20. *DA* [B], I, 129.
21. *Ibid.*, 135.

yields to its idlest cravings, and instead of guiding it, as the legislature intended that he should do, he merely follows its bidding."[22] Only a president like George Washington was able to resist this temptation and to provide the leadership necessary to protect the people from their own passions. These prospects are dim, muses Tocqueville with melancholy, at a time "when political morality is relaxed and when great men are rare."[23] This pessimistic observation reflects Tocqueville's witness of the first populist American president, Andrew Jackson, and the era of democratization.[24] Nevertheless, it shows Tocqueville's conviction that the fortune of the American republic depends, to a high degree, on the quality of presidential leadership.

The preceding examination of Tocqueville's statements on the American government shows that his skeptical view on the conduct of foreign affairs is not based on the provisions of the Constitution. On the contrary, he argues that the American president enjoys powerful foreign policy prerogatives, but has no opportunity to use them. Thus it is not the constitutional system of checks and balances, but the *habits, ideas* and *customs* of the democratic society which he considers to be an impediment to the conduct of foreign relations.

Conduct of Foreign Affairs in the American Democracy

The conduct of foreign affairs is the last aspect of Tocqueville's analysis of the defects and weaknesses of the American government. The real advantages which American society derives from a democratic government are dealt with in another chapter. Therefore the conduct of foreign relations from the outset is not counted under the peculiar qualities of the American democracy. Tocqueville's discussion of the weakness of American foreign policy is, as in most of his examination, executed with an eye to the European and in particular to the French situation.[25]

Tocqueville first considers the disadvantages of universal suffrage: "On my arrival in the United States I was surprised to find so much distinguished talent among the citizens and so little among the heads of the government. It is a constant fact that at the present day the ablest men in the United States

22. *DA* [B], I, 143.
23. *Ibid.*
24. See Arthur M. Schlesinger, Jr., *The Age of Jackson* (Boston: Little, Brown, 1945).
25. *DA* [B], I, 206 and Melvin Richter, "Comparative Political Analysis in Montesquieu and Tocqueville," *Comparative Politics*, 1 (January 1969), 129-160.

are rarely placed at the head of affairs."[26] Universal suffrage, he observed, by no means guarantees the wisdom of the popular choice. Superiority is irksome for people living under the conditions of equality, the main characteristic of a democratic society, thus these people do not like distinguished politicians.[27] Excellent men do not want to confront this democratic instinct by running for office, "in which it is so difficult to retain their independence, or to advance without becoming servile."[28] The inability of a democratic society to put the best at the helm of government is certainly unfavorable for the conduct of foreign relations, which requires a special sophistication and talent. Tocqueville attributes the election of such exceptionally qualified political leaders as George Washington and Thomas Jefferson to the high spirits caused by independence and the creation of the new republic.

> In this general excitement distinguished men were ready to anticipate the call of the community, and the people clung to them for support and placed them at their head. But such events are rare, and it is from the ordinary course of affairs that our judgement must be formed.[29]

Tocqueville sees a remedy for this natural defect of democracies in more indirect elections by elected bodies. He advocates direct democracy only for the local level, but indirect elections for the higher offices of government. Elections by bodies more independent of public emotions would secure the quality of officeholders.

The development of the American government went in the opposite direction. In the twentieth century, the American republic experienced a rapid democratization of government institutions. Of great significance was the direct election of the Senate. A Senate with members of high seniority elected for a long term was seen by the founding fathers to fulfill the need for "some institution that will blend stability with liberty."[30] A legislative body with "sufficient permanency" would serve "as a defense to the people against their own temporary errors and delusions."[31] Because of the senators' higher degree of independence, the Constitution assigned the more important foreign policy powers of Congress to them.

The Constitution provided for the election of senators by state legislators. But the 17th Amendment, ratified in 1913, changed the Constitution to pro-

26. *DA* [B], I, 207.
27. *Ibid.*, 208.
28. *Ibid.*, 209.
29. *Ibid.*, 210.
30. *The Federalist Papers*, no. 63; 385.
31. *Ibid.*, 384.

vide for direct election. The change was part of the Progressive Era's movement toward more democratic control of government.

According to Tocqueville, the frequent elections that characterize American democracy prevent revolutions and provide stability, but also prevent any steady and consistent policy. "Taste for variety is one of the characteristic passions of democracy. Hence their legislation is strangely mutable."[32]

There are two aspects to the impact of elections on foreign relations: First, the frequent change of administrations, including a high number of political appointees, and the related change in the conduct of policies, might cause calamities and confusion abroad. Second, the period of elections also causes a tie-up of the acting government.

> The period which immediately precedes an election, and that during which the election is taking place, must always be considered as a national crisis, which is perilous in proportion to the internal embarrassments and the external dangers of the country.[33]

The United States has frequently experienced such awkward repercussions in periods of presidential transition; change of government can even inflict disastrous consequences on relations with other countries, friends and foes alike.

What efforts is a democratic government capable of making in the event of a national crisis? Tocqueville answers this question with caution.

> We must wait until the American people are obliged to put half their entire income at the disposal of the government, as was done by the English; or to send forth a twentieth part of its population to the field of battle, as was done by France.[34]

Such sacrifices were fortunately never necessary, even during two world wars. Tocqueville expresses his doubts about the capacity of democracies for sacrifice and endurance. A democratic people, he says, is more apt to feel than to reason. Only with a clear perception of the future founded upon reason is a distinctive choice about priorities attainable. But this quality, Tocqueville remarks, is frequently wanting in democracies.[35]

The positive effect of democracy is the strengthening of the general potentials of a society. It will be richer, more populous, and more prosperous than a despotic state under the same geographic conditions. But the weak-

32. *DA* [B], I, 213.
33. *Ibid.*, 136.
34. *Ibid.*, 236.
35. *Ibid.*, 237.

ness of a democracy is, that "it can never combine, upon a single point and at a given time, so much power as an aristocracy or an absolute monarchy."[36]

Is therefore John Adams right in saying: "Democracies never last long"? Tocqueville has no definitive answer to that, but he suggests that the relative weakness of democratic republics in critical times would be a great obstacle to the foundation of such a republic in Europe. He assumes that on the belligerent European continent a republic confronted with centralized monarchies would not survive.

After the United States experienced the democratic surge of the 1960s and 1970s—comparable to the time of the Jacksonian democracy—similar concerns were voiced. In 1975 Samuel Huntington observed:

> The U.S. government has given up the authority to draft its citizens into the armed forces and is now committed to providing the monetary incentives to attract volunteers with a stationary or declining percentage of the Gross National Product.... The question necessarily arises, however, of whether in the future, if a new threat to security should materialize, as it inevitably will at some point, the government will possess the authority to command the resources and the sacrifices necessary to meet that threat.... If American citizens challenge the authority of American government, why shouldn't unfriendly governments?... A decline in the governability of democracy at home means a decline in the influence of democracy abroad.[37]

In his time Tocqueville could still assert that the institutions of the presidency and the Senate are "in some degree to detach the general foreign policy of the Union from the direct control of the people."[38] That is, of course, no longer true; there are not two distinctive presidencies, one for domestic politics that faces serious congressional and public opinion obstacles and another unrestrained in the conduct of foreign policy.[39] Since the early 1970s both domestic and foreign policy processes have become very much alike. This democratization of foreign policy arose from the context of the Vietnam War and the abuse of presidential power in the Watergate affair. Congress assumed an influential role and frequently opposed the foreign policy of the executive.

Since democratization has included the making of foreign policy, we have to face Tocqueville's question, whether the practical wisdom and good sense of a democratic society is apt to influence the course of foreign

36. *Ibid.*, 238.
37. Michael J. Crozier, Samuel P. Huntington and Joji Watanuki, *The Crisis of Democracy. Report on the Governability of Democracies to the Trilateral Commission* (New York: New York University Press, 1975), 105-106.
38. *DA* [B], I, 241.
39. The two presidencies thesis was established by Aaron Wildavsky in the 1960's: "The Two Presidencies," *Trans-Action*, 4 (December 1966), 7-14.

relations. Tocqueville himself has no doubt that the good sense of a democratic society "may suffice to direct the ordinary course of society"[40] but not always—Tocqueville argues here with great caution—in the relations with foreign nations.

Tocqueville is an aristocrat by birth and instinct, and therefore has a natural distaste for the intimate and petty concerns of people in a democratic society.[41] How can citizens in the democratic age, who have to care for their economic well-being and are acting in small circles, judge the affairs of the world? From his view, that capacity must be beyond them. For Tocqueville it seems to be impossible that a diplomacy in the national interest and of a fixed design requiring secrecy and patience could be democratically controlled.

That the character of American democracy does not fit European power politics and geopolitical designs is best illustrated by the fate of foreign policy in the Nixon/Kissinger Administration. In his memoirs Henry Kissinger quotes Bismarck: "A sentimental policy knows no reciprocity," adding: "For sovereign nations, predictability is more crucial than spasmodic brilliance or idiosyncratic moralistic rhetoric."[42] Nations, writes this foremost disciple of European cabinet politics and practitioner of *realpolitik*, can only cooperate on a "level of shared geopolitical interest transcending philosophies and history."[43] The problem of the foreign policy design of President Nixon and his security adviser was that the politics of manipulating the balance of powers, which worked well with authoritarian regimes like the Soviet Union and China, created a "credibility gap" at home. After the bombing of Cambodia, Kissinger critically comments on the domestic crisis: "Debate was engulfed in mass passion."[44] This observation confirms Tocqueville's claim that democracies are unable to adhere to a "fixed design" of foreign policy, and to execute it in spite of serious obstacles. "The Administration," Kissinger writes, "was confronting an implacable enemy and an equally implacable domestic opposition."[45] Kissinger never traces any connection between the public's lack of trust and the means and ends of the policy by the administration he represented. The public is not an element that figures in this foreign policy approach, but

40. *DA* [B], I, 243.
41. See Herbert Dittgen, *Politik zwischen Freiheit und Despotismus. Alexis de Tocqueville und Karl Marx* (Freiburg and Munich: Alber, 1986), 18-24.
42. Henry Kissinger, *White House Years* (Boston and Toronto: Little, Brown, 1979), 1089.
43. *Idem.*
44. *Ibid.*, 511.
45. *Ibid.*, 517.

rather an impediment to that policy. Barbara Tuchman has clearly espoused the republican spirit that opposes such a concept of foreign policy. "A nation's strength," she writes, "lies ultimately in its self-esteem and confidence in what is right; and that whatever damages these damages the nation."[46]

Tocqueville finds in democratization, the equality of condition, the principle that was inevitably to be the fate of modern society.[47] But are the customs and inclinations of a democracy compatible with the conduct of a foreign policy in the national interest? Tocqueville's skepticism in that respect was echoed after World War II by Walter Lippmann and George F. Kennan. Are the people, as Lippmann put it, a dangerous master of decisions when the stakes are life and death?[48] James Bryce, who was the second foreign visitor to write a masterpiece on the American democracy, grappling with the same problem, the compatibility of democracy and foreign policy, gives a compelling answer to that question:

> In a democracy the People are entitled to determine the Ends or general aims of foreign policy. History shows that they do this at least as wisely as monarchs or oligarchies, or the small groups to whom, in democratic countries, the conduct of foreign relations has been left, and that they have evinced more respect for moral principles.[49]

The responsibility for the conduct of foreign relations lies with the government and the president. The Constitution provides the presidency with the necessary authority and independence to execute an effective leadership in foreign affairs. It also provides the instruments to prevent a policy which finds no approval in the public. The public debate on foreign policy gives the idea of the national interest its content and its legitimacy.[50] Carl Joachim Friedrich wrote: "The people, an infant giant, have been forcing bad policies, they have prevented good ones—good or bad, that is not according to some abstract or ideal standard but according to the peoples."[51]

Regarding the question of war and peace, a fundamental principle of a republican Constitution is to get the *sanction* of the citizens for this decision. The justification for this principle given by Immanuel Kant in his *Perpetual Peace* is a still valid and worthwhile reminder:

46. Barbara Tuchman, *Practicing History* (New York: Alfred A. Knopf, 1981), 226.
47. See *DA* [B], II, 352.
48. Walter Lippmann, *Essays in the Public Philosophy* (Boston and Toronto: Little, Brown, 1955), 20.
49. James Bryce, *Modern Democracies* (New York: Macmillan, 1921), II, 383.
50. Schlesinger, *The Cycles of American History*, 79.
51. Carl Joachim Friedrich, *Foreign Policy in the Making. The Search for a New Balance of Power* (New York: Norton, 1938), 88.

> Nothing is more natural than that they [the citizens] would think long before be-
> ginning such a terrible game, since they would have to call down on themselves
> all the horrors of war, such as, to fight themselves; to pay the cost of war out of
> their own pocket; miserably to repair the devastation it leaves behind.[52]

Tocqueville's aristocratic feelings are most evident when he considers the
attitudes of democracies towards war. The "violent and poetical excitement
of arms," he explains, is lost in a democratic society and its mild manners.
"Among civilized nations the warlike passions will become more rare and
less intense in proportion as social conditions are more equal."[53] He praises
the spirit of military glory and sees even a peculiar advantage of war for
democratic nations:

> I do not wish to speak ill of war: war almost always enlarges the mind of a people
> and raises their character. In some cases it is the only check to the excessive
> growth of certain propensities that naturally spring out of the equality of condi-
> tions, and it must be considered as a necessary corrective to certain inveterate dis-
> eases to which democratic communities are liable.[54]

But despite Tocqueville's aristocratic taste for heroic virtues and war as a
great event, he clearly anticipates the perils of war for the freedom of a
democratic nation . War, he remarks, must inevitably lead to a concentration
of power. He considers it to be the first axiom of political science, "that war
is the surest and the shortest means" to destroy the liberties of a democracy.[55] When it comes to the question of war, his aristocratic instinct and his
passion for liberty are obviously in indissoluble conflict.

Americanism and Foreign Policy

The American liberal society is based on certain and commonly held political values and beliefs. Equality, freedom, and inalienable rights—the basic
humanistic liberal principles developed out of the epoch of Enlightenment—
formed the American national consciousness and its political structure. This
did not escape the attention of Tocqueville. "Two things," he writes, "are
surprising in the United States: the mutability of the greater part of human

---

52. Immanuel Kant, *Perpetual Peace. A Philosophical Proposal* (London: Sweet and
     Maxwell, 1927), 26.
53. *DA* [B], II, 279. See also: Seymour Drescher, *Tocqueville and England* (Cambridge,
     Mass.: Harvard University Press, 1964), 152-169.
54. *DA* [B], II, 283.
55. *Ibid.*, 284.

actions, and the singular stability of certain principles."[56] This is surprising for the European observer, because, on the old continent, the opposite held true: human action is more fixed and the general principles of the society are part of the revolutionary process.

The basic values of the American republic, pronounced in the Declaration of Independence as life, liberty and the pursuit of happiness, have been called *Americanism* or the *American creed.*[57] Americanism was the rallying center for national unity and is the basis for the national consciousness and identity. Tocqueville compares American and European patriotism in his chapter on public spirit in the United States. He finds the "irritable patriotism" of the Americans embarrassing:

> You are not allowed to speak freely of private individuals or of the state, of the citizens or of the authorities, of public or private undertakings, or, in short, of anything at all except, perhaps, the climate and the soil; and even then Americans will be found ready to defend both as if they had co-operated in producing them.[58]

However embarrassing his personal experience with American self-rightness was, he drew a fine distinction between the instinctive patriotism of a monarchy and the reflecting patriotism of a republic. He describes the patriotism of the European nations as a kind of religion: "It does not reason, but it acts from the impulse of faith and sentiment."[59] In comparison, the patriotism of a republic is more rational: "It is perhaps less generous and less ardent, but it is more fruitful and more lasting: it springs from knowledge; it is nurtured by the laws; it grows by the exercise of civil rights; and, in the end, it is confounded with the personal interest of the citizen."[60] This distinction is significant in understanding the American democracy and its foreign policy. In contrast to European nationalism, the great and disparate American nation is not rooted in myths of history or ethnicity, but in the political ideas of the American creed. The Declaration by which Americans made themselves independent marked the birth of the first nation in history explicitly

56. *Ibid.,* 271.
57. Samuel P. Huntington, *American Politics: The Promise of Disharmony* (Cambridge, Mass.: Belknap Press of Harvard University Press, 1981) and Gunnar Myrdal, *An American Dilemma. The Negro Problem and Modern Democracy* (New York: Harper and Brothers, 1944), 3-25. Hamilton also used the phrase "the standard of our political creed." *The Federalist Papers,* no. 24; 157.
58. *DA* [B], I, 253.
59. *Ibid.,* 251.
60. *Idem.*

grounded not on tradition, or loyalty to tradition, but on appeal to universal principles of political right.[61]

Because American nationalism is permeated by the American creed and its recognition of universal inalienable human rights, it becomes international in its essence.[62] That the basic principle of freedom will also characterize the influence of America in the world is reflected in Tocqueville's famous prediction at the end of the first volume of *Democracy in America*, in which he compares the different principles of the Russian and American society and their common destiny to sway the globe. The one has freedom as the principle means of action; the other, servitude.[63]

Tocqueville considers the democratic instinct to be the greatest hindrance to the conduct of a patient and far-sighted foreign policy. But when the United States stepped into international politics, her confidence in unique character and the mission of the republic proved to be a greater obstacle in the game of nations. Americans tend to be pragmatic but at the same time they are, as Tocqueville observed, addicted to the use of general ideas.[64] The tendency to think in simplistic and heroic schemes leads to the dream of quick, dramatic and heroic actions in foreign policy. Americans see the world not in geopolitical terms but in terms of friendship and enmity. These are the main reasons why the United States, addicted to a kind of "High Noon" style of international diplomacy, has often failed in the complex world.[65]

The American creed, the idealism of a redeemer nation, is present in most foreign policy declarations, in Wilson's Fourteen Points, in Roosevelt's Four Freedoms, in the Truman Doctrine and in what was called the Reagan Doctrine. For all wars and interventions, Americanism has been the ideological foundation and moral justification. The belief in the special mission of Americanism, the certainty of being different in the world and the view of the American republic as a model or a beacon was already expressed by Thomas Jefferson. On leaving the White House he reminded the Washington citizens of the destiny of "this solitary republic of the world, the only monument of human rights, and the sole depository of the sacred fire of freedom and self-government, from hence it is to be lighted up in other

---

61. Thomas L. Pangle, *The Spirit of Modern Republicanism. The Moral Vision of the American Founders and the Philosophy of Locke* (Chicago: The University of Chicago Press, 1988), 278.
62. See Myrdal, *An American Dilemma*, 6.
63. *DA* [B], I, 452.
64. *DA* [B], II, 15. Myrdal made the same observation (4).
65. See Stanley Hoffmann, *Dead Ends. American Foreign Policy in the New Cold War* (Cambridge, Mass.: Ballinger, 1983), 105.

regions of the earth, if other regions of the earth shall ever become susceptible of its benign influence."[66] This conviction was echoed in 1962 by John F. Kennedy: "Our nation was commissioned by history to be either an observer of freedom's failure or the cause of its success."

To be sure, there have been periods in American history when Americanism and the faith in its exceptionalism were misused by "Know-Nothings" and "Huey Longs" or were degenerated to imperialistic missions, to jingoism and ideological witch hunts at home. It is also true that the weaknesses of the American government, which Tocqueville elucidated with great instinct and clarity, such as unfitness for secrecy, impatience, poor coordination, and impetuous shifts of opinion, have frequently hampered or even damaged the conduct of foreign relations. American diplomacy, as one experienced diplomat writes, seems at times to be more a part of the problem than of the solution, but he adds, to recommend changing this aspect is to recommend the destruction of democracy.[67] With all its defects and failures, the American democracy and its manifest interest in the human rights of others continue to generate hope and expectations.

Conclusions

Is a democratic foreign policy possible? This question does not need much deliberation. Modern history has shown that democracies have been successful in the world arena and continue to be so. The United States was, after World War II, faced with the task of taking the role of a dominant world power. The confrontation with the Soviet Union during the Cold War made necessary global military commitments, which were sustained despite strong domestic opposition. The success of George F. Kennan's concept of containment, a strategy that required a "long-term, patient, but firm and vigilant" policy, refutes the Tocquevillian doubts about the efforts democracies are capable of making.

Is a democratic foreign policy desirable? Democracies have failed and committed follies. American foreign policy has oscillated between extroversion and introversion, between the role of a missionary and a sheriff, thus being confronted with the task of balancing different impulses and interests.

66. Jefferson to the citizens of Washington, March 4, 1809, in Andrew A. Lipscomb and Albert E. Bergh eds., *Writings of Jefferson* (Washington, D.C., 1903), XVI, 347.
67. David D. Newsom, *Diplomacy and the American Democracy* (Bloomington and Indianapolis: Indiana University Press, 1988), 218.

But Tocqueville himself identifies the principal merit of democracy when he praises its ability to learn and correct errors. "Though a democracy is more liable to error than a monarch or a body of nobles," he writes, "the chances of its regaining the right path when once it has acknowledged its mistake are greater also; because it is rarely embarrassed by interests that conflict with those of the majority and resist the authority of reason." He concludes: "The great privilege of the Americans does not consist in being more enlightened than other nations, but in being able to repair the faults they may commit."[68] The most important factors for the ability to correct a wrong course of politics are the constitutional checks on power and the responsiveness and accountability of the government to the people. There is compelling evidence in American history of the twentieth century for this capacity to draw lessons from the experience of the past. The attack on Pearl Harbor convinced the American people to go to war, and after that experience a new isolationism was hardly conceivable. The Senate rejected the League of Nations, but then the United States became a primary sponsor and supporter of the United Nations. The prevalent American approach to foreign policy has not been that of Stephen Decatur: "Our country, right or wrong," but that of Carl Schurz: "Our Country, right or wrong. When right, to be kept right; when wrong to be put right."[69]

There has always been disappointment because the American institutions and their domestic and foreign policies did not match the expectations of the American creed on which they are based. But the fact that Americanism is rooted in the universal rights of man is also cause for great hope. Because republics are based on the rights of the people and public justice, there is reasonable hope for international law and international justice, if only, to use Kant's picture of his *Perpetual Peace*, in gradual but unending approximation.

68. *DA* [B], I, 239.
69. Huntington, *American Politics*, 241.

[6]

Tocqueville and the Historical Sociology of State

Pierre Birnbaum

The work of Alexis de Tocqueville is in many ways at the origin of contemporary political sociology. Tocqueville is, in fact, one of the very first to point to the possible emergence of an atomized mass society, and to reflect on the formation of a depoliticizing consensus. This consensus is compatible, in many respects, with a flourishing pluralism which is capable of limiting the arbitrary: a principle which, from Dahl to Lipset, will be at the heart of American political sociology. Tocqueville's reflection on the import of individualism thus remains classical, insofar as it emphasizes one of the dangers of an egalitarian democratization which destroys the collective forms of social solidarity. But Tocqueville also opens the way for a sociology of bureaucracy and administration by placing, at the center of his comparative research of forms of government, the centralization/decentralization opposition from which he deduces the despotism/liberty opposition and in function of which he constructs his theory of the factors propitious to the triggering of the Revolution.

One would like to begin however by emphasizing on the one hand, that Tocqueville's commentators, specially those who study his political sociology, never ponder the possible presence in his work of a potential theory of state. One finds very little indication of this kind in Drescher, Lively, Lamberti, or Whitney Pope,[1] to take just a few examples. Significantly,

---

1. See Jack Lively, *The Social and Political Thought of Alexis de Tocqueville* (Oxford: Clarendon Press, 1965). Seymour Drescher, *Dilemmas of Democracy. Tocqueville and Modernization* (Pittsburgh: University of Pittsburgh Press, 1968). Jean-Claude Lamberti, *Tocqueville et les deux "Démocraties"* (Paris: Presses Universitaires de

91

when Preston King presents Tocqueville as one of the main theoreticians opposed to state control, thus introducing the concept of state into the general discussion of the author of *Democracy in America*, he does this, in reality, to apprehend very classically, in terms of centralization and even morality, the centralization/decentralization opposition which, in his eyes, rests only on an ethical point of view.[2] This marks the extent to which the commentators of Tocqueville have failed to introduce the concept of state into their analyses of his work. Most of the work done on Tocqueville, often written in the English-speaking world, predates the late sixties renaissance in these same societies, of a sociology of state. Political sociologists still reasoned at that time, in terms of consensus, of elitism, of pluralism, of participation, of groups, and were not aware of phenomenons connected to power and, a fortiori, to the state.

On the other hand, the sociologists of state have, for the most part, in the last fifteen years, completely neglected the work of Tocqueville in their analyses and have turned instead to Marx or, most often, to Weber. This is the case, in particular, with Immanuel Wallerstein, who never cites Tocqueville in his book *Capitalisme et économie-monde,*[3] however much he emphasizes the opposition between France and England in the seventeenth and eighteenth century in terms of state types. In a similar Marxist perspective, oriented this time toward the study of the consequences of the end of the Middle-Ages, Perry Anderson, in his book on *L'Etat absolutiste,*[4] cites Bodin or Hobbes but remains silent about Tocqueville. We know that the sociology of state is also characterized by its call for a return to history in order to account for the phenomenon of state and, in this perspective, one might have expected to encounter incessantly the name of Tocqueville. Again, however, Tocqueville is almost never mentioned in the collective work at the origin of new thought on the state, *The Formation of National States in Western Europe,*[5] edited by Charles Tilly. Nor is he mentioned by other authors as innovative in their thinking as Strayer or Kenneth Dyson (*Les origines médiévales de l'Etat moderne* and *The State Tradition in*

France, 1983). Whitney Pope, *Alexis de Tocqueville. His Social and Political Theory* (London: Sage, 1986).

2.   Preston King, *Fear of Power: An Analysis of Anti-Stalinism in Three French Writers* (London: Frank Cass, 1967), 13, 33.

3.   Immanuel Wallerstein, *Capitalisme et économie-monde* (Paris: Flammarion, 1980).

4.   Perry Anderson, *L'Etat absolutiste* (Paris: Maspéro, 1978).

5.   Charles Tilly, *The Formation of National States in Western Europe* (Princeton, N.J.: Princeton University Press, 1975).

Western Europe).[6] This is especially surprising, as these authors examine the role of the king in France in his control over the provinces, the birth of a bureaucracy, etc., in contrast to the emergence of a center in England around which strong loyalty quickly rallies: all themes that are so familiar to Tocqueville. And although R. Bendix devotes well-written pages to Tocqueville in his book *Nation-Building and Citizenship*[7] and analyzes the "great transformation" brought about by the birth of citizenship and the subsequent mass entrance of citizens into the public arena, he nevertheless turns away, neglecting Tocqueville when he comes to his comparative study of the formation of the nation-state and of the development of bureaucracy in the Western world! In the same way, strangely enough, an author as knowledgeable about the works of Tocqueville as Gianfranco Poggi, who has devoted numerous and fascinating pages to him,[8] makes no mention of his name when he comes to write *The Development of the Modern State*, as if the move to a perspective centering on the state implied at the same time a complete abandonment of Tocqueville to the advantage, once again, of Weber.[9]

Let us evoke here a last example of this strange and paradoxical destiny of Tocqueville by quickly examining the work of Theda Skocpol, an author who has played a crucial role in the contemporary reemergence of a historical sociology of state. In her first book, *States and Social Revolutions*, Skocpol makes almost no use of Tocqueville although she analyzes, in a very Tocquevillian fashion, the beginning of revolutions: this she studies through the example of France in 1789, where a bureaucratized state is fighting a war against an enemy who has the advantage of a more modern economic potential, and attempts to reform itself, but encounters, in the process, the resistance of an aristocracy that has itself lost control over the local powers and peasant communities under the centralizing action of the state. Under these conditions, collective, revolutionary action is inevitable, and it leads to the reinforcement of the state.[10] Tocqueville would only have approved this analysis, as well as Skocpol's consideration of the state as a

6. Joseph Strayer, *Les origines médiévales de l'Etat moderne* (Paris: Payot, 1979). Kenneth Dyson, *The State Tradition in Western Europe* (Oxford: Martin Robertson, 1980).
7. Reinhard Bendix, *Nation-Building and Citizenship* (Berkeley, Cal.: University of California Press, 1969).
8. Gianfranco Poggi, "Tocqueville e lo staendestaat. Lettura sociologica della seconda parte della *Démocratie*," *Rassegna Italiana di Sociologia*, 12 (1971), 395-427.
9. Gianfranco Poggi, *The Development of the Modern State* (London: Hutchinson, 1978).
10. Theda Skocpol, *States and Social Revolutions* (Cambridge: Cambridge University Press, 1979).

"macro-structrure" challenging the theory of the "political arena." For Skocpol, as for Tocqueville, the state becomes a specific variable, the intervention of which allows one to understand social change. Yet, between *States and Social Revolutions* (1979) and *Bringing the State Back In* (1985), a collaborative book co-edited by Skocpol, a profound evolution has taken place, for in this second book, Tocqueville, who was neglected when Skocpol specifically sought to elaborate a position in the framework of the Marxism influential in political sociology, is now fully acknowledged. Let it be said that the intellectual scene has changed with the decline of Marxism and the domination of a comparative sociology oriented toward the diversity of history: the "Tocquevillian model" (Skocpol) that confers a most dominant role on the state acquires its letters of nobility and is presented as an agent with a decisive, however unintentional, impact on the instigation of collective action and the advent of decisive stakes. To explain 1789, Skocpol adopts very explicitly the theses of *The Old Regime and the Revolution* and points out that "the consequences of the action of the state are at the heart of Tocqueville's demonstration even if he has not described sufficiently the activity and the goals of those who act at the heart of the state itself."[11] Furthermore, many studies of this collaborative book are explicitly presented as relevant to the Tocquevillian analysis of the state.[12] This radical shift from the figure of Tocqueville, the unrecognized, to Tocqueville, a key author of contemporary political sociology, demonstrates, in itself, the extent to which the frames of reference of Anglo-Saxon political sociology of state have undergone profound change in recent years. This change from Dahl to Lipset, and then from Marx to Poulantzas, now pushes political sociology to rediscover Tocqueville, who, though he is often assimilated to Weber as a sort of precursor, is, in fact, the uncontested theoretician both of the state and of bureaucracy.

In reality, this rediscovery, interesting though it is, remains insufficient and overly schematic, as it does not involve an intimate knowledge of the work of Tocqueville. Thus it is time for the Tocqueville specialists, who have long neglected his theory of the state, to examine it thoroughly. We would propose several avenues of possible research.

We know that Tocqueville distinguishes between political centralization, which he finds compatible with democracy, and administrative centralization, which carries, according to him, a potential despotism. The first concerns general political affairs or foreign policy, the second, domination of

11.   Peter Evans, Dietrich Rueschmeyer, and Theda Skocpol, *Bringing the State Back In* (Cambridge: Cambridge University Press, 1985), 21.
12.   *Ibid.*, 253 et sq.

the entire territory by "a central power" through a hierarchical bureaucratic organization that destroys the communal autonomy in which Tocqueville sees the foundations of democracy and the principal barrier against the arbitrary.

For Tocqueville, the first form of centralization is found in England as well as the United States while the second form is realized in France, from the time of the Old Regime to the modern era, thus provoking the beginning of revolutionary periods. A first ambiguity must be addressed: the theory of the state cannot be limited simply to an analysis of administrative centralization. Certainly a strong state presents itself as a machine of hierarchical roles occupied by functionaries and, in this sense, every strong state constitutes a centralized bureaucracy. However, it is not only involved in this dimension of institutionalization. It is also involved, for example, in a process of differentiation that separates the state from the ruling class and from religion (thus presupposing the implementation of a complete secularism) and from the identities put into play by parties and pressure groups. In the public arena, the state thus constructs a citizenship that looks for universalism, the construction of which is the concern of its own public schools in which one acquires a political socialization of state.

In a note for a draft of *Democracy in America*, Tocqueville writes:

> The French centralizers use the word *state* in an unusual way. Often this is the only difference between us. The state, they say, in the century in which we live and the centuries into which we shall enter, should be involved in many things. Agreed. But by *state*, they almost always mean the executive power alone, acting without the help or the guarantee of the legislative and judiciary powers. This is where we no longer understand each other.[13]

Tocqueville is well aware that the usage of the word *state* in the French example cannot simply be identical with the word to which one may have recourse when examining the political power in other societies. He then explains this notion in the spirit of Montesquieu, as a lawyer attentive to the separation of powers, and not according to an analysis of the historical specificity of a state that succeeds in pushing as far as possible the process of institutionalization and of differentiation that we have already discussed. In another note for the draft of his book, Tocqueville adds: "The French think that centralization is French. They are mistaken; it is democratic."[14] He thus moves even further from a historical sociology of the construction, in France, of a state that is not only centralized but also "strong."

13. *DA* [N], II, 256.
14. *Ibid.* 268.

Tocqueville's commentators have not tried to approach his work from this type of framework. They have preferred to preserve the centralization/decentralization axis, and have paid little attention to the relatively frequent usage of the term state in his many writings. From the first pages of *The Old Regime and the Revolution*, in his text on the *Social and Political State of France*, he uses the notion of state again and again to analyze the strategies of the clergy, of the nobility, of the poor: for him, the nobles "conducted the affairs of the state," the aristocracy meant to "lead the entire state," possess themselves of "the fortune of the state," "France had a state religion," etc.[15] In *Democracy in America*, for example, Tocqueville also makes relatively frequent use of this concept: already in the introduction, he evokes the influence of money on the "affairs of the state," the strategy of the king which consists in having "the lower classes participate in the state;" he evokes the way in which, with the emergence of associations, "the state would be sheltered from tyranny and licentiousness," for society is not immobile in a "democratic state."[16] This is to underline that the "new political science" that he seeks to build in order to account for a "new world"[17] must be in every way well aware of the state. It is true, however, that in his mind the term *state* merges with notions of administration, centralization, despotism and of the arbitrary while it remains, simultaneously, capable of describing countries that are profoundly democratic, like the United States or England, in which he notes, nonetheless, that the state remains "weak,"[18] opposed to France in the extreme where "one had not seen such a power in the world since the fall of the Roman Empire."[19] In this last example, "the state suddenly achieves the extreme limit of its force, while private individuals let themselves fall, in a matter of minutes, to the depths of weakness."[20] Tocqueville, one can see, uses the term *state* to describe examples of very dissimilar political powers with profound differences, the first being particularly "weak," the second, on the contrary, remarkably "strong."

For several years now, contemporary political sociology has taken to opposing "strong" and "weak" states. Following the distinctions proposed by Peter Nettl and that we have ourselves expounded,[21] one marks the degree to

15. *L'Ancien Régime et la Révolution*, *OC*, II:1, 36, 39, 41, 53, 62, etc.
16. *DA* [N], I, 5, 11.
17. *Ibid.*, 9.
18. *Ibid.*, 90.
19. *L'Ancien Régime et la Révolution*, 85.
20. *DA* [N], II, 246.
21. Peter Nettl, "The State as a Conceptual Variable," *World Politics* 20:4 (July 1968), 559-592. Bertrand Badie and Pierre Birnbaum, *Sociologie de l'Etat* (Paris: Grasset, 1979). Pierre Birnbaum, *States and Collective Action* (Cambridge: Cambridge University Press, 1988).

which France, on the one hand, England and the United States, on the other, represent the ideal, typical forms of state, either strong or weak. This comparative perspective is very close to that proposed by Tocqueville. It is different, however, in that Tocqueville reasons above all in terms of centralization/decentralization, which can easily describe the political powers that are very centralized but not those that are differentiated, and that cannot, consequently, easily be referred to as state. In contrast, Tocqueville still uses the notion of state when he examines, for example, the case of England where, according to him, a strong political centralization coexists with a complete absence of administrative centralization. For him, "the state, there, seems to move as a single man who raises immense masses to his will and carries whither he desires the full force of his power. The England that has done such great things for fifty years has no administrative centralization." There are many researchers in political science who, in contrast to Tocqueville, recognize the quasi-absence of all state in England or in the United States of the nineteenth, even of the beginning of the twentieth century. Tocqueville does sometimes recognize this fact when he insists that in the United States "society acts by itself. There is no power save at its heart." Why, then, does he persist in using the concept of state, which implies a complete differentiation marking the borders of state-controlled space vis-à-vis the most diverse identities of society?

In reality, beyond this non systematic approach to the state, one finds in Tocqueville many elements prefiguring contemporary theories that highlight the different types of state. It is the "national character,"[22] as Tocqueville rediscovers, that produces so many exceptional circumstances, so many, as he incessantly repeats, that the Unites States or France become quasi-unique societies by their type of construction of the political. And contemporary political sociology, inspired by a comparative approach, echoes this affirmation by showing the extent to which the cultural code proper to each given society produces a completely distinct type of state, despite the processes of export and import through which a type of state finds itself reproduced in societies of particular cultural codes.[23]

As Tocqueville notes from America in a letter to his brother Edouard:

> We are truly in another world here; here political passions are only on the surface. The true passion, the only kind that deeply stirs the human heart, the passion that one finds every day, is the acquisition of wealth, and there are a thousand ways of acquiring it without disturbing the state. One needs to be very blind in my opinion to want to compare this country with Europe and to adapt what works in one to

22. See, for example, *DA* [N], I, 25.
23. Bertrand Badie, *Les deux Etats* (Paris: Fayard, 1988).

the other; I believed this before leaving France; I think it all the more now that I'm able to survey the society in the midst of which I live; this is a people of salesmen who take an interest in public affairs only when their work allows them the leisure.[24]

The Americans, those "solemn men, occupied by the serious interests of life," seek only to maximize their own "material pleasure" by applying "the doctrine of interest well understood." As Tocqueville also notes:

In the United States, as soon as a citizen has any knowledge and any resources, he looks to enrich himself in commerce and in industry.... All that he wants from the state is for it not to come and trouble him in his labors and for it to insure his profit. In European societies, when a man begins to feel his strength and to expand his desires, the first idea that comes to him is to find a public position.

And, in a shorter note, he says: "In America, every man wants to rise through industry or commerce. In France, as soon as he desires to rise above his status, he asks for a public position."[25] By opening the way for comparative research on the sociology of elites founded on the variable of the state, Tocqueville prefigures in a remarkable way the work of Sombart or that of Lipset. The weaker the state, the fewer are its functionaries, for then the state is not the space of legitimacy or social power: this is an economic "aristocracy"—the arrival of which Tocqueville fears—which occupies the position of power and prevents the differentiation of the state. This analysis has been confirmed in recent times by such politicists as Wright Mills, Baltzell, or William Domhoff[26] in their many works. The model proposed by Tocqueville thus introduces us to the negative correlation between state and ruling class: the weaker the state, the stronger the establishment; and inversely, the stronger the state, the more it is able to impose its own power and to break the prior unity of the ruling class.[27]

When, on the other hand, the strong state predominates, the market loses its preeminence and the political-administrative elite incarnates the only recognized legitimacy. The institutionalization of the state is marked by the formation of a system of very rigid roles that separates functionaries from other elites. As Tocqueville remarks, prefiguring the work of historians such as Denis Richet or that of sociologists such as Marie-Christine Kessler or Ezra Suleiman, "those who work in public service, almost all bourgeois, al-

24. Cited in *DA* [N], II, 119.
25. *Ibi*d., 208.
26. See William Domhoff, *Who Rules America Now?* (Englewood Cliffs, N.J.: Prentice-Hall, 1983).
27. For an analysis of the American ruling class in terms of a weak state and for a general presentation of the relations between the elites in the United States, see Pierre Birnbaum, "Etat et élite: l'exemple américain," *Pouvoirs*, 29 (1984).

ready form a class that has its own spirit, its own traditions, virtues, honor, its own pride."[28] They constitute, most particularly in societies where there is a strong state, "a nation within each nation"[29] and are isolated from society at large in that they are supposed to act rationally in the name of the general interest. One notes thus in the Unites States "the absence of what we call at home the government or the administration" because "there exists nowhere a center on which the rays of administrative power converge,"[30] the public workers there are "confused in the midst of the crowd of citizens, [and] they have neither palace nor guards, nor ceremonial costumes." Their work stability is uncertain because of the application of a spoil system which implies that they "are only in power for a moment."[31] For Tocqueville, on the contrary,

> under the Old Regime as in our time, there was no city, town or village, no hamlet in France, hospital, factory, convent or school that could have an independent will in its particular affairs, that could administer its own goods according to its will. Therefore, as today, the administration held all of the French under its supervision.[32]

In another declaration, he exclaims:

> Among all of the most absolute rulers of Europe, I challenge anyone to find a *single* one who had such a multitude of functionaries at hand and could act in such a constant and direct way, not only on the affairs of the state but on the interests, however small, of its citizens.[33]

Tocqueville shows us here the extent to which the notion of state goes far beyond administrative centralization, for it implies at this point not only public possession of the school system that allows for the control of the political socialization (thus escaping the upper class), but also, for example, the control of an important part of the apparatus of economic production through nationalizations that further marginalize the role of the market. This point also clarifies Tocqueville's usage of the term "despotism"[34] to describe the functioning of this strong state: it could also be seen in relation to the Bonapartist model analyzed by Marx in the *Eighteenth Brumaire of Louis Bonaparte*, in which the explanation, from the mode of production, uncovers

28. *L'Ancien Régime et la Révolution*, 133.
29. *DA* [N], II, 253.
30. *Ibid.*, 56, 59.
31. *Ibid.*, 156, 159.
32. *L'Ancien Régime et la Révolution*, 122.
33. *Ecrits et discours politiques*, *OC*, III:2, 107.
34. See James T. Schleifer, *The Making of Tocqueville's Democracy in America* (Chapel Hill, N.C.: University of North Carolina Press, 1980) 173-187.

the logic of a strong state that holds, in the words of Marx (which are also those of Tocqueville), "all" of the classes of society "under supervision." This point seems crucial, as it demonstrates that authors as opposed in their views as Marx and Tocqueville agree when it comes to recognizing the specificity of a strong, France-like state: the structure of such a state is such that it often functions, from one period to the next, in a "Bonapartist" way.[35] The Americans, on the other hand, "having from the beginning governed themselves, never needed to hold the state responsible for their supervision."[36]

One could also, in the framework of this text, draw attention to the quasi presence in the work of Tocqueville of a theory of state that rests on a comparison between the meaning of citizenship in one society and in another. One could describe at greater length the way in which he examines the role of religion in the construction of state. This last point deserves ample discussion insofar as, for the theoreticians of state, religion exercises a decisive influence over the emergence of a particular mode of state. One knows that the construction of a strong state in France appears largely in response to the force of the Catholic church, organized as a bureaucratic and centralized structure. The pretension of the church to manage both spirit and territory provokes, in response, a differentiation of the state that is virtually complete at the beginning of the twentieth century. In the United States, on the other hand, the many churches and Protestant sects which fall under the scrutiny of Tocqueville create values: to what extent, then, is the presence of a weak state, of a strong democracy linked to Protestantism and to the individualism to which it gives rise? We know that Robert Bellah and Seymour Lipset agree explicitly with Tocqueville when Tocqueville finds Protestantism crucial to the birth of American consensus and describes the affinity between liberalism, democracy and Protestantism.[37] It remains to be seen how Tocqueville, the practising Catholic, can imagine transposing recommendations favorable to the return of a weak state and to a strong democracy onto a society as eminently Catholic as France. Tocqueville thinks that Catholicism would be better adapted to democracy in the end, once the church had been separated from the state, but this argument, which Doris Goldstein finds "weak,"[38] is not, in fact, sufficient for those who

---

35. See Pierre Birnbaum, *Les sommets de l'Etat* (Paris: Seuil, 1977) ch. 1.
36 . *DA* [N], II, 247.
37. Robert Bellah, "Civil Religion in America," *Daedalus*, 96:1 (Winter 1967), 1-21. Seymour Lipset, *The First New Nation* (Garden City, N.Y.: Doubleday, 1963).
38. Doris Goldstein, *Trial of Faith. Religion and Politics in Tocqueville's Thought* (New York: Elsevier, 1975), 102.

question the possibilities of transforming one type of state into a society of an opposing dominant cultural code.

In conclusion, we would inquire as to the extent to which the evolution of these states conforms to the predictions of Tocqueville. By a remarkable intuition, the author of *Democracy in America*[39] thought that the state would become partially strong in the United States. The sociology of state has recently drawn attention to the growth of a new state in American society that rests, predominantly, on the system of judiciary courts and on parties (Skowroneck)[40] and has demonstrated, furthermore, how certain sectors of this state which seem "weak," such as the Department of Foreign Affairs or the Departments of Industry and Agriculture, in reality reveal themselves to be stronger and stronger over time (Krasner, Finegold and Skocpol, Ikenberry).[41] This new approach to the state in the United States questions in part the theory of Tocqueville, and we might ask if democracy is, in fact, threatened, not by industrial power, as Tocqueville feared, but instead by the centralization and the state control that seemed to him to be proper to Europe and to France most particularly. Conversely, certain still fragile changes that are taking place in France today seem to be important steps toward a decentralization that raises questions about the presence of a strong state. The laws passed by the socialist government in 1982 advocate for the first time a Girondine conception of the state to the benefit, certainly, of the local politicians. However, with the end of prefects and the a priori control of expenses by the central administration,[42] a crucial element of the strong state has been changed. If local culture remains "subjugated" and unfavorable to the flourishing of associative, American-like democracy,[43] the Jacobinic nature of the strong state is nevertheless put into question at the very moment when the market and liberal ideology are triumphing at a national level. Thus in the United States as in France, the analysis of contemporary transformations

---

39. *DA* [N], I, 65. The author shows that "there are several states in which one begins to see traces of an administrative centralization. The state of New York is the furthest along in this direction," 65.
40. Stephen Skowroneck, *Building a New American State* (Cambridge: Cambridge University Press, 1982).
41. Stephen Krasner, *Defending National Interest* (Princeton, N.J.: Princeton University Press, 1978). K. Finegold and Theda Skocpol, "State Capacity and Economic Intervention in the Early New Deal," *Political Science Quarterly*, 97:2 (Summer 1982), 255-278. John Ikenberry, *Reasons of State. Oil Capacities and the Capacities of the American Government* (Ithaca, N.Y.: Cornell University Press, 1988). See also Marie-France Toinet ed., *L'Etat en Amérique* (Paris: Presses de la Fondation Nationale des Sciences Politiques, 1989).
42. See, for example, Jacques Rondin, *Le sacre des notables* (Paris: Fayard, 1985).
43. Patrice Quantin, "Une ville en France: qui participe?," in Albert Mabileau, *Les citoyens et la politique locale* (Paris: Pédone, 1987).

of state, which are in reality rather limited,[44] testifies to the lasting and fertile character of Tocqueville's intuitions concerning the comparative analysis of state types.

(Translated by Elisabeth Rottenberg)

44. See Pierre Birnbaum, "L'impossible Etat à l'américaine," in *L'Etat de la France* (Paris: La Découverte, 1989).

[7]

Tocqueville: A Phenomenology of the Social

Claude Lefort

Few authors have Tocqueville's ability to convince one of the soundness of their project. The clarity of exposition, the methodical usage of comparison, the concern with formulating the nature of his project at the beginning of his exposition and reformulating it at different stages of the argument, the ability to summarize here and there an entire development in a conclusion; often the conspicuous processes of demonstration leads the reader to conclude that Tocqueville has perfect mastery over his subject. Although he warns us that he plans to show the effects of the equality of conditions without turning the latter into the only cause for the present state of the world, he suggests, by the path thus delineated, that he reaches his goal. What goal: to assess the virtues and vices of democracy, to discern the forms that democracy can take in different nations and varying circumstances, to locate the advances and regressions of humanity under the effects of a democratic revolution, to detect the dangers that it carries with it? It is certain that the image of the scale enters into such a picture, and with it the image of the judge. Tocqueville says it himself: that he wished to paint and to judge. However, I doubt whether one can hold him to this image.

In *Democracy in America*, Tocqueville is a master of the art of contrast. Modernity stands out against the background of the Old Regime; America stands out against the European world; the physiognomy of democracy is revealed only when it is compared to aristocracy, its opposite; the effects of the equality of conditions are measured in relation to the opposite effects of inequality. When he does not posit oppositions, Tocqueville makes rigorous distinctions, or rather breaks concepts apart: a line is clearly drawn between equality and freedom, between the social state and the political institution. Thus he clarifies the picture and creates the distance necessary to judge. However, one must, I think, admire him more for his sense of the ambiguous and the complex, his preoccupation with the initial principles of his exposition, his power to decipher the particular fact and to draw from it a truth that puts the logic of his argument in question.

Let us take the notion of democratic revolution. In one sense, it stands for a break between the old and the modern. Although the revolution takes shape over time, there comes a moment when it reveals more than a discontinuity, a contrast between two modes of temporality. On the one hand, the actions of men, their institutions and their beliefs are inscribed within the element of immortality: however diverse the given societies, they are all busy assuring themselves permanence. On the other hand, the modern world is devoted to change. It lives, knows that it lives, and wants to live amidst an incessant upheaval of experience.

We are thus confronted, Tocqueville will not hesitate to say, with two incomparable humanities that shed light on each other. But this is only one aspect of his thought. From the very beginning of his book, he considers the democratic revolution to be *irresistible*. It seems we have only to take action and to discover the means by which it is possible to control its course. Between these two incomparable humanities we have no choice: time has *become* irreversible. Yet is this a simple acknowledgment? And is it enough to call on Providence to convince us of the inevitability of change? There is no doubt that Tocqueville believes in a discovery that puts into question the very notion of humanity, the individual and society. That the other should appear to one as a fellow man, that the individual possesses by nature the right to decide his fate; that society as such emerges from the diversity of networks of dependence or from particular communities, as the idea of a sovereign people arises: these are not simple facts, but signs of the advent of a truth which cannot be contested except by putting a limit to thought.

If, then, one cannot go back, it is because one does not have the power to reject the idea of individual freedom as something human. It is not the dominant opinion that prevents us from having this power; an exigency constitutive of mind now compels us not to. Furthermore, when we form an image of the dominant opinion that shapes the thoughts of each citizen, we assert our freedom proper. In this regard, Tocqueville's originality is double. On the one hand, unlike a number of his contemporaries, he does not combine the democratic notion, the modern notion—which he does not fear to call the just notion of freedom—with a theory of progress.[1] He believes in the perfectibility of man, but he is aware in the highest degree of the ambivalence of the effects of all innovation, even if innovation is universally significant. The certainty that accompanies the idea of individual and political rights does not exempt one from examining the consequences of its inscription on reality and in the life of societies.

If Tocqueville does not share the theses of Machiavelli according to which there is a constant amount of good and evil from one period to the next, Tocqueville suggests, in his wake, that there is no good without evil, and that every gain carries with it a loss. On the other hand, although he attributes the discovery of the unity of the human race to a spiritual revolution, that of Christianity, he observes—in conformity with tradition, yet with an emphasis on the character of the social state at the time of the Roman Empire—that the quality of being equally weak before the prince predisposes men "to receive the universal truths that Christianity teaches." In other words, a new idea, though it brings revelation, is efficacious only when it fits into a definite environment at a particular time. Tocqueville cannot be accused of historicism or sociologism: what is just does not depend for its truth on a time or a form of society.

The advent of truth allows men to think what was previously unthinkable—what was unthinkable, for example, for the Greeks, as demonstrated by their conception of slavery—but this truth must take shape in the social. And when the truth seems almost natural, one will not be able to conclude that the men who had not yet recognized it were inferior in other regards to modern men. Tocqueville brings both of these ideas together. It is important to understand the American world in itself through its guiding principles (which leads him to say that one would need to burn all books in order to grasp the new); however, this American world does not become clear except by its contrast with the old world.

In large part, the opposition between old and modern concurs with that between aristocracy and democracy. The former is, as everyone knows, at the heart of his reflection and is expressed time and time again (more than ten times to be exact). The contrast is most deeply felt in the chapter on *individualism*. On the one side, is found: permanence from one generation to the next; an intensity of social links at the heart of social classes, a gradation that allows each to see above him another who can protect him and beneath him someone from whom he can demand support; the general disposition of men

---

1. "Etat social et politique de la France," in *L'Ancien Régime et la Révolution, OC*, II:1, 62.

to conceive of "something that is placed outside of them and often to forget themselves."

On the other side one finds contrasting conditions: the extreme mobility of families who rise or fall or change constantly; a rupture in the web of time; an increased awareness of the ability to be self-sufficient and free of debt. The contrast can be summed up in the famous formulation: "aristocracy turned all citizens into a long chain that moved from peasant to king; democracy breaks the chain and separates each link."[2] However, in the middle of the chapter, Tocqueville slips in a remark about the times of aristocracy: "it is true that, in these same centuries, the notion of likeness is obscure."[3] He adds to this remark when he explains that "the very image of society was obscure."[4] The consequences of this remark lead to a break in the symmetry between the two types opposed. In the aristocratic world, at least as it is described by Tocqueville, the relations between men are shaped locally and are both social and political.

In the step by step articulation of the networks of dependence, these relations are regulated for the most part at the heart of the seigniorial domain, of the commune or guild. On the other hand, and this is a central argument for Tocqueville (that one finds in Marx in another form although his premises and conclusions are very different), democracy implies a disjunction between the social and the political. As conditions become more equal and men recognize each other as fellow beings, society is more pronounced and gains in autonomy. Yet this argument lends itself to two conflicting interpretations, both of which are to be found in the text, and to which I shall presently turn. According to the first, society rises above men while the personal ties maintained between them are undone; they see themselves subordinated to this "vast being."

According to the second, because political action and political institutions are circumscribed and the government has only a relative legitimacy that is always put into question, energy that is specifically social can be liberated, and civil society becomes a place of creation. Thus Tocqueville says of democratic government that he "praises it more for what it makes one do than for what it does."[5] And returning to the thesis that opposed the government by the most fit to that which remains at the mercy of the whims of the greatest number, he does not hesitate to declare that

2.   *DA* [N], II, 98.
3.   *Idem.*
4.   *DA* [N], II, 276.
5.   *DA* [N], I, 191.

democracy does not give the people government that is the most fit, but it accomplishes what such a government is powerless to do: it produces a nervous activity in the entire social body, an overabundant force, an energy that can *never* exist without it [my emphasis] and which, if circumstances happen to be a little favorable, gives rise to great things.[6]

Democracy thus constitutes the anti-type of aristocracy when Tocqueville seeks to find in it the seeds of a new genre of despotism; it represents, on the other hand, an original type that cannot be known by its opposite when he seeks to find in it signs of a new genre of freedom. Thus we must ask another question: is Tocqueville entirely certain that democracy retains nothing of aristocracy? Certain passages prevent us from affirming this.

Let it be said that Tocqueville is not only gifted in the art of contrast, but is also a master of surprise; he reverses perspectives in order to overthrow formerly well-established truths. His artful writing keeps the reader constantly on the alert, demands mobility of perception and thought and prevents him from securing any position of certainty.

The section entitled "On the Spirit of Law in the United States and How it Serves as a Counterweight to Democracy" is one of the most striking examples in how it sheds a new light on the subject at hand. Tocqueville's remarks in this section are not a digression. Chapter VIII, in which they are to be found, discusses "On That Which Tempers the Tyranny of the Majority in the United States" and related to what precedes it: "On the Omnipotence of the Majority in the United States and its Effects." The earlier chapter is cited too often to be taken up here yet again. It contains a violent critique of American democracy and of democracy in general. Unstable, arbitrary, formidable in its material and moral force, the majority seems to have overcome the obstacles encountered in the past by despotic princes or by the Inquisition. Yet this terrible picture becomes completely muddled when Tocqueville introduces the jurists. As he describes their inclinations, their habits, one sees their influence grow. They wield competence, have a sense of permanence and forms, and in addition their action is considerable. Due to the institution of a people's jury,

the judiciary language becomes... in a way the common language; the spirit of law, that originates in schools and courts slowly spreads beyond its confines; it infiltrates, so to speak, all of society, and descends into the lowest ranks, and the people as a whole end up adopting some of the habits and the tastes of the magistrate.[7]

6. *Idem.*
7. *DA* [N], I, 211.

But jurists exert their power not only because of the jury; Tocqueville observes earlier that "they fill the legislatures and are at the head of administrations." And, in the end, their power is immense: it "envelops the entire society, permeates each of the classes that compose it, works it in secret, influences it unbeknownst to it and finally shapes it according to its desires."

What remains of the omnipotence of the majority? In any case it is striking that Tocqueville should characterize the spirit of law as aristocratic: "the body of jurists forms the only aristocratic element able without effort to blend in with the natural elements of democracy and to combine with them successfully and lastingly."[8] *Without effort?* These words require further attention, for they suggest a connivance between the general traits of democracy and at least some aristocratic traits. It seems to me, however, that such a passage in Tocqueville demonstrates once again how difficult it is to reduce democracy to a social state. The power of the jurists would not appear so extraordinary to him if he could acknowledge that democracy implies a distinction between opinion and right.

Tocqueville's writing is, for me, one of the most singular art forms. It sometimes seems that the author moves away from the theses he posits without knowing it. On the other hand, there are moments where the sequence of points of view is very deliberate. There is nothing more remarkable than the analysis of the function of associations in American life. The second part of the second volume opens with a new examination of the relations of equality and freedom. I have already alluded to this text. Judging that there exists an extreme point where equality and freedom merge, Tocqueville denies this cleavage of the social and the political. But he immediately says that there are a thousand other forms of equality and separates the social state from political institutions once again. He then devotes two chapters to individualism in order to describe one of the major effects of equality: the definite isolation of man at the heart of society. Here he introduces the thesis according to which the Americans fight individualism with free institutions.

But what are these institutions? At first the emphasis is placed upon local political freedoms. The most important is to be found in the political life that the legislators see fit to give each portion of the territory. However, in the following section, this collective activity seems to be only one aspect of a larger phenomenon, the phenomenon of association that is the most produc-

8.   *Ibid.,* 208.

tive art form, or what the author calls "the mother science." He presents civil associations as the most indispensable:

> If the men who live in a democracy have neither the right nor the desire to unite toward political goals,—he observes—their independence would run great risks, but they would preserve their wealth and enlightenment for a long time; however, if they did not acquire the ability to associate in ordinary life, the civilization itself would be in danger.[9]

It is in defending this right to association that Tocqueville differs from his contemporaries who, noting the weakness and the incompetence of the individuals in society, think only to render the government more skillful and more active, that is, to subordinate social life to the workings of power. Tocqueville reinforces his argument by revealing, in a new chapter, the role of newspapers. Because men are no longer closely tied to each other, only the newspaper gives them "a way of speaking to each other every day without seeing one another and of proceeding together without being united."[10]

Though at first he judges its role only in general terms, he does not hesitate thereafter to demonstrate its political function. His remarks on the press thus introduce an analysis of the relation between political associations and civil associations. At present, it appears that where political association is prohibited, civil association is rare, that one supports the other. Moreover, political association generalizes the "desire and custom of association," and may be considered "one of the big schools that is free and where citizens come to learn the general theory of association." This is followed by a judgment that, without denying the importance of local associations, nevertheless reverses the priority:

> when citizens develop the ability and custom of associating for all things, they will associate just as freely for small things as for important ones. But if they can only associate for small things they will lose the desire and the capacity to do so.[11]

Tocqueville then introduces his famous formulation: "thus, in reveling in a dangerous freedom, Americans learn the art of reducing the perils of freedom." And in order to convince the reader of the depth of his conviction, after having agreed that a nation might prefer to impose a limit on the right to association, he concludes:

---

9. *DA* [N], II, 104.
10. *Ibid.*, 108.
11. *Ibid.*, 112.

but it is better for it to know precisely what these goods cost. To save a man's life, I understand that one may cut off his arm, but I do want not to be told that he will be as skillful as he would have been had he not been one-armed.[12]

If I choose to recall these well-known words on associations, it is because they show how, after having separated the social from the political, Tocqueville is able to bring them together again.

I would have liked to question the Tocquevillian notion of equality of conditions and the dual movement that sometimes leads one to separate and sometimes to join the desire for equality and the desire for freedom. Such is the analysis of the effects of the equality of conditions—independence, isolation, likeness and equality—that we are always subject to doubt. If Tocqueville's aim is to show how freedom becomes servitude, he nevertheless also encourages us to know the opportunities that democracy offers for political and individual freedoms.

I would like to return, in conclusion, to a question that I asked earlier. The ambiguities, even the contradictions of analysis: are they unintentional, or should the frequent reversals of perspective be seen as deliberate? On second thought, I am not sure whether such a question is entirely relevant. The art of Tocqueville's writing seems to me to be in the service of an exploration of democratic society and simultaneously an exploration of the *social flesh. Flesh.* I advance this term which I borrow from Merleau-Ponty, to designate a differentiated environment that develops through its own internal and palpable division, in all of its parts. Tocqueville lets himself be guided by the exigency of his investigation. He explores the social tissue minutely without fear of discovering contradictory properties in it. I would venture to say that he makes *cuts* in this tissue and looks in each of its parts for the possibilities that it contains, that is, with the knowledge that in reality "everything holds together." Thus he does not hesitate to draw all of the possible consequences from individualism—which does not mean that the dynamism of democracy can be limited to that of individualism. Or else he draws all of the possible consequences from the new function of public opinion—which does not mean that he simply condones the tyranny of the majority. Or else he examines the final effects of the power of state growth, without, however, adopting the thesis of a democratic despotism (I will remind, in passing, that he challenges this notion expressly).

On the other hand, his exploration requires the formulation of general ideas and, more precisely, of conceptual oppositions, such as those between equality and hierarchy, freedom and servitude, authority and self-

12. *Ibid.*, 113.

affirmation, society and the individual, religious belief and unbelief, etc. The overlapping of language and experience is such that he must clarify the meaning of words to get at the things themselves.

But this clarification cannot remain of a purely theoretical order. This is why clarity is needed for the description of a society in gestation: the democratic society. His concepts do not refer to essences; they allow one to recognize the important articulations in function of which the political, social, moral and intellectual phenomena work together at the heart of one unique configuration.

Thus Tocqueville's project seems to me to be inspired by phenomenology, in the broad sense of the term. In the *Phenomenology of Perception*, Merleau-Ponty quotes Husserl's formulation: "experience that is still silent must be brought to the pure expression of its proper meaning." However, still close to Marxism, he makes the following comment to justify the application of this formulation to the knowledge of history and the political:

> In every civilization, one must discover the *idea* in a Hegelian sense, that is, not a physical-mathematical law, accessible to objective thought, but the formula of a unique relation in regard to one's fellow being, to the nature of time and to death, a particular way of giving form to the world that the historian must be able to recover and to assume.

Later Merleau-Ponty would radically critique this mystique of the totality that appears in his preface. Yet it is striking that Tocqueville should announce this critique. Certainly he attempts to bring the democratic experience to the pure expression of its proper meaning; certainly he attempts to unmask a particular way of forming the world; however, he discovers that experience has more than one meaning and works at grasping the opposite aspects of the same phenomenon and at understanding how the oppositions refer from one phenomenon to the other.

In conclusion, I would assert that, whatever the reservations may be to certain analyses and certain of Tocqueville's judgments, whatever may be the limits of his research, his work still has current value. But one could say that our contemporaries often lose the sense of ambiguity. Everything that happens in their eyes happens as if society had no depth, as if they could see it in one fell swoop, as if they could be satisfied with the celebration of the market or the critique of the state-providence or the condemnation of individualism or the condemnation of mass culture or the glorification of social movements.

It is to Tocqueville's credit that in examining every new phenomenon he found to be characteristic of democracy, in examining the democratic revolution to which he was a witness, he discovered its counterpart and, when he could, the counterpart of that counterpart—counterpart of the positive and counterpart of the negative. His merit is thus that he preserves the indeterminacy of history.

(Translated by Elisabeth Rottenberg)

[8]

The Question of Fraternity in *Democracy in America*

Francesco M. De Sanctis

By people at the time, the French Revolution was seen as a radical solution to the continuity of European tradition. Through the beheading of Louis Capet, the Revolution appears as a symbol of an era which heralded for some an epoch of revolutions and fratricidal battles. "When it cut off the head of Louis XVI"—wrote Balzac—"the Revolution cut off the head of all fathers." As for the value systems brought into question through the metaphor of patricide, it is perhaps possible to consider fraternity as yet another metaphor representing the problem of new social relationships and new types of authority, to be created in the style and way of life dictated by the times themselves.

Over and above this setting, a critical viewpoint begins to rear its head regarding the legacy of what was now no longer merely a theoretical and rationalistic natural law. This legacy was inadequate for the new social reality which had emancipated itself from the Old Regime. Beyond the fulfillment of principles which had been elaborated out of two centuries of theorizing on equality and liberty (natural rights), the Revolution also seemed to announce a new notion of human coexistence. Of course such a notion had been freed from any interests, contracts and individualism which it had previously subsumed and out of which society itself had served as an instrument for the fulfillment of an individual and egotistical life scheme. This process, which was primarily ethical in nature and to a lesser extent juridical and political, seems to be attributable to fraternity. It is on this very point that men who were now free and equal began to question the traditional divisions of humanity based on either economical or religious grounds that had been translated into differences of race, creed and class.

113

Compared to equality and liberty, fraternity, while establishing itself as the referent for a new "generation" of rights (social rights), cannot declare itself as a right. Fraternity concerns a more personal and more elementary sphere of identity than equality because it deeply binds the Revolution to the universal matrix of evangelical precepts which, when secularized, are replaced by the fundamental rights of men and citizens based upon the presupposition of responsible life in common.

The evangelical bidding to love one another as brothers seems to deny, as indeed does the third principle of the Revolution, the condition of brotherhood in its negative context, which is originally characterized as being rooted in envy springing from the pretension that brothers should be equal. Such envy is fatal to solidarity. Thus fraternity seen in terms of equality/love, a dichotomy towards which all forms of universal brotherhood and solidarity aspire, could well be in opposition to a vision of fraternity in terms of equality/envy. This way of interpreting and of living fraternity, a widespread condition in an "orphan" society of masses, rather than providing a remedy for modern freedom, could be considered as a further danger to society itself. A quote from the well-known essay *Auf dem Weg zur vaterlosen Gesellschaft* by Alexander Mitscherlich illustrates the theme developed in this paper:

> A society of the masses... creates an innumerable army of rival and envious brothers. Their main conflict is not characterized by oedipal rivalry which disputes a father's privileges of power and freedom, but by fraternal envy towards one's neighbor, the competitor who has had more than oneself.

Compared to equality and liberty, Tocqueville does not appear to be directly interested in the third principle of the Revolution. Fraternity is not an explicit theme in *Democracy in America*; to speak about it is thus only possible by attributing to certain passages the function of signals from which the implicit position of the author with regards to the problem can be obtained. This is due to his original ambivalence regarding equality, a presupposition of the condition itself.

My attempt to outline Tocqueville's view of fraternity is closely linked to the problem of equality. Fraternity, with the ambivalence I am attributing to it, includes important aspects of Tocqueville's intellectual and pragmatic attitude as the product of the condition of equality in democratic man. Despite the breadth of its effects, equality in Tocqueville's view of modernity is essentially presented in two ways, i.e. equality as a factual condition of democratic man (a socio-cultural phenomenon) and equality as a right or an aspiration (a juridical and political problem). I have attempted to elaborate Tocqueville's possible position, which might well regard fraternity as an inherent dimension of equality (as a factual condition), considering it a vice or a virtue of that very condition and, therefore, the moral interface of the socio-cultural phenomenon which characterizes modernity.

The Decline of Fraternity

However, if it is true that Tocqueville is not explicitly interested in fraternity as a problem linked to democracy, it is also true that he explores another topic which implicitly points back to it: the decline of paternity as the politico-ethical principle of aristocracy. This decline seems to create an outlet for an attempt to interpret modernity in the light of fraternity. Fraternity, therefore, emerges from a condition (= democracy) which is constitutionally orphan of that very principle and imposes itself as a statute which implicitly regulates relationships between men—heirs *uti singuli* of their own position entrusted to the equality of conditions.

In the well-known chapter of the first part of *Democracy in America*, Tocqueville sets out to illustrate the social condition of Anglo-Americans as an example of the democratic social state *par excellence*. This chapter, in fact, expatiates upon the socio-political function of hereditary rights and implicitly upon the family as an institution able to represent, as a device which conserves and transmits or else modifies and revolutionizes the economic, social, juridical, political and consequently psycho-anthropological structures of the entire order of society.

The end of the "family spirit" which Tocqueville examines in this chapter is, in fact, essentially the end of the supremacy of paternity—and egalitarian right of succession can be seen as a signal of this end. The equality which such a right introduces among brothers abrogates the code of structured social relationships, i.e. the paternal code. Equality among brothers, whether proclaimed or promised by the right of equal succession, reveals or determines "a revolution within property" which changes both structure and nature—yet, according to Tocqueville, acts in depth "upon the soul" of the brothers-owners by modifying their "passions" and their intellectual and pragmatic attitudes. Such equality, therefore, deprives the socio-political scene of a paternal figure in which the authority of aristocracy can legitimize itself. What is more, by suppressing any power to perpetuate the paternal privilege within the social structure, equality imposes fraternity as the form and style of democratic coexistence.

Furthermore, according to Tocqueville, the "family spirit" is a specific type of sociality which is able to create immediate ties between men, over and above any autonomous or individual choice. These ties are special but not universal and are essentially ties of supra and subordination which are able to create a "natural" resistance to despotism. Democracy renders both these aspects troublesome as, with the spread of equality/fraternity, those ties are no longer immediate, and resistance is no longer natural.

> For as long as there was family spirit the man who fought tyranny was never alone; around him he found the support of clients, hereditary friends and those close to him. And had this support been lacking, he still felt supported by his ancestors and animated by his descendants.[1]

With the extinction of the politico-ethical role of the paternal figure around whose authority the "family spirit" had radiated, thus defining the aristocratic world structure, a new society of brothers in a situation of equality now predominates. This new social structure is based upon uniformity but not upon unity. Indeed, the dispersion of property and of the social power connected with it is related to the estrangement of the components of fraternal society, which pushes man towards individualism and solitude. Democratic man, constitutionally deprived of that "spirit of family" which had outlined the pluralism and polyarchy of aristocracy, is placed in a present which is unrelated to the times and generation which had preceded him and which will follow him. The modern feeling that democratic man inherits with fraternity (= individualism), being inextricably bound to the end of the aristocratic family ethos, imposes a change in social structure and behavior and consequently also in mental attitudes. As Tocqueville writes:

> In democratic peoples, new families are always arising out of nothingness, others are always falling into it, and all those families that remain change face; time leaves nothing unchanged, and the vestiges of generations are erased. One easily forgets those who preceded one, and one has no idea as to those who will follow. Only those who are close are of interest to us.... Thus not only does democracy make each man forget his ancestors, but it hides his descendants from him and separates him from his contemporaries: it always brings him back to himself and threatens to finally enclose him entirely within the solitude of his own heart.[2]

At the end of chapter VIII of the third part of the second *Democracy*, which is dedicated to the influence of democracy on the family, Tocqueville senses that he has reached a turning point in his ideas on feelings and customs

1.   *DA* [N], I, 243.
2.   *DA* [N], II, 98.

which regard modernity. This turning point allows him to summarize the most salient features of his work on the era and its future. He writes:

> I do not think that it is impossible to enclose within a single sentence the entire meaning of this chapter and of several others that precede it. Democracy loosens social ties, but it strengthens natural ties. It brings relatives closer together and, at the same time, separates citizens.[3]

Thus the family spirit in which the principle of aristocratic paternity is meaningful bears no relation to the private or "natural" sphere, but to the public and social sphere instead. Therefore, the chapter dedicated to the family specifically sets out to illustrate a singular tendency of democracy through a process which might well be defined as *naturalization of institutions via the neutralization of parental authority*, and in which parental authority is brought back to its simple task of generating and rearing offspring. The significant result of this process, which here, too, highlights the nature of history, essentially consists of privileging within itself affective and private ties rather than institutional and public ones. However, if in its natural function of human reproduction this process represents the civilization and refinement of institutions, it does not produce the same effects in the reproduction of citizens. In fact, to the extent to which the ties created by the democratic family appear to be based mainly on "intimacy" and "free sympathy," they do not seem to be a breeding ground for political virtue but rather for a fraternal type of society in which, according to Tocqueville, "in the eyes of the law, the father is only a richer and more aged citizen than his sons"; and such a reduction of paternal status to a fraternal dimension legitimizes a situation "in which the arm of the government seeks out every individual man in the crowd in order to bend him separately to its common laws."[4]

Another feature of democratic equality which, in combination with the aspect already mentioned bears remarkable similarity to fraternity, is also worth underlining. According to Tocqueville, "the general notion of likeness,"[5] which had been obscured in the aristocratic era, could only be brought to light by democracy. Democracy introduces the beginning of an era of universal likeness which determines a new way of feeling and interpreting human relationships. Democracy renders man unable to sense notable differences not only between himself and his neighbor in general, but also between himself and the enemy or the foreigner.

3. *DA* [N], II, 168.
4. *DA* [N], II, 166.
5. *DA* [N], II, 98.

When ranks are almost equal in a people, when all men think and feel in just about the same way, each of them can easily judge the feelings of all the others: he glances at himself; this is enough. There is thus no misery that he cannot easily perceive and which a secret instinct cannot uncover. In vain should they be strangers or enemies: imagination immediately puts him in their place. It adds something personal to his pity, and makes him suffer when the body of his fellow being is being torn to pieces.6

This "sensitivity" towards the human species is unknown to aristocracy because its institutions, writes Tocqueville, "do not create any real sympathy; because real sympathy exists only between similar people; and, in the aristocratic centuries, one only finds similar people among the members of one's own class."7 However, such universal and progressive similarity (so universal that Tocqueville feared that "variety would disappear from the human race"8) together with democracy allows for a certain ubiquity of "family air" which generates sympathy, or, in other words "general compassion for all members of the human race."9 But due to the sufferings of less fortunate brothers, it also generates envy towards those who are more fortunate. As is well known, envy is, for Tocqueville, an archetypically fraternal sentiment which is universally and typically democratic.

If we return to the "family" metaphor in which the different role of each of its components can be seen to represent different forms of socio-political order, then the end of aristocracy is the father's death replaced by a fraternal society—yet fraternal only because it is constitutionally orphan of a hierarchically uniting, reassuring, protective figure and not because fraternity is regarded as a cohabitative value. This is the reason that democratic society does not, on the one hand, necessarily produce an *état de société* or on the other makes man search for a substitute to compensate for the loss of this father figure. Let us briefly examine these last two points.

The Idea of Society

The existence of equality as the most important condition of an *état social* for Tocqueville is not necessarily indicative of the existence of an ulterior condition which can be defined as *état de société*. Good examples of this can be found in the condition of the physical isolation of pioneers in the wilderness of the American west and in the moral isolation of individuals

6.   *DA* [N], II, 147.
7.   *DA* [N], II, 146.
8.   *DA* [N], II, 191.
9.   *DA* [N], II, 147.

belonging to a people still troubled by the effects of a violent democratic revolution such as the French one. In both examples we recognize that the requirement of the democratic *état social* (= equality) is present, but not yet the *état de société*. The word "society," in fact, in Tocqueville's terminology has two fundamental meanings. The first meaning is ample and generic: society is merely an apt term to describe a global condition of coexistence leaving out of consideration its cohesive structure or values which regulate lifestyles. According to this meaning Tocqueville writes indifferently about aristocratic or democratic society. The second meaning is more specific and quasi-prescriptive: society is a form of coexistence governed by values which are not exclusive to one person or to a particular group of individuals yet which are generally agreed and which unite the attitude of individuals towards a common life. These attitudes determine the *forma mentis* of its members. In this sense, aristocracy, due to its pluralistic and polycentric socio-political structure and to its values centered on the "family spirit" and on the concept of honor learned from this particularistic spirit, is unable to express a unitary and general concept of man.

> In the aristocratic centuries which have preceded ours, there have been certain very powerful figures and weak social authority. Even the image of the society was vague, and was constantly lost among the different powers which ruled the citizens.[10]

Elsewhere we read:

> In an aristocratic society, each class has its own opinions, ideas, laws, morals, its separate existence. Thus, the men who make up a certain class, do not in any way resemble those from other classes; they do not have the same way of thinking, of feeling, and they barely believe that they belong to the same race.[11]

Thus, the very image of society and its conception as an abstract entity absorbing individuals and groups who are part of it are possible only by a social democratic condition whose opinions, feelings, customs and rights make up a common patrimony, run on the basis of a fraternal code of living. However, the constitutive ambivalence of fraternity creates the crucial problem of modernity: in passing from aristocracy to democracy (in which universal likeness promotes sympathy without ties, compassion without duty, yet where envy spreads with the claim and passion of equality) what would hold together men who were now fraternally emancipated from a paternal figure? In such a situation, greatly worsened during a revolutionary transition, will interest aimed at material well-being and rational and economical

10. *DA* [N], II, 276.
11. *DA* [N], II, 146.

premeditation aimed at the satisfaction of needs and passions guarantee an *état de société*? We can begin to find an answer to these questions in the first *Democracy*. When Tocqueville describes the social and political function of religion in the American democracy, he bestows upon it a paradigmatic value for democracy in general and in particular for a democracy in which family spirit has been destroyed along with religious spirit.

> Religion is much more of a necessity in a republic... than in a monarchy... and in democratic republics most of all. How can a society fail to perish if, when political ties loosen, moral ties are not strengthened?[12]

It will not be possible to examine here all the questions which this problem poses within Tocqueville's work, and not least relating to his much repeated conviction that democratic man is unable to establish morals without religion. According to Tocqueville, man's lot of solitude and independence renders him incapable of establishing ultimate grounds for actions and behavior. What is of interest to our topic is also implicit in the last quotation where it was said (alluding to Montesquieu's typology of government forms) that both monarchy and aristocratic republics (i.e. forms of socio-political life dominated by the family spirit and paternal code) create cohesion among men through direct political ties.[13] The weakening of such ties creates an alternative. On the one hand, as equality and likeness are universal, we see the opening up of the possibility of founding a tie among men based on a moral dimension which tends towards universality. On the other hand, there is the possibility of social disintegration brought about through anomie, anarchy or despotism.

It must be stressed that Tocqueville's interest is not that of an ideal social solidarity lost on the threshold between old community and modern society and that his interest does not lie in the ideal of social harmony which eliminates conflict. Tocqueville's concern lies in the evaluation of conditions in which the state of society becomes possible, such as the condition of recognition and common reference to man as such. An essential prerequisite of this *état de société*, then, is the end of family spirit, paternity and particularism, in exchange for a link between men based on material and spiritual similarity, i.e. upon fraternal features which democracy imposes upon mankind by means of equality of conditions. In my opinion it is here

---

12. *DA* [N], I, 229.
13. With regards to ties which united men in aristocracy we read in the second part of *Democracy in America* that they "are not born of natural law, but of political law." *DA* [N], II, 146.

that Tocqueville is seeking for the *homo democraticus* a problematic moral tie that no law can abstractly impose.

Democratic Replacements

These considerations lead us on to the second point, the replacements which can make up for the disappearance of the paternal figure. Fraternal democracy, as I have tried to define it, is almost obligated to substitute God for the departed father, in order to fulfill its own potential values. Or it could also entrust itself to a central power with uniform governmental and administrative organization unified in the state, the form which social power takes in democracy (a power which was previously divided among fathers-masters). This possibility, too, is merely an outcome of the constitutional duplicity of democratic man in his condition of orphan torn between the desire for independence and the search for a master.[14] What troubles Tocqueville throughout his work is not so much the question of anarchy, which would however presuppose developed and mature, or at least self-confident individuals, but the ambivalence of democratic man with regards to authority and power (to which it is linked), without which even a fraternal type of society would become problematic. Thus, what interests our writer is not whether or not authority exists within a mature democracy—this is to say, a democracy which has overcome the stage of transition and its struggles and the disillusionment which its revolutionary and violent nature produces with regard to the values of citizenship—but rather where this authority should be placed, who it will be given to and upon what type of legitimacy it will be able to depend, once the family spirit and paternal code which had once legitimized it have waned. When equality and the immediate and instinctive fraternity which accompany it are established within social relations, according to Tocqueville "the idea of rights inherent to certain individuals disappears rapidly from the minds of men; the idea of all-powerful rights, thus unique to society, come to take its place."[15] In a situation of fraternal equalitarianism, the individual is offended by any inequality and is practically cheered by the common subordination to a despot.

> No great inequality offends the eyes when all conditions are unequal; while the smallest difference seems shocking in the midst of general uniformity; the sight of it becomes increasingly unbearable as the uniformity becomes more complete....

14. *DA* [N], II, 239-240, 278.
15. *DA* [N], II, 241.

> Democratic man only obeys his neighbor who is his equal with great repugnance; he refuses to acknowledge in his neighbor a greater natural intelligence than his own; he doubts his own fairness and sees with jealousy his neighbor's power; he fears it and scorns it; at every instant he loves to make him feel the common dependency in which they both have the same master.[16]

As is well known, Tocqueville's real worry is always and only the despotism which in modernity can take possession of the social power now unified in the state. If we refer to *Democracy in America*, we find several examples of possible despotism, ranging from majority despotism to despotism of faction,[17] from a plebeian Caesar to the tutor-state, with this last perhaps being the most degraded form of fraternal democracy (seeking a new master who can reassure it in its incurable narcissism in the face of crude, new reality). This form of state fulfils the "new despotism" foreseen by Tocqueville in the future of democracy as a possible outcome of modernity. It is not only freed from all feelings of envy, but also demanded by individuals as:

> a power... absolute, detailed, regular, provident and gentle. It would resemble paternal power if, like such power, its object were to prepare men for adulthood; but, on the contrary, it seeks only to keep them in childhood forever.[18]

It is within this context that God, or rather religion, represents a necessary substitute for the departed father by satisfying the democratic man's need for reassurance in those fundamental spiritual and intellectual areas which govern important fields of human action. Religion provides democratic man with a way of facing the difficulty of modern freedom in social areas (principally politics and economics) which religion itself, placed by the modern age within its natural limits, may free, leaving them to the autonomy of reason. This is why, according to Tocqueville, due to the insecurity, the mobility and risks which characterize it, democratic independence either saves religion or else leads to the loss of freedom. It is impossible to achieve independence at the same time in all sectors of intellectual, moral, theoretical and practical life. It is also difficult to achieve it both at a political and social level at the same time:

> When authority in religious matters no longer exists, any more than it does in political matters, men soon become frightened, faced with the sight of this limitless independence, this perpetual agitation... everything worries and tires them. Since everything is in a state of fluctuation in the intellectual world, they want everything to be firm and stable at least in the material world, and, because they can no longer return to their former beliefs, they choose a master. Personally, I doubt that man can ever endure complete religious independence and total political freedom

16. *DA* [N], II, 244.
17. *DA* [N], II, 128.
18. *DA* [N], II, 265.

simultaneously; I tend to think that, if man has no faith, then he must serve, and, if he is free, he must believe.[19]

In addition to the compensational substitute for the father figure, there does exist an alternative corresponding solution which enables democratic man to live in fraternity. Of the two pre-existing solutions one accepts without criticism the condition of the democratic age, and the other allows a mature choice of a dimension of possible freedom.

The first solution, which increases the stunted narcissism of immature fraternity and which can be seen as the source of the political apathy of infantile hedonism, is represented by the *petits cotéries*.[20] These are small cliques which are perfectly homogeneous with individualism and whose demands for well-being allow democratic despotism to legitimize its all pervasive tendencies owing to the fact that such groups are unable to set up any form of participation or resistance to central power. On the other hand, within the political dimension of these groups, fraternity can be a rational and critical choice which aims at correcting the natural weakness of the individual. In fact, within a democracy, the individual, even when he is socially emancipated from ties of status, does not have, according to Tocqueville, sufficient means to develop individually in a politically responsible way. This is because he now only represents himself and his own personal interests and thus he possesses a civil life, but not a political one.[21] Fraternity, in the immediacy of its egalitarian application, gives no spontaneous help through which man can rise above the limitations of individualism. "A nation"—writes Tocqueville—"in which individuals lose the power to do great things independently, without acquiring the ability to achieve them in groups, would soon return to barbarism."[22] Thus only the difficult "art" of political association can positively correct the effects of fraternity by displacing democratic man from his congenital narcissism to a desire of security, rendering him able to assume in a mature way the responsibility of political action. This is clearly stated in chapter VII of the second part of the 1840 *Democracy*:

> A political association brings a multitude of individuals out of their self-absorption; however separated they may be naturally by age, intellect, fortune, it brings them together and puts them in contact with each other. They meet once and learn to find each other again forever.[23]

19. *DA* [N], II, 33-34.
20. *DA* [N], II, 181.
21. "In private life, every man can, if he must, imagine that he is capable of being self-sufficient. In political life, he could never imagine it." *DA* [N], II, 110.
22. *DA* [N], II, 104.
23. *DA* [N], II, 111.

Of course, political associations present pathological aspects too: the despotism of faction described in chap. XIV of the second part of the 1840 *Democracy*. However, this form of despotism is founded outside the association itself and within a social sphere where there is a sense of political apathy and emotional indifference towards the *res publica* in general as well as a sort of fear of freedom and the conflicts which it entails.[24] This means that the same political associations, and especially parties, cannot be vehicles of political freedom where there is a common condition of spiritual estrangement from politics owing to the desire for material well-being and an exaggerated love for order and security.

> When the majority of citizens are preoccupied with their own private affairs, the smallest political party should not despair of becoming a political leader. For it is not rare to see, on the vast stage of this world, as well as on those of our theaters, a multitude of men represented by a few. They speak in the name of an absent or inattentive crowd; alone, they act in the middle of a universal stagnation; they have everything at their disposal, according to their whims, they change laws and tyrannize customs, to their liking; and it is astonishing to see how a great nation can fall into a small number of weak and unworthy hands.[25]

The strength of aristocracy had lain in the natural coherence of inequality-paternity upon which the state was founded as well as upon the "family spirit" which pervaded political life. On the contrary, equality-fraternity, which defines the social state of man, lacking in auctoritas and power, naturally tends to estrange itself from political life and to alienate all social power unifying the state and making it a representation of the unrepresentable unity of brothers (who are now politically represented as an undifferentiated "mass" or "crowd").

In order to save democratic freedom on its way to becoming universal and to producing abstract and mass fraternity, an artifice is needed. The expedient of association seems to be for Tocqueville something which flaws the abstract generalization of fraternity, a device through which (in the modern age) each person can test his own insignificance against a crowd of equals. By means of political association, a part of politically spendable social power can be artificially recuperated. This takes place without giving up fraternity, but rather strengthening it beyond natural differences. Association allows for a choice to be made towards a concrete objective based upon common and specific needs, interests and ideas. A typical feature of aristocracy is thus retrieved: the spirit of participation/resistance to power, together

24. *DA* [N], II, 127.
25. *DA* [N], II, 128.

with the institutional clash which is necessary for the acquisition and conservation of liberty. According to Tocqueville, liberty has its focal point in the political sphere. This occurs above all in democracy. From the political sphere, liberty radiates out into all environments of modernity, including economic life.

It is upon this point regarding modern life that I should like to conclude this paper.

The Industrial and Commercial Mentality

According to Tocqueville, the most significant elements of social order are those which cannot be modified without radically threatening the whole of society. However, there is a nucleus within society which, when tampered with, can cause it to change its nature and become distorted. A large part of this nucleus is made up of the property/mentality/system of production plexus, founded upon equality, within which the understanding of feelings and customs and of the intellectual and political spheres of democratic man are revealed. There are two main phenomena which accompany the democratization of the modern world: the change in property and relations with things and people connected with it and the universalization of work.[26] The mobilization and monetizing of property mobilizes and eradicates individual positions while each person has to face the problem of satisfying his own needs. Thus, the freedom from work in a democracy cannot be attributed to a certain status, order or class.

In theory, property is accessible to everyone, just as, in theory, all forms of work and ways of earning are accessible. Essentially, these elements too were thought to be monetizable in the same way as property, which could be made private.[27]

In this context the old difference between master and servant is abolished and obedience within a relationship becomes voluntary and provisional, as at any moment, writes Tocqueville, "the servant can, and hopes to become master; the servant is therefore not essentially different from the master."[28]

26. "Among democratic nations... the idea of work, as a necessary, natural and honest condition, offers itself... from all sides to the human mind." *DA* [N], II, 135.
27. "Equality does not only bring back into favor the idea of work, it revives the idea of work bringing profit" (*idem*); and, elsewhere, Tocqueville underlines that in a democracy, political activity itself can be conceived as a job with its own form of remuneration in the form of salary.
28. *DA* [N], II, 157.

Despite real inequality, despite richness and poverty, command and obedience, the distance between the two is *casual.*

> Public opinion, which is based upon the ordinary order of things, brings them towards the same level and creates a sort of imaginary equality…. In the depth of their souls, master and servant no longer perceive any profound differences between themselves.[29]

Even in the sphere of the legitimacy of obedience, the end of the family spirit which gave everyone a role before their birth, while not managing to eradicate "real inequality," allows the element of fraternal likeness to emerge over and above the actual condition of life. This attitude towards all differences in economic or political social rank is rooted in a prerequisite element of the socio-anthropological constitution of democratic man to which a special form of mental productivity can be added. In his notes on his journey in America, Tocqueville already considers the industrial and commercial mentality (which determines the American character) the psychological equipment which is necessary to be able to live and produce in a democracy, a mentality which, as in America, is also apparent in agriculture, modifying the relationship between man and the land. Democracy, therefore, grows with a homogeneous way of understanding and producing material and spiritual goods which then generate the cultural and spiritual world of modernity in which democratic man is formed. "Democracy" writes Tocqueville in chapter XIV of the first part of the 1840 *Democracy*, which is significantly entitled *De l'industrie littéraire*, "introduces the industrial spirit into the heart of literature."[30]

The nucleus determined by equality/fraternity, freedom in property and labour, and industrial mentality is so characteristic of the democratic world, so peculiar to the man who lives there, that it is dangerous to undermine its internal coherence. Therefore, Tocqueville sees the reemergence of democracy, at this level, as pathological—because, just at this level, the very principle of democracy is at stake. The aristocracy which he sees looming in the "large industry" seems to be like a "detour" of modernity through which the democratic trend is halted and inverted, reproposing in a deviant way diversion, variegation, antipathy, indifference and extraneousness among men who have now become *brothers of common destinies and expectation.* The social, economic and cultural phenomena introduced by this type of industry represent for Tocqueville "a large and unhappy exception"[31] which outlines

29. *Idem.*
30. *DA* [N], II, 64.
31. *DA* [N], II, 163.

a "small society" around industry itself. This "small society" upsets the structural laws of the material and spiritual form of society by establishing "a monster in the middle of the social condition." The great capitalist, according to Tocqueville, despite appearances, is totally incapable of historically repeating the aristocratic role because his power is only manifest in a relationship of exploitation of workers and not in a rapport of socio-political protection and responsibility. On the other hand, workers, in an era of widespread education, individual independence, well-being and both horizontal and vertical mobility, seem more and more to resemble brutes. They lack independence ("they are... almost at the mercy of their masters"[32]), their salaries fall steadily compared to the steady growth of wealth, and they are forever tied to their socio-economic condition.

> This state of dependency and misery, in which a part of the industrial population currently finds itself, is exceptional and contrary to everything that surrounds it; but, for this very reason, it is even more serious, and more deserving of the particular attention of the legislator; because it is very difficult, when the whole society is changing, to keep one class motionless, and force several to peaceably endure their needs and desires when most people are continuously starting on new paths towards fortune.[33]

If this small society based on inequality and externality represents within democratic society an exception to democracy's tendency towards levelling and pacifying to the extreme the stagnation of all political passion and initiative, then its relationship with the revolution will be equally unusual. As Tocqueville explicitly states, when one lives in a democratic society, what is revolutionary is certainly not equality but inequality.

> If America ever experiences any large revolutions, they will be brought about by the presence of Blacks on the soil of the United States: that is to say that it will not be the equality of conditions, but, on the contrary, their inequality which will give birth to them.[34]

If, therefore, passively accepted fraternity in its abstract universality is a source of political apathy, of social anomie, of individualism and alienation of citizenship, then the removal of fraternity, as is manifest in the relationship between great industrialists and workers, represents the limit of survival of a democracy, as modernity has shown us. Social revolution, which seems to belong to the exploited classes who have no hope of improving their lot, represents, according to Tocqueville, together with military dictatorship and various forms of democratic despotism, the limit of a foreseeable democracy

32. *DA* [N], II, 164.
33. *Idem.*
34. *DA* [N], II, 214.

and the elimination of the principles of the French Revolution and not their fulfillment. Tocqueville begins to outline these ideas from the forties onwards, especially in speeches given before and after 1848.

To conclude this outline of Tocqueville's possible attitude towards the third principle of Revolution in *Democracy in America*, we could perhaps ask ourselves the following question: what happens in a fraternal society to the maternal code? The question arises perhaps from the fact that motherhood is generally the archetypical background from which fraternity emerges and legitimizes itself as the referent of psycho-anthropological and socio-political structures which characterize significant eras and forms of society. Little is written in *Democracy* regarding this question. In the first *Democracy*, the mother is defined as the holder and transmitter of customs, the pedagogical value of which in American democracy is emphasized by Tocqueville. Where American conditions do not hold—for example, in a situation like France where the Revolution has deprived the country of customs and replaced them with a period of stunted transition while awaiting democracy—the maternal role remains subject to this spiritual condition. In the second *Democracy*, motherhood is seen as being strictly connected to the role of wife and as a radical modification of the condition of the American woman. The social role of motherhood is limited to the family circle and totally subjected to the will of the husband. Tocqueville explores the female condition in pioneering families, seeing such families as a feasible model for the American family in general. Considering the essentially private position of the maternal role, apart from a quick mention of their relationship with customs, which should not, however, be ignored, there do not seem to be any links with the public sphere of democratic fraternity.

On the other hand, with regard to the *état d'esprit* of democratic man, inclined towards well-being, security and tranquillity to the extent of being tendentially alien to political passion and to the risks of freedom—and above all, to revolutionary passions—democratic man is prone to allowing himself to be cared for and fed by the enormous protective uterus of mass society which is the state. The state, in the form of that "new despotism" which is meek, meticulous, helpful and providential, and which is described in the final pages of the second *Democracy*, is seen to care for men who have regressed to childhood because they are unable, after the death of Father, to become responsible brothers of others. In a similar spiritual condition, we find the presence of negative attitudes generally attributed to the social effects of the maternal code; but they are too few to allow further discussion.

(French quotations translated by Beth Bakeman)

[9]

Pauperism and Democracy. Alexis de Tocqueville and Nassau Senior

Hugh Brogan

On 11 January 1837 Alexis de Tocqueville wrote from Paris to his friend Nassau Senior in London to thank him for a present:

> You could not have sent me anything that I should have liked better than your outline of political economy. I have often realized that I lack adequate understanding of this important branch of human science, and I have many times reflected that you were the man most capable of supplying my wants. Everything you publish is very valuable to me, but what you write on political economy is so most of all.[1]

This avowal so impressed Minnie Simpson, Senior's daughter and the first editor of the Tocqueville-Senior correspondence, that she headed the page on which it appeared "ignorance of Political Economy".[2] She had allowed herself to be deceived by a typical specimen of Tocquevillian unction. Tocqueville, as is demonstrated by one of the latest volumes of his *Oeuvres complètes* and pointed out by its editor,[3] was well acquainted with the writings of Jean-Baptise Say and Alban de Villeneuve-Bargemont. It is doubtful if the recipient of the letter, Minnie's father, was taken in. For his friendship with Tocqueville had begun in what may be called a haze of applied economics, and it was to be years before it got onto a different footing. This paper attempts to sketch the place of Senior's investigations in Tocqueville's thought, and to evaluate the ensemble.

1. *OC*, VI:2, 79.
2. M. C. M. Simpson ed., *Correspondence and Conversations of Alexis de Tocqueville with Nassau William Senior* (London: Henry S. King and Co., 1872), II, 17.
3. *OC*, XVI, 24, 118, 142-143 (footnote), 425-434.

The two men met during Tocqueville's first visit to London, in 1833. According to Minnie Simpson he walked into Senior's chambers at Lincoln's Inn with no other introduction than the words, "I am Alexis de Tocqueville and I come to make your acquaintance."[4] There is no reason to question this story, but of itself it does not explain why Tocqueville sought out Senior. Perhaps the idea was put into his head by Richard Whately, the Archbishop of Dublin, whom he met at a dinner party, for Whately, himself an economist, had been Senior's tutor at Oxford.[5] Tocqueville, whose obsessive interest in local administration was one of his most enduring characteristics,[6] may have heard from Whately that his friend Senior was at that very time engaged in reforming the English poor law. Tocqueville had already noticed a placard at a political meeting which read "Poor Laws in Ireland! Better Wages in England!"[7] Two weeks later, as the guest of Lord Radnor at Longford Castle, near Salisbury, he attended a petty sessions where he saw the unreformed poor law in action, and had at least two serious conversations on the subject with his host. An approach to Nassau Senior fitted in very well with these preoccupations.

Tocqueville's charm and intelligence conquered the economist in a moment, and the publication of the first part of the *Democracy* in 1835 did the rest. Senior received an early presentation copy. He hastened to assure the author that he had read it with great interest, delight, and (he hoped) instruction, and found it to be one of the most remarkable books of the age. He volunteered help to get it reviewed in England, and made a string of comments on various points of political economy in the second volume.[8] Tocqueville responded gratefully, then in March wrote to say that he had been commissioned to write an article on pauperism. He asked Senior to send him a copy of the Poor Law Amendment Act, which had become law the year before, a request with which Senior immediately complied. This was one of the most important intellectual gifts that Tocqueville ever received, perhaps comparable to his discovery of *The Federalist* during his visit to the United States.

For the Act was an outstanding piece of legislation, just as much as were the other great statutes of the Grey ministry—the Act abolishing slavery in the British Empire, the Municipal Corporations Act, the Reform Act itself. Like the Report of the Royal Commission which preceded it, it was largely the work of Nassau Senior and Edwin Chadwick, the disciple of Jeremy

4.   *Correspondence and Conversations*, I, iii.
5.   See letter to Gustave de Beaumont, August 13, 1833, *OC*, VIII:1, 126.
6.   This interest was first awakened in America in 1832, and was still evident twenty-four years later, in the *Ancien Régime*.
7.   *Voyages en Angleterre*, *OC*, V:2, 12, note dated August 15, 1833.
8.   Senior to Tocqueville, February 17, 1835, *OC*, VI:2, 66-68.

Bentham, and as such brought to bear on the problem of pauperism the combined insights, or at any rate opinions, of classical economics and utilitarianism. Report and law came into being because the twin problems of over-population and under-employment (really the same thing) in the countryside were imposing what was felt as an intolerable strain on the system of poor relief which the country gentry had administered since the reign of Elizabeth I; and in the Report, if not in the Act, we can see the first faint sketch of a British welfare state, for the commissioners, less heartless than is commonly supposed, concerned themselves not only with the able-bodied unemployed, but with relief for the indigent sick and elderly, and with the care and education of pauper children. To Senior, who possessed much of the expert's contempt for the amateur, the principal achievement of the Act seems to have been its replacement of gentry administration with a more democratic system supervised from London.[9] To the English upper and middle classes the law was welcome because it made labour more mobile and gratified their eternal hankering to cut taxes and reduce expenditure on the unfortunate. To the rural and urban working classes alike the law, with its ban on outdoor relief, its fearsome workhouses and its propensity to strip the poor of their last possessions and break up their families, was a horror, long and passionately resented, and one of the chief objects of attack by the Chartist movement. Perhaps, in the very long run, the chief effect of the law was to deepen the gulf of hostility and incomprehension between the classes which is still one of the worst banes of British life.

For Tocqueville none of these considerations (certainly not the two last) were what mattered. Confronted with this formidable document he went to work in his usual manner, reading carefully and making extensive notes in which he summarized the details of the new law and jotted down his reflections on its significance. Then, it appears, he went back to work on his pauperism article, presumably finishing it before sailing for England with Gustave de Beaumont on April 21, 1835.[10] It is these notes, the article on

9. *Correspondence and Conversations*, I, 203-204; also *OC*, VI:2, 334.
10. The editors of the *Voyages en Angleterre* identify Tocqueville's notes on the new poor law as "contemporains" with his 1835 journey to England (*OC*, V:2, 221), which in a loose sense is certainly true; but the English translator of that volume took the word to imply that the notes were actually made in England. This seems most unlikely. There is a close parallel between one passage of the notes and one in the *Mémoire sur le paupérisme* (*OC*, V:2, 229 and *OC*, XVI, 137). We know that Tocqueville was working on the *Mémoire* in early March, 1835 (*OC*, VI:2, 73-74) and that Senior on 18 March sent him the copy of the poor law which is still preserved in the library at the château de Tocqueville. There being no reason why Tocqueville should delay, he presumably read the document at once. He did not set out for England for another month.

pauperism itself (with an incomplete successor) and the records of some subsequent conversations that tell us plainly what he made of Senior's law.

Two main themes emerge from these materials. First, Tocqueville immediately saw the bearing of the new poor law on one of his favorite topics: "The law of 14 August 1834 has *centralized*[11] the administration of the poor into the hands of three functionaries called *Poor Law Commissioners* (for England and Wales). They are appointed by the king."[12] He was pleased to note that by what he saw as a characteristically English and American device any tendency to tyranny in these arrangements was checked by the fact that the Boards of Guardians were elected by the rate-payers, and could only be removed by the courts, but the mere fact of even so limited a degree of centralization acted on him like a fire-bell. On his first visit to England, in 1833, John Bowring had assured him that British administration was radically decentralized and that this was the secret of British progress: the idea had gone straight into the first part of the *Democracy*.[13] It now struck Tocqueville that a centralizing tendency might after all be at work in Britain, and he raised the matter with his translator, Henry Reeve, when he returned to England in 1835. Reeve instantly confirmed the notion ("You have seen our new poor law") and threw in the thought that the prison system was probably going to be centralized along the same lines.[14] After this conversation Tocqueville wrote excitedly in his notebook:

> Centralization—a democratic instinct—the instinct of a society which is beginning to shake off the mediaeval system of individualism . Prepares the ground for despotism.
> Why is centralization so much more habitual in democracy? A big question to be *dug out* in the third volume of my book, if I can fit it in—a *leading* question.[15]

He carried this preoccupation with him into conversations with Lord Minto and John Stuart Mill[16]—who confirmed the idea that centralization was increasing in England, but hoped it would not go too far[17]—to Birmingham and to Manchester, developing his thoughts more and more fully as he went

11. Tocqueville's emphasis.
12. *OC*, V:2, 229.
13. *OC*, V:2, 31-32 and DA, [N], I, 69-80.
14. OC V:2, 49, note dated May 11, 1835.
15. *Idem*. Tocqueville's emphases.
16. But not, so far as we know, to Senior, although the two men met eight times during Tocqueville's visit to London. Only two of their conversations are recorded: one about Ireland, in which Tocqueville listened to Senior questioning John Revans, and one, recorded by Camille de Cavour and Beaumont, in which Senior at last convinced Tocqueville that there was no necessary connection between democracy and peasant smallholding.
17. *OC*, V:2, 53-54.

along, until the way was open before him which led to the last *partie* of the *Democracy,* in which his conception of centralization received its definitive treatment. The Act of 1834 was thus, for him, the seed of a mighty tree.

But if it stimulated a train of thought which fed into the *Democracy,* it lay, much more immediately, behind the *Mémoires sur le paupérisme.* The views expressed therein form the second theme.

We know nothing of the circumstances which led to the commission from the Société Royale Académique de Cherbourg, of which Tocqueville was the newest member, to write on pauperism, but it is not unreasonable to guess that his was the choice of subject, since at various times he had already taken many notes on it, of which the first *Mémoire* bears traces on almost every page. Just as, during his investigation of American democracy, Tocqueville's lively intelligence had, willy-nilly, accumulated information on many topics that were, however fascinating, so remotely connected to his main subject that he had much difficulty in fitting them into his literary scheme, so his investigation of the English aristocracy in 1833 had thrown up material that was even more intractable. There was no room for the English Poor Law in the first part of the *Democracy,* and the *Système pénitentiaire,* which included an appendix on American pauperism that might have been extended as a result of Tocqueville's English investigations, had already been published. Rather than abandon so much good work Tocqueville (we may guess) decided to take advantage of an invitation from the Cherbourg academy to write an entirely fresh study, and having advised his countrymen about prisons and democracy, now set out to teach them about indigence; and whereas he had used American researches as the foundation of his first two books, his new work would be based on the inquiries he had carried out in England. But this time he was handicapping himself severely. He had to write in a hurry, and by his own standards his investigations had been superficial. No wonder he appealed for help to Senior; but Senior was the last person to give him the help he really needed. For Tocqueville's problem was that he had already acquired all the prejudices and misconceptions which disfigured Senior's 1833 Report on the poor law.

When Tocqueville studied the provisions of the new law he was struck forcibly, more even than by its centralizing potential, by its central principle: that of making relief as unpleasant as possible to the recipients. Under the old poor law the workhouses had been comparatively comfortable places; indeed they gave their inmates a standard of living that was actually better than that of many employed farm laborers. Outdoor relief (i.e. doles of money; food and other necessities supplied for consumption in the pauper's home, rather than in the workhouse) was also universal. The architects of the new law, Senior and Chadwick, were determined that these absurdities (as they saw them) be stamped out, otherwise there was no inducement to make a pauper seek work. So they set up the notorious standard of "less eligibility." At all costs the workhouses must be made less agreeable than the world outside, so that the paupers would loathe their status and take every change of finding employment. Outdoor relief must be abolished. Tocqueville entirely approved of this rigor. As late as 1851, when discussing the question of a French poor law with Senior, he was to say, "If we give this right we must of course make this relief disagreeable; we must separate families, make the workhouse a prison, and our charity repulsive."[18] But both in 1851 and in 1835, in the first *Mémoire,* he went even further than his friend, doubting if any right to relief should be granted to the unemployed (which makes his belated assertion that France ought after all to have a poor law rather vacuous).[19] To Senior it seemed self-evident that the unemployed should not be left to beg or starve; such had been a principle of English law since the seventeenth century. Tocqueville insisted that the principle itself was wrong, and would ensure that any new poor law would end up as corrupt, corrupting and expensive to the tax-payer as the old one had been:

> To want to establish a law which comes to the help of the indigent on a regulated, permanent, uniform basis, without expecting the number of paupers to increase, or their idleness to grow with their needs, their indolence with their vices, is to plant an acorn and then to be astonished that a stalk appears, followed by flowers, later by leaves, and at last by more acorns which, cast far and wide, end one fine day by calling up a green forest from the bowels of the earth.[20]

So rather than grant the right to relief, Tocqueville, in a second essay on pauperism,[21] proposed to set up local savings banks, which would take over the functions of the state-supported *monts de piété* (or pawnshops), so that the poor would lend to the poor (and the rich, I must observe, remain untroubled). He supported the establishment of voluntary parish associations (a truly Tocquevillean notion) for the suppression of begging and vagabondage.

18. *Correspondence and Conversations*, I, 204-205; *OC*, VI:2, 334.
19. *Idem.* Tocqueville did believe in the need for *une charité publique* to deal with the problems of orphans, old age, sickness and lunacy (*OC*, XVI, 138); perhaps that is what he meant by poor law. His disbelief in public relief for the able-bodied was general among English economists in the 1820s; they were all for abolishing the poor law entirely. I do not think that Senior ever took so draconian a view: he was too practical a politician.
20. *OC*, XVI, 137.
21. This sequel to the first *Mémoire* was publicly promised, and Tocqueville nearly finished it in 1837; but he broke off, apparently daunted by the immense problems he was tackling. See *OC*, XVI, 140-157. The essay remained unpublished until 1989.

He thought that perhaps one day the time would be ripe for co-operatives as a means of dealing with industrial unemployment. Above all he advocated the equal division of the land among the peasantry who worked it: once that was done, no agricultural laborer need ever starve. He was glad to think that, thanks to the Revolution, such an agrarian reform had already taken place in France; and he held up the drunken improvidence of the English farm laborer as a horrid example of what happened when all land was allowed to accumulate in the hands of the rich.[22]

These remedies were offered in good faith, but they were totally insufficient for the social problem that tormented the nineteenth century. Mass poverty and degradation in England were acute during the eighteen-twenties, thirties and forties, and gave rise to an immense literature, as well as to the Chartist movement, Disraeli's "Young England" group, the Anti-Corn Law League, Christian Socialism and the huge exertions of Evangelical philanthropy, in short, to all the most vital expressions of the day. Other European countries too would in due course feel the impact of a rising population and the industrial revolution. Tocqueville knew it. His essays on pauperism (in the course of which he used the phrase "the two nations," made famous a few years later by Disraeli)[23] were based almost entirely on English experience, and repeated (mostly) English arguments; but they were designed for application in France. No publicist under the July Monarchy could for a moment forget the class antagonisms which threatened not only the regime but, some thought, the fabric of society itself. During his visit to England in 1835 Tocqueville had observed sardonically that "The whole of English society is based on the privilege of money" and that "The English have left but two rights to the poor: the right to be subject to the same legislation as the rich, and the right to become the equals of the rich by acquiring equal wealth"; and even these rights were more apparent than real.[24] From England he had travelled to Ireland, where for more than a month he had studied minutely a miserably poor rural society: his notes still have shock value as a picture of human suffering. Yet his response to the challenge of urban squalor, rural destitution and their causes was pitifully inadequate.

He was in part, no doubt, the victim of outdated analysis, much as was Senior himself. Malthusian political economy, the new poor law, even the first attacks on the corn laws, were all part of the great post-Waterloo reform

---

22. This passage contains several of the points made by Tocqueville to Senior in letters, and in the conversation witnessed by Cavour (see supra, footnote 16).
23. *OC*, XVI, 132. Disraeli's novel, *Sybil* (1845) was subtitled "The Two Nations,"which were revealed to be the rich and the poor.
24. *OC*, V:2, 63-64.

movement which was itself a response to conditions that had been maturing, if that is the word, for at least a generation. The inadequacy of this early liberalism was amply demonstrated in the great economic crisis of the late thirties which in turn produced the agitations of the forties and the victory of free trade. But so little did Nassau Senior perceive the meaning of what was happening that he argued zealously against the Ten-Hour Act on behalf of the factory-owners, putting forward his famous argument that cotton mills only made a profit for their owners during the last (i.e. twelfth) hour of labour, and that therefore any curtailment of the working day would be ruinous to the industry and all involved in it. Fortunately his argument was fallacious, and the Factory Act went through in 1847, but meanwhile his influence on Tocqueville, such as it was, could not be very beneficial.[25]

Nevertheless it will not do to lay all the blame for Tocqueville's attitude at the economist's door. He had formed his doctrine on poverty long before he met Senior; it achieved finality, at latest, during the American journey.[26]

That journey, it is not perhaps often enough remembered, was officially an enquiry into American prisons, and its purpose was to find out if the penitentiaries of New York and Pennsylvania were effective in redeeming convicts by turning them into decent honest men. In the *Système pénitentiaire aux Etats-Unis* Tocqueville attributed modern crime to frustrated abilities and economic distress, and remarked that prisons commonly completed the work of corruption that poverty began. For him, crime and poverty were but two aspects of the same problem, and he did not believe that state-directed charity was the way to tackle either. In this, his first published work, he was already invoking the specter of the old English poor law, which he perhaps first heard about from John Spencer of Canandaigua:

> In England they thought they could choke the well of misery and crime by giving work or money to every unfortunate; and now we see that every day the number of paupers and criminals in that country increases.[27]

(Incidentally, this passage shows how widespread was the Senior-Chadwickian view of the old poor law even before their report was written or published.) Tocqueville was to make the same point at much greater

25. Senior's views on the Factory Act are conveniently summarized in S. Leon Levy, *Nassau W. Senior*, new edition (Newton Abbot: David & Charles, 1970) 103-116. It was while Tocqueville was working on the second pauperism essay that he received Senior's *Outline of Political Economy* and the *Report of the Commission on the Poor Law*, though he did not immediately read these works (see *OC*, VI:2, 79). But he cites the Report at *OC*, XVI, 133.
26. See the appendix on American pauperism, *Du système pénitentiaire aux Etats-Unis*, *OC*, IV:1, 319-322.
27. *Ibid.*, 152.

length two years later, in the first *Mémoire sur le paupérisme,* where he also laid bare the bleak view of human nature which lay behind his social policies:

> Man, like all organized animals, has a natural craving for idleness. However there are two motives which drive him to work: the need to live and the desire to improve his standard of living. Experience has demonstrated that most men can be driven to work only by the first of these motives, the second being powerful only over a small number.[28]

As for manual laborers,

> Among the lower classes, who abandon themselves most readily to every intemperate excess and like to live as if each day had not its morrow? Who in everything show least foresight? Who make premature and imprudent marriages which seem to have no purpose but that of multiplying the number of the world's unfortunates?[29]

And so on. Françoise Mélonio, the editor of the *Mélanges,* does well to stigmatize such views, in a footnote, as commonplace.[30] This sort of thing was indeed what passed for social science in the circles in which Tocqueville grew up and spent most of his life. To be fair, the experience of the great Revolution and the Terror makes such opinions unsurprising. But unsurprising or not they resemble all too clearly what privileged groups have always tended to assert about the unprivileged, and in particular resemble what, at that very time, American slaveholders were asserting of their slaves. They have no more and no less validity than that. On the whole, they amount to this, that Tocqueville believed the poor to be idle, thriftless and immoral, and proposed to regulate their lives in such a way as to reform their characters. He differed from Nassau Senior only as to the best means to adopt. He was conscientiously benevolent, but it did not occur to him, or to his friend, that the proletarians might have their own view of their problems, which might be worth listening to, might indeed have greater value than his own. For the great prophet of democracy at heart disliked and feared the workers, if not individually, then as a class. It is a common error.

Tocqueville was never compelled to face the inadequacy of his sociology. His sketch of industrial Manchester is justly famous, but not for nothing is it called "*Outer* appearance of Manchester" [my emphasis] and, as Seymour Drescher pointed out long ago, in neither Birmingham nor Manchester did he interview working men: he got all his information about social relations

28. *OC*, XVI, 128.
29. *Ibid.*, second *Mémoire sur le paupérisme*, 142.
30. *Ibid.*, 131-132, footnote 16.

and conditions from members of the middle class—lawyers, manufacturers, an assistant poor law commissioner.[31] Even in Ireland his informants were of the same stripe; he did not get near enough to the people to learn to respect them, either collectively or individually, and even if he had, he might not have applied the lessons of rural Ireland to industrial England, or to Paris and Lyon. He never interviewed any occupant of a workhouse, as he had interviewed prisoners in Philadelphia.[32] His views and actions in 1848 were to spring from this defect in his understanding; and here is laid bare the chief weakness of his thought.

Everyone agrees that from beginning to end *Democracy in America* is an attempt—it might almost be called a backward looking attempt—to come to terms with the political and social transformations that followed the French Revolution. Tocqueville was an aristocrat who believed that democracy had come to stay and that it need not entail the loss of those values which the traditions of his class, nation and church had taught him to hold dear. Political equality need not mean the loss of political liberty; majority rule need not mean majority tyranny; the rule of the many, with all its dangers (dangers which he explored at length) need not entail the death of culture. I do not dispute any of these propositions, or the fascination of Tocqueville's handling of them. But they do not exhaust democracy as a topic. It might even be argued—indeed, it frequently *has* been argued—that they leave the most important question about democratic political relations untouched. Curiously, the author of *Democracy in America* seems to be unaware of the full meaning of his most important term: equality. I put it like that because as the author of the pauperism essays, of the *Souvenirs* and of the *Ancien Régime,* Tocqueville showed himself acutely aware of the great problem of his day, which was not, *Is a middle class republic a prudent and necessary political experiment?* but, *Are changing material conditions making violent revolution inevitable?* The challenge of mass poverty and class war was felt acutely in France and England. Tocqueville, whose parents had narrowly escaped death in the Terror, was not likely to overlook it, indeed it was one of the forces which drove him to write. He wanted to show that democracy was not a synonym for mob rule or a Jacobin dictatorship, and thanks to his American investigations was able to do so convincingly. But somehow, in

31. Seymour Drescher, *Tocqueville and England* (Cambridge, Mass.: Harvard University Press, 1964) 66-67.
32. These interviews are essential reading for all students of Tocqueville's social attitudes. (See *OC*, IV:1, 329-341, and the fuller originals at Yale.) It is significant that he commends solitary confinement on the Philadelphia model because, among other things, it breaks a prisoner's spirit and makes him wholly amenable to discipline. *OC*, IV:1, 189-190.

writing *Democracy,* this fundamental issue dropped out of sight as he expounded the manners of a modern, liberal, commercial society. He seems to have been misled by his wishes into supposing that the successful American experiment, the outcome of exceptional American circumstances, was a sufficient exemplar for Europe. His propaganda was too successful: it persuaded him himself. Hence his bitter disillusionment when the Revolution of 1848 broke out:

> I passed the best of my youth in the midst of a society which seemed to be becoming once again prosperous and great while once again becoming free; there I conceived the idea of a moderate, orderly freedom, restrained by religion, custom and law; I was charmed by the thought of such a liberty; it became the whole passion of my life; I felt that nothing could console me if I lost it, and now I saw plainly that I must give it up.[33]

He might boast, in the preface to the twelfth edition of the *Democracy,* which he brought out in the course of 1848, that the great and sudden events of the year had not taken him by surprise (which was not entirely true) and urge the merits of his prophetic book for a France which was struggling to establish an orderly, rather than a turbulent, Republic: one which should be peaceful rather than bellicose, liberal rather than repressive, and respectful of, rather than inimical to, the sacred rights of property;[34] but his claim to the attention of his countrymen is not quite convincing. The second part of the *Democracy* had not been the only great work issued in 1840, and it was to the author of *Qu'est-ce que la propriété?* rather than to Tocqueville that the men of 1848 turned. For Proudhon had asserted that equality meant political and *economic* justice, meant an equal right *in* property, and that, failing such equality—failing the redistribution of land among all citizens—property was only theft, and the state only a defence of the rich against the poor. In some ways Tocqueville and Proudhon resemble each other (notably, in their insistence on the moral and political value of agrarian reform), and although Tocqueville emphatically rejected the socialists of 1848, he could not answer them. He saw the ethical necessity of equality (or at least, he inferred that it was the will of God),[35] but his conception of it was comparatively insipid, little more than a variant of what we have of late learned to call civic humanism, impressive to him only because it challenged the ideas which had sustained the monarchies of Europe for so long. For Tocqueville, equality meant no more than that which subsisted between all male members of the prosperous classes in the United States, where the great problem of social

33. *Souvenirs, OC,* XII, 86.
34. *OC,* I:1, xi, iii-iv.
35. *OC,* I:1, 4-5.

stratification and differentiation was as yet, on the whole, below the horizon (except in the slave states). The study of America thus enabled him to evade the heart of the egalitarian challenge which, as Proudhon made so plain, was essentially moral. According to Proudhon it was not enough for aristocrats to share power with *bourgeois* and then join them in a conspiracy to control and manipulate the lives of the peasants and workers, always in the name of their own best interests: a complete transformation of the social order was required, and that in turn could only arise from a change in men's hearts and minds. Tocqueville rejected such ideas as unscientific, but he was too intelligent not to feel the full force of the socialist critique. He tried to ward it off with the frail dogmas of Nassau Senior's political economy, but in his heart of hearts he suspected that they were nonsense—hence the most remarkable passage in the *Souvenirs:*

> ...when I consider the marvelous diversity, not only of human laws, but of the principles behind the laws, and the diverse forms that, even today, and whatever people may say, the right of property has taken and still takes on this earth, I am tempted to believe that what we call necessary institutions are often no more that institutions to which we are used, and that when it comes to the constitution of society the scope of the possible is much vaster that can be conceived by men living each in a particular society.[36]

If my account of Tocqueville's attitudes to pauperism, then, is correct, it follows that we must be careful not to make an idol of the second *Democracy,* even on this occasion. It is too clearly no more, if no less, than a tract for the upper classes of the July Monarchy. Rather we must remain alert to its limitations. For otherwise we may forget, as Tocqueville in the end was not allowed to, that the great question of human equality is still unresolved. Then we ourselves might be guilty of being brilliant about the marginal. We need to learn, as Tocqueville, sprung from the *noblesse,* never did, the lesson which Proudhon, son of the people, tried to teach: that equality means justice, and that to attain justice we must, at the very least, listen to the poor rather than theorize about them, and be prepared to subordinate our wishes to theirs, for otherwise what are we but robbers of their necessity? The political economy on which Tocqueville and Senior agreed was not much more than a rationalization of the class interests which had emerged at a particular moment of social evolution. If proof of that proposition is required, I need only point to the present state of my own country, where something very like Seniorism has been applied strenuously for the past twelve years. The result of the experiment has been to demonstrate that while, no doubt, the state may be ruined if too much money

36. *OC*, XII, 96-97.

is given to the poor it can, even more certainly, be ruined even faster, if too much is given to the rich. In Britain, we do not yet sufficiently realize either true equality of opportunity or equality of condition; I am not sure how many of us really aspire to those ideals. Yet without them, what is democracy but a cruel sham? Without them, how can we avoid our own 1848 and, beyond it, our own 1851?

[10]

Tocqueville and American Literary Critics

Cushing Strout

Tocqueville's *Democracy in America* wavers between alarming prophecies about democracy in general and more sanguine comments about America in particular. What he sought in his book, as he confessed to his friend Kergorlay, was "less the complete picture of that foreign society than its contrasts and resemblances to our own."[1] There is on the one hand the possible coming, especially in Europe, of a "democratic despotism" marked by bureaucratic paternalism and the alienation of the citizen from political participation and potency. Modern American conditions have made that vision seem pertinent to many sociologists. There is on the other hand the America with some antibodies against the diseases of modernity because, in contrast to Europe, it has effectively integrated two traditionally distinct elements: "the spirit of Religion and the spirit of Liberty."[2] Many modern historians have reflected on that idea.

There is another Tocquevillean theme equally influential, but known mainly to American literary critics. His prophecies about democratic litera-

---

1. Letter to Louis de Kergorlay, October 18, 1847, in Alexis de Tocqueville, *Letters on Politics and Society*, Roger Boesche ed., James Toupin and Roger Boesche trans. (Berkeley, Cal.: University of California Press, 1985), 191. See Cushing Strout, "Tocqueville's Duality: Describing America and Thinking of Europe," *American Quarterly*, 21 (Spring 1969), 87-99.
2. Tocqueville's formulation is the epigraph for a study of recent relations between politics and religion by Robert Booth Fowler in *Unconventional Partners: Religion and Liberal Culture in the United States* (Grand Rapids, Mich.: Eerdmans, 1989). I made an extensive historical analysis of Tocqueville's ideas about American religion in *The New Heavens and New Earth: Political Religion in America* (New York: Harper and Row, 1974).

ture would have a remarkable career, beginning a century after he made them. This French influence was quite different from the recent proposals to treat all ideas about society, politics, and history as mere appearances that veil the ultimate reality of what Hayden White has called "figurative characterizations." French thinkers and their American devotees have made everything a matter of tropes, as if in keeping with Professor Higgins's dictum in *My Fair Lady* that "the French don't care what you do actually, so long as you pronounce it properly."[3] These two French influences illustrate Marcel Proust's maxim that "every generation of critics does nothing but take the opposite of the truths accepted by their predecessors."[4] The current fashion is to make us mistrust the coherence of texts, continuity in literature, or even the pertinence of any historical point of reference outside the maze of textual readings.[5] Tocqueville, on the other hand, was called into service earlier because critics thought he helped us to see the contours of our national literary tradition, even though his terms actually referred to an ideal type of democracy.

Help was needed. After all, even a liberal novelist like H. G. Wells, as late as 1941, thought it was absurd for any scholar to call himself a professor of *American* literature.[6] Our subject was still a poor country cousin in English departments until the Tocqueville-quoting critics put it on the intellectual map in a decisive way—with a crucial assist from the war, which made our writers attractive to European intellectuals, repelled by fascism. A Frenchman was, in this sense, our literary Godfather.

I first set out on literary studies very much under the influence of Tocqueville's literary prophecies. I was led to them by W. H. Auden's long poem *New Year Letter*. One of his notes strongly impressed me. "The American literary tradition," it ran, "Poe, Emerson, Hawthorne, Melville, Henry James, T. S. Eliot, is much nearer to Dostoievski than to Tolstoi. It is a literature of lonely people. Most American books might well start like

3. Hayden White, "The Historical Text as Literary Artifact," *Clio*, 3:3 (1974), 299; Cushing Strout, "The Fortunes of Telling," in *The Veracious Imagination: Essays on American History, Literature, and Biography* (Middletown, Conn.: Wesleyan University Press, 1981), 13.
4. Marcel Proust, *The Maxims of Marcel Proust*, Justin O'Brien ed. and trans. (New York: Columbia University Press, 1948), #354, 185.
5. Some French intellectuals in the 50th issue of *Le débat* (May-August 1988) have themselves made a trenchant critique of the reduction of reality to language, beginning with Structuralism. See the searching account by Thomas G. Pavel, "The Present Debate: News from France," *Diacritics* (Spring 1989), 17-32. For the orientation, influence, and confusions of deconstruction see John M. Ellis, *Against Deconstruction* (Princeton, N.J.: Princeton University Press, 1989).
6. Fred Lewis Pattee, *Penn State Yankee* (State College: Pennsylvania State College Press, 1953), 165.

Moby Dick, 'Call me Ishmael.'... Most American novels are parables, their settings even when they pretend to be realistic, symbolic settings for a timeless and unlocated (because internal) psychomachia."[7] This passage has a Tocquevillean ring. When I returned from the war in Europe to Williams College, I wrote an honors thesis in 1947 called "A Literature of Lonely People," and I cited Tocqueville on the danger that democratic poets, finding nothing ideal "in what is real and true" would "range at last to purely imaginary regions." (His prediction now seems more accurate about much "postmodern" fiction than about the canonical novelists I wrote about.[8]) Three years later a scholar observed that Tocqueville's contemporary prestige was linked particularly to his literary prophecies.[9]

Tocqueville's reflections on literature are generated by his method of using what Max Weber would call "ideal types." They refer not to an empirical America, but to a conceptual distinction between aristocracy and democracy. It is roughly identified for literary purposes with the distinction between classicism and romanticism. Tocqueville put it this way: "All that belongs to the existence of the human race taken as a whole, to its vicissitudes and its future, becomes an abundant mine of poetry." The lines that American critics would often cite assert that democratic poets will not feed on "persons and achievements," on "legends or the memorials of old traditions," or on supernatural beings, but rather on "passions and ideas," on "man himself, taken aloof from his country and his age and standing in the presence of Nature and God." The prosaic nature of democratic society will make the poet look beyond appearances in order to explore "the hidden depths in the immaterial nature of man" and so "to throw light on some of the obscurer recesses of the human heart."[10]

Contemporary American literature, he noted, was English in substance and form. It would some day, however, have a character "peculiarly its

---

7. W. H. Auden, *New Year Letter* (London: Faber and Faber, 1941), 153. This connection between Auden and Tocqueville also impressed Harry Levin. See his *The Power of Blackness* (New York: Vintage Books, 1960), 17-18.

8. Commenting on the post-modern emphasis on life as fiction, Charles Caramello has noted how this literary fashion evades history. See *Silverless Mirrors: Book, Self, and Postmodern American Fiction* (Gainesville, Fla.: University Presses of Florida, 1983), 91.

9. Reino Virtanen, "Tocqueville on a Democratic Literature," *The French Review*, 23 (1950), 214-215. He notes that Tocqueville's prophecy applies to Emerson and Whitman better than to either Hawthorne or Henry James. *Ibid.*, 218.

10. Alexis de Tocqueville, *DA* [B], II, 75-76. André Jardin points out that Tocqueville's idea about democratic literature is similar to one in Lamartine's preface to *Jocelyn*. See *Tocqueville: A Biography*, Lydia Davis and Robert Hemenway trans. (New York: Farrar Straus Giroux, 1988), 259. The important difference, however, is that Lamartine emphasizes that man knows that he is part of an "interdependent" unity.

own," and he thought it possible "to trace this character beforehand."[11] He then launched into his familiar antithesis between democracy and aristocracy. His abstract distinction would be applied to our literature because our critics saw his polarity as a difference between American and English literature. A brilliant generalizer, he nevertheless conceded that "an abstract word is like a box with a false bottom; you may put in it what ideas you please and take them out again unobserved."[12] He admitted that he had done some conjuring himself with the idea of equality by personifying it; and he often forgot (as our literary critics did) his own warnings about distinguishing America in particular from democracy in general.

Tocqueville was compelled to speculate because his countrymen knew "much about Messrs. W. Irving and Cooper, a little about Dr. Channing. We have heard of some others," he added, "but without ever being able to judge them." He wrote an American collector of books to ask for extensive information about "the movement of ideas in the United States and the resultant literary development." He confessed: "It is a gap which I would like to fill, but I admit on this point I am almost as much at a loss as my readers."[13] He never received an answer. Consequently, the only literary examples he cites in his great book on America are works by Byron, Chateaubriand, and Lamartine.

In 1941 when F. O. Matthiessen in his *American Renaissance* introduced Tocqueville's idea into the discussion of classic American writers, he applied it in a limited and persuasive way to Emerson and Whitman.[14] But others soon extravagantly expanded the application of Tocqueville's idea. Lionel Trilling, when asked in 1951 to write on "the British idea in literature," was at first dismayed at the prospect of having to betray "that living multiplicity of manners and matters, of temperaments and wills, which makes the glory of English letters." He found a way to deal with it by considering the idea in comparison with American literature, which he saw in Tocquevillean terms as defined "by its tendency to transcend or circumvent

11. The George Lawrence translation of this passage in the 1966 edition of *Democracy in America* incorrectly has Tocqueville saying: "No one can guess that character beforehand." *DA* [M-L], 439. The French version [5th ed. (Paris: Pagnerre, 1848), III, 110], as Vincent Giroud, Curator of Modern Books and Manuscripts at the Beinecke Rare Book and Manuscript Library, has helpfully written me, is: "Il n'est pas impossible de tracer ce caractère à l'avance."
12. *DA* [B], II, 56, 69-70.
13. James T. Schleifer, "Tocqueville and American Literature: A Newly Acquired Letter," *Yale University Library Gazette*, 54 (1980), 133.
14. Katherine Harrison earlier cited Whitman as proof of Tocqueville's prescience in "A French Forecast of American Literature," *South Atlantic Quarterly*, 25 (1926), 350-360.

the social fact and to concentrate upon the individual in relation to himself, to God, or to the cosmos." If the social fact did appear, it was seen as "alien and hostile to the true spiritual and moral life."[15] This second point was Trilling's own.

His persuasive example was Kipling's socialized Kim, for whom the discovery of his ancestry is his destiny, in contrast to Mark Twain's Huck, for whom the discovery of his father's death brings only relief at his "greater safety in his isolate freedom." Only in the English book was initiation into society seen as "possible, fascinating, and desirable."[16] D. H. Lawrence had seen "the end of the humanistic social personality" in our literature, and when it came to the "easily usable social tradition of literature" and the isolation of our great literary figures, it seemed to Trilling that Tocqueville "speaks more immediately than any American across the American decades."[17] Four years later Auden, also citing Tocqueville, would use Oliver Twist and Huck to define a similar Anglo-American difference.[18]

This comparison was a critic's version of the familiar complaint by Hawthorne, Cooper, and James that American society as a literary subject was thin by comparison with English and European thickness. This contrast seemed to warrant identifying an American fictional tradition, different from the novel, called "the romance," a term Hawthorne himself had used to describe his stories. Philip Rahv, editor of *Partisan Review*, agreed with the genteel literary historian Barrett Wendell that our early literature was a record of "the national inexperience" marked by "instinctive disregard of actual fact."[19] For Rahv as for Trilling, the contrast between mythicizing romance and realistic novel was typified in the difference between Hawthorne and Henry James. Other critics, especially Trilling's colleague Richard Chase, developed the theme so that metaphysical symbolism and mythicized

15. Lionel Trilling, "An American View of English Literature," in *Speaking of Literature and Society*, Diana Trilling ed. (New York: Harcourt Brace Jovanovich, 1980), 261.
16. *Ibid.*, 262. Cf. also Irving Howe, "The Pleasures of *Kim*," in Quentin Anderson, Stephen Donadio, and Steven Marcus eds., *Art, Politics, and Will*: Essays in Honor of Lionel Trilling (New York: Basic Books, 1977), 157.
17. Trilling, *ibid.*, 264; "Family Album," *ibid.*, 238.
18. W. H. Auden and David Daiches, "The Anglo-American Difference: Two Views," *Anchor Review*, 1 (1955), 211-212, 219.
19. Philip Rahv, "The Cult of Experience in American Writing," in Rahv, *Essays on Literature and Politics 1932-1972*, Arabel J. Porter and Andrew J. Dvosin eds. (Boston: Houghton Mifflin, 1978), 14. The essay was published originally in 1940. An anthology of American literature, first published in 1855, called *The Scarlet Letter* "a psychological romance" that even the "hardiest Mrs. Malaprop" would never call "a novel." Evert A. Duyckinck and George L. Duyckinck, *Cyclopaedia of American Literature* (New York: Charles Scribner, 1866), IV, 504.

characters became the hallmarks of American nationality in literature. Chase found in the idea of the romance a way of praising "the peculiar narrow profundity" of American classics while accusing them at the same time of lacking "a sense of history" as well as "a sense of society and culture."[20] This charge reached its Anglophile apogee in Marius Bewley's argument that the American literary artist dieted on "democratic abstractions" that have "no social context."[21]

Trilling pointed out in 1958 that the decline of English power and the new sense of American destiny after the second world war had given us the ability to think of our literature as being "a separate entity, with its own special qualities which existed of and by themselves, with its own history peculiar to itself, with its own kind of development." It seemed to him that "all the world," and perhaps the English most of all, recognized this national difference. As if to prove his point, the *Times Literary Supplement* asserted for English readers that their fiction,

> more than we ever realize until we set it against American, is rooted deeply in society; man for the English novelist is social man... and though the society may be criticized or rebelled against, it remains inescapable.[22]

There is, however, only a half-truth in this vaunted Anglo-American difference, one that Anthony Trollope and Nathaniel Hawthorne saw in each other. The American preferred the Englishman's novels for being "solid and substantial" in the "realist" mode, while Trollope, an admirer of Hawthorne, asserted that American literary creations are "more given to the speculative,—less given to the realistic,—than are those of English literature. On our side of the water," he added, "we deal more with beef and ale, and less with dreams."[23] But the dreams often mixed the speculative with the social.

20. Richard Chase, "The Classic Literature: Art and Idea," in Arthur M. Schlesinger, Jr. and Morton White eds., *Paths of American Thought*, (Boston: Houghton Mifflin, 1963), 54. Strangely enough, Chase himself criticized "myth-criticism" for not taking time and place seriously. See his *The American Novel and Its Tradition* (New York: Doubleday, 1957), Appendix II, 245-246.
21. Marius Bewley, *The Eccentric Design: Form in the Classic American Novel* (New York: Columbia University Press, 1959), 15.
22. "Reflections on a Lost Cause: English Literature and American Education," *ibid.*, 348; "The Limits of the Possible," *The American Imagination: A Critical Survey of the Arts from the Times Literary Supplement* (New York, 1960), 36.
23. Quoted in F. O. Matthiessen, *American Renaissance: Art and Expression in the Age of Emerson and Whitman* (New York: Oxford University Press, 1941), 235, 236. Nicolaus Mills, while he did not abandon the Tocquevillian themes, much narrowed the contrast between American "romancers" and English "novelists" by closely comparing several examples of their work. See *American and English Fiction in the Nineteenth Century: An Antigenre Critique and Comparison* (Bloomington, Ind.: University of Indiana Press, 1973), passim.

While Trilling saw that our writers do not show social initiation in a positive light, a social theme in the work of Hawthorne, Cooper, Twain, and Melville does exist, often taking the form (as A. N. Kaul has argued) of a search for a more satisfying form of community life.[24]

The thirty-year history of Tocqueville's literary prophecy has exposed its limitations by the evolving qualifications and modifications. R. W. B. Lewis's Tocquevillean idea of the American Adam as a figure "at home only in the presence of nature and God" saw him, nevertheless, as being "thrust by circumstances into an actual world and an actual age." This recognition of time, place, and history contrasted with Charles Feidelson's argument that American symbolism's "characteristic subject is its own equivocal method."[25] Daniel Hoffman in *Form and Fable in American Fiction* spoke of the romance as "an ahistorical depiction of the individual's discovery of his own identity in a world where his essential self is inviolate and independent of such involvements in history." The actual American, he claimed, had "neither a class nor a history to fix his place in society, neither priest nor church to ameliorate his relation to the immensities." Tocqueville, who made so much out of the influence and pervasiveness of American churches, would have been astonished at this hyperbolic development of his theme. Yet even Hoffman admitted at the back door what he had driven out the front, "the continuity of culture and the struggles of history." He conceded that the American fictional hero "must define himself in conflict with... a society reflecting the American inheritance of European culture and its burden of historical responsibility."[26] This inheritance has been the persistent burden of "the international theme" in our fiction of the bewildered American abroad, a story frequently told by Irving, Cooper, Hawthorne, Howells, and James, and even occasionally by Melville and Twain, not to mention the more modern examples of Hemingway, Lewis, Fitzgerald, Wolfe, and Malamud.

---

24. A. N. Kaul, *The American Vision: Actual and Ideal Society in Nineteenth-Century Fiction* (New Haven, Conn.: Yale University Press, 1963), ch. 2. James Gould Cozzons is the rarity of an American novelist who (in *The Just and the Unjust* and *Guard of Honor*) does see social initiation positively, but Trilling never discusses him.
25. R. W. B. Lewis, *The American Adam: Innocence, Tragedy, and Tradition in the Nineteenth Century* (Chicago: University of Chicago Press, 1955), 89; Charles Feidelson, *Symbolism in American Literature* (Chicago: University of Chicago Press, 1953, 1966), 73.
26. Daniel Hoffman, *Form and Fable in American Fiction* (New York: Oxford University Press, 1965), x, xii, 7, 9. For "the international theme" in American fiction see Cushing Strout, *The American Image of the Old World* (New York: Harper and Row, 1963).

Richard Poirier in *A World Elsewhere* expanded on Feidelson's idea of American classic novelists as proto-modernists by seeing them as creating through language "an essentially imaginative environment." His chief example, however, was an Englishman, D. H. Lawrence; and, as Warner Berthoff has pointed out, "'America' figures here as an almost completely unanalyzed historical integer." Nevertheless, Poirier had the good sense to challenge the romance/novel distinction on the solid ground that "none of the interesting American novelists can be placed on either side of this dichotomy."27 By the end of the 1960's Joel Porte's *The Romance in America* took for granted the validity of the tradition I have been describing, but he improved it by adding race and history to the large concerns that the romancers used their fictions to explore.28

In 1971 Trilling's colleague Quentin Anderson in *The Imperial Self* was still citing Tocqueville and Trilling, but Anderson was aware that American critics had been ignoring society and history in their intoxication with myth and symbol. He pointed out that our political founding fathers, after all, were not beguiled by abstractions and used a concrete vocabulary that "posited rooted oppositions between warring social interests."29 Even more revisionary, however, was his turning upside down Trilling's often-cited contrast between Hawthorne, the abstract romancer, and James, the social novelist. For Anderson "the compelling character of history, generational order, places and things" was as absent in James as it was in Emerson and Whitman, while Hawthorne, on the other hand, in his profound awareness of "the constraints of associated life," was more akin to Jane Austen, George Eliot, or Anthony Trollope than he was to the late James.30 Six years later Myra Jehlen also revised the "desocialized" theme by pointing out that classic isolated protagonists, such as Natty Bumppo, Hester Prynne, Captain Ahab, Huckleberry Finn, and Isabel Archer, illustrate an authorial moral: "all fail in the end to create their private worlds and their failure sounds dire

---

27. Richard Poirier, *A World Elsewhere: The Place of Style in American Literature* (New York: Oxford University Press, 1966), 16; Warner Berthoff, "Ambitious Scheme," *Commentary*, 44 (October 1967), 111.
28. Joel Porte, *The Romance in America: Studies in Cooper, Poe, Hawthorne, Melville, and James* (Middletown, Conn.: Wesleyan University Press, 1969), x.
29. Quentin Anderson, *The Imperial Self: An Essay in American Literary and Cultural History* (New York: Knopf, 1971), 39.
30. *Ibid.*, 77, 223. Trilling himself changed his mind about Hawthorne, finding that for him the world was "ineluctably *there*." Trilling, "Hawthorne in Our Time," in *Beyond Culture: Essays on Literature and Learning* (New York: Viking Press, 1965), 199.

warning of the dangers of isolation and solipsism."[31] An English critic
pointed out that while the protagonists of our classic fiction from Deerslayer
to Invisible Man were not fully a part of their society, yet "to be outside society is not to be immune to its claims," as these characters discover,
"shuttling to and fro" between "a desire for order and a desire for freedom, a
responsibility to the self and a responsibility to society."[32]

The 1980s marked a turn away from the Tocquevillean image of our literature because issues of race and gender had become politically salient.[33]
The Tocqueville-quoting fashion tended to forget that symbolism could be
"a method for exploring historical and cultural issues rather than for transcending them."[34] Melville's *Benito Cereno* is densely packed with symbolism, for example, but it is closely based on an account of an actual slave
mutiny. The novella exposes the cultural and political significance of
Northern racial and republican prejudices in the context of the crisis in the
1850s over the question of the expansion of slavery. Over a century later
Melville's story would serve Robert Lowell in addressing a modern racial
crisis through his rewritten version for the dramatic trilogy *The Old Glory*.[35]
True, Hawthorne spoke of his "psychological romances" as a means of discovering "the truth of the human heart," yet they also notably exploited New
England legends and memorable events, elements that Tocqueville identified

---

31. Myra Jehlen, "New World Epics: The Novel and the Middle-Class in America,"
    Salmagundi, 36 (1977), 50. My undergraduate thesis made a compatible argument
    that our classic stories underscored the need to plunge into what first appears as
    "'the destructive element'—experience, society, affection." *A Literature of Lonely
    People*, 102.
32. C. W. E. Bigsby, *The Second Black Renaissance: Essays in Black Literature*
    (Westport, Conn.: Greenwood Press, 1980), 66, 145.
33. For the polemical argument, addressed mainly to Trilling, that the theory of the ro-
    mance has produced a canon of white, middle-class, male Anglo-Saxons, one that
    ignores Edith Wharton, Willa Cather, and Ellen Glasgow, see Nina Baym,
    "Melodramas of Beset Manhood: How Theories of American Fiction Exclude
    Women Authors," *American Quarterly*, 33 (1981), 123-139. Denis Donoghue cites
    Tocqueville's passage about the sources of poetry in democracy and also Trilling
    and Poirier on the literary sense that "value is not here and now but in 'a world else-
    where.'" His evidence, however, is the readiness of ordinary Americans to believe
    the worst of institutions and the professions—the result of a more recent "adversary
    culture" of suspicion. See his "The True Sentiments of America," in Leslie
    Berlowitz, Denis Donoghue, and Louis Menand eds., *America in Theory*, (New
    York: Oxford University Press, 1988), 236, 238.
34. Cushing Strout, "Tocqueville and the Idea of an American Literature (1941-1971),
    New Literary History, 18 (1986), 123.
35. See my discussion of *Benito Cereno* and *The Old Glory* in *Making American
    Tradition: Visions and Revisions from Ben Franklin to Alice Walker* (New
    Brunswick, N.J.: Rutgers University Press, 1990), 111-114.

with aristocratic literature, but which Hawthorne had closely studied and thoroughly made his own.[36]

These steadily accumulating qualifications to the Tocquevillean theme correct its distortions without detracting from Tocqueville's genius. It is a mark of his historical subtlety that he acknowledged in a draft "the great difficulty in untangling what... is democratic, commercial, English, and puritan" in America.[37] This discrimination is more valuable than the "desocialized" theme because historically minded writers like Hawthorne and Cooper wrestled with the same problem in their work. Tocqueville, like our classic novelists, was also sensitive to issues of race and gender, topics which are now all the rage in contemporary criticism. A current critic indicts "prevailing perspectives on American literature" for minimizing social and historical contexts. They were no longer prevailing, however, when he published his book, but it is ironical that he should quote Tocqueville to show that there are always many "connections between the social and political condition of a people and the inspiration of its writers."[38] Quoting Tocqueville to undermine a "desocialized" tradition that was fond of quoting him is proof of his vitality. We have come full circle.

36. The preface to *The House of the Seven Gables* is characteristic. See Cushing Strout, "From Trilling to Anderson: The Strange History of Tocqueville's Idea of a Democratic Poetry," *American Quarterly*, 24 (1972), 601-606. The best examination of Hawthorne's extraordinary historical sense is in Michael J. Colacurcio, *The Province of Piety: Moral History in Hawthorne's Early Tales* (Cambridge, Mass.: Harvard University Press, 1984).
37. Quoted from one of Tocqueville's notes by Sean Wilentz, "On Tocqueville and Jacksonian America," in Abraham S. Eisenstadt ed., *Reconsidering Tocqueville's Democracy in America* (New Brunswick, N.J.: Rutgers University Press, 1988), 224. See *DA* [N], II, 5.
38. Quoted in Russell Reising, *The Unusable Past: Theory and the Study of American Literature* (New York: Methuen, 1986), 34. He cites the 1945 edition, but his quotation is actually from the George Lawrence translation (*DA* [M-L]).

[11]

Democratic Literature: Tocqueville's Poetological Reflections and Dreams

Gisela Schlüter

In 1840, Tocqueville forecast with regard to American letters that modern literature would be democratic literature. His concept of "democratic literature" is familiar to Tocqueville scholars, but has to a large extent been ignored in literary studies, or to put it more precisely, in the theory of literature and its history. What Tocqueville says about "democratic literature" may seem original, brilliant, even ingenious, to the Tocqueville scholar, but to literary scholars with a historical interest, Tocqueville's expositions seem abstract in the negative sense of the word, much too speculative, or even trivial.

So let us attempt to do historical justice to Tocqueville's theory of a "democratic literature" by putting it back in its contexts: on the one hand in the context of Tocqueville's theory of democracy, on the other hand in the context of post-revolutionary discourse on the "democratization of literature." In this way Tocqueville researchers can demonstrate the merits of the Tocquevillian concept to those in the field of literary studies, and, conversely, have its historical relativity explained to them. Let us first of all allow the skeptical literary scholar to speak; he will submit Tocqueville's theses to a critical historical examination. Then we shall grant a hearing to the Tocqueville scholar's speech for the defense.

First of all, the literary scholar will say, it is important to distinguish within the Tocquevillian concept of a "democratic literature"—and the history of this concept has still to be clarified—between literary-sociological and, in the narrow sense of the word, poetological statements. As part of his attempt to create a politological morphology of literature, Tocqueville uses literary-sociological arguments in Chapters XIII (entitled "Literary Physiognomy of Democratic Centuries"), XIV ("Of the Literary Industry") and XIX ("Some Observations on the Theater of Democratic Nations"), but argues poetologically in Chapters XVII ("Of Some Sources of Poetry in Democratic Nations") and XVIII ("Why American Writers and Orators Are Sometimes Turgid"), stylistically and linguistically in Chapter XVI ("How American Democracy Has Changed the English Language").

The literary scholar will first point out that the literary-sociological point of view has dominated French literary theory since 1789. Post-revolutionary literature, especially romantic literature, with such famous names as Mme de Staël, Benjamin Constant, Victor Hugo, Stendhal, Chateaubriand and Balzac, to name but a few, defines itself in political categories corresponding to its political situation and intention.

In addition to this general remark, the literary scholar will also be able to prove that Tocqueville's distinction between *littérature démocratique* and *littérature aristocratique* is part of a broad conceptual tradition, i.e. it takes up ideas of "political literature" which had been circulating between the French Revolution and the July Monarchy. For example, there had been calls for a *littérature républicaine* around 1789, a concept that can be found in Mme de Staël's writings; it was intended to make literature work towards the introduction of Republicanism. With the transition to social issues after 1830, *littérature républicaine* is replaced by socially committed literature— the concepts of *art social, art progressif, littérature populaire*, etc., are in circulation everywhere. The attempts to define literature according to its political intention lead to an entire catalogue of new semipolitical concepts in post-revolutionary literary theory.

The developing industrial society, the literary scholar will continue, generates trivial commercial literature, characterized from the early 1830s onwards as *littérature industrielle* and analyzed in 1839, i.e. shortly before the appearance of the first volume of *Democracy in America*, by Sainte-Beuve in his article entitled "De la littérature industrielle." Tocqueville's reflections on *littérature industrielle* and *littérature démocratique* sound partly like an echo of Sainte-Beuve's article, in which he criticized commercialized and democratized contemporary literature:

> With our electoral and industrial morals, everyone, at least once in his life, will have had his page, his discourse, his prospectus, his toast—will have been, in short, an author. From there to writing a pamphlet is but a small step. Why not me as well? each asks himself.

Incidentally, Sainte-Beuve may also be thinking here of the genre *littérature des ouvriers*, which was in vogue during the July Monarchy. He continues:

One must resign oneself to new customs, to the invasion of literary democracy as to the accession of all other democracies. Small matter that this seems more vocal in literature.[1]

Are we not at this point, the literary scholar will ask the Tocqueville scholar, already at the center of Tocqueville's reflections? Isn't Tocqueville simply taking up what everybody was saying, especially after 1830, about *littérature démocratique* being commercial mass literature? Is he not adapting the stereotyped arguments of the *literati* and feature writers, according to whom the tendency in a democratic society is for everybody to write for everybody—and about everybody: *littérature de tous*, according to Janin in 1834 in his "Manifeste de la jeune littérature," *littérature à la portée de tous, littérature de tous les jours*.[2] Is he not simply joining in the chorus of those, in particular Désiré Nisard, who complain in unison about the mediocrity, the low level of contemporary literature, and so harshly judge the "proletariat of thought"[3] and the "workers in books"?[4] And finally: can one not hear remarks everywhere in the France of the July Monarchy saying much the same thing as Tocqueville says in his notorious ignorance, supposing American literature to be typically "democratic literature"? Had not America become for *literati* and literary critics the symbol of philistine rationality, "people of attempted sorrow," as Victor Hugo said in 1835, "nation of chance, without root, without past, without history and without art,"[5] and in the same year, Philarète Chasles: "The muse does not reveal herself.... Such is the American muse"[6]? Mme de Staël, John Bristed, James Fenimore Cooper, Achille Murat, Thomas Hamilton, and in particular Tocqueville's travelling companion Gustave de Beaumont, had all prior to Tocqueville judged American literature to be nonexistent, deficient or inferior, and put this down to the materialism, utilitarianism, *esprit positif* of the United States, as well as to the strong fixation on English literature. And had not Tocqueville's contemporaries, insofar as they admitted the existence of literature in

1. Ch. -A. Sainte-Beuve, "De la littérature industrielle," in *Portraits contemporains* (Paris: Lévy Frères, 1870), II, 454.
2. Jules Janin, "Manifeste de la jeune littérature.—Réponse à M. Nisard," in *Revue de Paris*, 1 (1834), 21, 24.
3. Charles Louandre, "Statistique littéraire: la poésie depuis 1830," in *Revue des Deux Mondes*, 30 (April 1, 1842), 997.
4. Alfred de Vigny, "Du mot carrière des lettres," in *Oeuvres complètes*, Fernand Baldensperger ed. (Paris: Gallimard, 1950), I, 942.
5. Victor Hugo, "A Alphonse Rabbe, mort le 31 décembre 1829," in Victor Hugo, *Les Chants du crépuscule. Les Voix intérieures. Les Rayons et les ombres*, Pierre Albouy ed. (Paris: Gallimard, 1983), 77.
6. Philarète Chasles, "De la Littérature dans l'Amérique du Nord," *Revue des Deux Mondes*, 4th series, 3 (1835), 177, 195.

America, made identical diagnoses, such as Achille Murat: "Everyone is a *literatus* in the United States,"[7] and Philarète Chasles: "all these poets resemble each other, they lack originality"[8]?

What, therefore, the literary scholar will then ask, are the distinguishing features of Tocqueville's analyses and forecasts in the dense literary-critical context outlined above? Is Tocqueville able to disentangle those aspects which were being treated as equivalent in the regrettably confused discourse of that time on the criticism of culture, in order to explain the alleged decline of civilization: democracy, industrialization, the American way of life? The way of life whose entire democratic monstrosity was demonstrated for Harriet Martineau in 1837 by the fact that in the USA "every factory child carries its umbrella; and pig-drivers wear spectacles."[9] Is the skepticism present in the criticism of culture of these years not more adequately articulated in the passing ironic *aperçu* of someone like Heinrich Heine than in the ambitious theories of his French contemporaries, and in particular of Tocqueville?

The Tocqueville scholar will have to concede to the literary scholar the relevance of the contexts expounded above. He will not be able to completely deny the relevance of Barbey d'Aurevilly's dictum: "everyone's ideas create this thinker's originality."[10] But he will insist on the necessity of keeping Tocqueville's entire theory of "democratic literature" in mind, of bearing in mind the entire politological context of this theory; according to him, Tocqueville's theory is superior to other competing approaches and seems to be a suitable tool for removing deficiencies in contemporary theories of "democratic literature," allowing the development of a virtually complete model, for Tocqueville with his theory of democracy laid the foundations for a model of this kind. The theorems put forward by the others, in contrast, are simply strung together eclectically, or, to put it another way, Tocqueville has constructed his theory on his own carefully selected foundation, tailored to the needs of the builder, whereas others have simply erected their buildings on *lieux communs,* common land, due to their lack of a properly formulated theory of democracy.

The Tocqueville scholar will make it clear first of all that Tocqueville makes differing statements in 1835 and 1840 on the literature of democratic societies and these correspond to the shifts of emphasis within his theory of

---

7.   Achille Murat, *Esquisse morale et politique des Etats-Unis de l'Amérique du Nord* (Paris: Crochard, 1832), 380.
8.   Philarète Chasles, "De la littérature dans l'Amérique du Nord," 179.
9.   Harriet Martineau, *Society in America* (London: Saunders and Ottley, 1837), I, 16.
10. Jules Barbey d'Aurevilly, "Alexis de Tocqueville," in *Les oeuvres et les hommes, XIXe siècle* (Paris: A. Lemerre, 1892), 178.

democracy. In 1835, Tocqueville—in line with the emphasis on "democratic despotism"—had, in the opinion he pronounced on the end of liberty in view of the *tyrannie de la majorité*, also given his verdict on literature:

> If America has not yet had great writers, we needn't look far for reasons: no literary genius exists without freedom of mind [*liberté d'esprit*], and there is no freedom of mind in America.[11]

In the 1835 version, state power, the *tyrannie de la majorité*, destroys the individuality of the author; it silences him by removing his individuality or his otherness, incorporates him into the majority:

> He cedes, he finally folds under each day's effort, and returns to silence, as if he felt the remorse of speaking true.[12]

In 1840, on the other hand, Tocqueville admits that there will be American literature in the future. The author will become part of the masses, which are now no longer understood as a repressive majority but as a totality. To the extent that democratic, faceless society is reflected in "democratic literature," it reflects on itself. In 1880, Zola defined the "accession of democracy... in letters" as "works born of the crowd and for the crowd."[13] According to Tocqueville:

> In democratic societies, where men are all very small and strongly similar, each, in envisaging himself, sees in an instant all the others.[14]

Starting from this reductionist approach, Tocqueville constructs his literary theory; using this approach as his starting point he develops his poetological statements about the "sources of poetry in the democratic centuries." This is where his originality really lies, as the Tocqueville scholar will try to explain to the literary scholar. The latter may at this point express his doubts concerning Tocqueville's tendency to use suggestive psychology instead of factual arguments.

But let us turn first of all to Tocqueville's literary sociology: its advantage over the competing approaches already mentioned, from Mme de Staël to Balzac, results, according to the Tocqueville scholar, from Tocqueville's efforts to be theoretically rigorous, corresponding to the methodological necessity as postulated in 1835 "to push each of his ideas in all their theoretical

---

11. *DA* [N], I, 200.
12. *Idem.*
13. Emile Zola, *Le roman expérimental*, Aime Guedj ed. (Paris : Garnier-Flammarion, 1971), 200 ("L'argent dans la littérature").
14. *DA* [N], II, 74.

consequences, and often until the limits of the false and impassable."[15] This rigor, incidentally, led Heine to paint the following brief portrait of Tocqueville:

> Mr. Tocqueville deserves praise for pursuing his thoughts so steadfastly; he is a man with brain but little heart who pursues the arguments of his logic all the way to the freezing point; his speeches too have a certain frosty glitter, like cut ice.[16]

Tocqueville intensifies the opposition between "aristocratic" and "democratic" literature to a sharp antithesis: aristocratic society has a formative influence on literature at the level of author, work, public and poetics just as democratic society does. More precisely: traditionalism as an historical principle of the pre-revolutionary society of the *Ancien Régime* corresponds to classicism as its literary principle—just as conversely the literary principle of modernism corresponds to the post-revolutionary historical principle of innovation:

> I am supposing an aristocratic people, in whose society one cultivates letters; works of intelligence, just as affairs of government, are here regulated by a sovereign class. Literature, like political existence, is almost entirely concentrated in this class, or in those which most closely border it. This for me is sufficient to give the key to all the rest.[17]

The literature of aristocratic societies is produced and received by a homogeneous vehicle of culture: the "socio-cultural alliance" (Erich Kohler) of *noblesse* and a small segment of the *tiers état*. Not only literary production but also reception is exclusive, restricted to these classes, for it assumes awareness of tradition, education, knowledge: the permanence of the political and social dominance of these classes ensures the permanent existence of an identical vehicle of culture and an identical system of rules over long periods of time—for the aristocracy possesses "a monopoly of traditions."[18] Permanent cultural obligations and norms and the principle of *repos* give a culture maturity.

Authority, stability, continuity, traditionalism as hallmarks of the—schematically outlined—"aristocratic centuries," these "correspond to"—I have taken the liberty of putting this expression "correspond to" in quotation marks, as I have certain reservations about a literary sociology which operates with analogies—the exclusivity, normativeness, conventionality, classi-

---

15. *DA* [N], I, 16.
16. H. Heine, *Werke und Briefe in 10 Bänden*, Hans Kaufman ed. (Berlin and Weimar: Aufbau, 1972) VI, 547 et sq.
17. *DA* [N], II, 61.
18. E. Duclerc, "Aristocratie," in *Dictionnaire politique*, E. Duclerc and Pagnerre ed. (Paris, 1842), 93.

cism of the *littérature aristocratique*, "literature in which everything is regulated and coordinated in advance." [19]

"Let us now return this portrait and consider the reverse": "Let us transport ourselves to the heart of a democracy." [20] The characteristics of "democratic literature" are now developed in direct opposition to those of "aristocratic literature"—a rigorously contrastive procedure with certain risks—for antithesis is according to Nietzsche, "the narrow gate through which error likes to sneak to truth." [21]

In democratic societies, vehicles of culture no longer exist:

> There does not exist in America a class in which the predilection for intellectual pleasures transmits itself with such ease and hereditary leisure. [22]

The new "democratic nobility": "the manufacturers' aristocracy of our days," [23] does not have a class character, due to a lack of tradition, and for this reason cannot assume the vacant position of a vehicle of culture:

> To tell the truth, although one may have wealth, the wealthy *class* does not truly exist, for this wealth has neither a common spirit nor common objects, neither common traditions nor hopes. [24]

"Democratic literature" has its anonymous origin and its anonymous goal in the masses. It is not exclusive, as "aristocratic literature" used to be, but is vulgar in this sense. As vehicles of culture no longer exist, there are no normative authorities or binding systems of rules, either:

> In these nations, literature will therefore only know with difficulty to be subjected to narrow rules. [25]

"Aristocratic literature" had perverted esthetic innovation within its closed esthetic system of rules into mannerism. The esthetic form of "democratic literature," on the other hand, threatens to run wild as a result of its underlying esthetic disorderliness. Tocqueville continues: "and it is virtually impossible for letters to be subjected to permanent rules." [26]

Placed in a traditionless society which has no awareness of history, the democratic writer, exiled as it were in his present, despises the principle of

19. *DA* [N], II, 61.
20. *Ibid.*, 62.
21. F. Nietzsche, *Menschliches, Allzumenschliches*, Krit. Gesamtausgabe, Giorgio Colli and Mazzimo Montinari eds., (Berlin: De Gruyter, 1967) IV:2, 165.
22. *DA* [N], I, 43.
23. *DA* [N], II, 142.
24. *Idem.*
25. *DA* [N], II, 62.
26. *Idem.*

tradition and makes arbitrary use of tradition's reserves. Traditions cannot grow any more, especially as the aristocratic principle of *repos* has been replaced by the democratic one of mobility.

What "corresponds" (with the same reservation) to the social mobility, instability, discontinuity, loss of tradition and the readiness to innovate of the "democratic centuries" is the multifacetedness, independence, lack of tradition of "democratic literature." It is released to Modernism.

Now the Tocqueville scholar would have to point out at this juncture that Tocqueville's theory of literature only becomes transparent when two different emphases in his theory of democracy are taken into account. The basic semantic explanations of the concept by James T. Schleifer,[27] Jean-Claude Lamberti,[28] and Francesco De Sanctis[29] cannot be dealt with here.

Let us rather make a heuristic distinction between two concepts of democracy which seems sufficient to clarify his theory of literature: on the one hand, democracy produces and guarantees plurality and mobility, and one could talk of the pluralistic version of this concept in this connection. On the other hand, democracy results in uniformity and stagnation as a consequence of egalitarianism; let us call this aspect the totalitarian version—a version which, incidentally, takes its inspiration from the *mal du siècle* of the early Lamennais. These two types of democracy, or these two sides of democratic societies, correspond to two different mentalities, described by Tocqueville as "agitation" and "monotony" and by De Sanctis very aptly as "fretta e malinconia."[30] At this point we should take into account the fact that underlying the literary-sociological deduction of the principle of modernism is the pluralistic concept. It is the plurality and mobility of a society which produces a modern esthetics—in the sense of the disappearance of the system of esthetic rules and in the sense of actualism as an esthetic reflection of a changing reality. Literary-sociological deduction of the modernism principle within the framework of the dichotomy of "democratic" and "aristocratic" literature now allows Tocqueville to set out his reflections, which are actually poetological, in the chapter "Of Some Sources of Poetry in Democratic Nations," which incidentally takes up considerations similar to Gustave de Beaumont's in his 1835 novel *Marie,*

27. James T. Schleifer, *The Making of Tocqueville's "Democracy in America"* (Chapel Hill, N.C.: University of North Carolina Press, 1980).
28. Jean-Claude Lamberti, *Tocqueville et les deux "Démocraties"* (Paris: Presses Universitaires de France, 1983).
29. Francesco De Sanctis, *Tempo di democrazia: Alexis de Tocqueville* (Naples: Edizioni Scientifiche Italiane, 1986).
30. *Ibid.*, 370.

ou l'esclavage aux Etats-Unis: "Poetry, in my eyes, is the search for and painting of the ideal."[31]

This fundamental orientation of poetry towards the Ideal of Beauty is problematic in democratic societies, for the "democratic imagination" tends to orient itself towards the Real instead of the Ideal of Beauty: "The imagination... devotes itself almost exclusively to the conception of the useful and the representation of the real."[32]

Now if Tocqueville had, on the basis of this observation, been able to conceive of democratic literature as realistic literature—from this point of view there would have been interesting perspectives; he could have provided a politological preliminary to Balzac's "Avant-propos" to the *Comédie humaine* and anticipated the self-perception of someone like Courbet, who announced in 1861: "Realism is the democratic art."[33] Realism will seek to legitimize itself using the "spirit of democracy" in the same way as Hugo interpreted Romanticism as arising from the "spirit of liberalism" ("Romanticism, all considered, is nothing but liberalism in literature"[34]). But Tocqueville had not yet conceived of democratic literature as realistic literature in principle; he had not yet seen realism as a solution to the esthetic crisis created by modern democratic society.

Allow me to interrupt you, the literary scholar will say. With reference to art, Tocqueville accepted "the Real" as a solution of this kind; he says with reference to democratic painters that "in place of the ideal, they pose the real."[35] So if Tocqueville in the chapter "Of Some Sources of Poetry" excludes "the Real" from literature, then the reason is that first of all his argument is genre-specific in this poetological chapter, i.e. with reference to lyric poetry, and secondly, he takes as his basis a classically inspired definition of lyric poetry, according to which poetry is only that which is dedicated to the Ideal. So it is problematic to apply his poetological statements on *poésie démocratique* to literature in general, and it is impossible to derive a complete esthetic program from it. One has to concede, the literary scholar will continue, that Tocqueville does not provide a complete theory of esthetics, but rather puts forward various theses for painting and literature, and within literature again for the various genres. If these differences—which

31. *DA* [N], II, 73.
32. *Ibid.*, 74.
33. Courbet on the occasion of a congress in Antwerp, quoted by R. Lauer, "Der europäische Realismus," in *Neues Handbuch der Literaturwissenschaft*, R. Lauer ed., (Wiesbaden: Akademische Verlagsgesellschaft Athenaion, 1980), XVII, 13.
34. Victor Hugo, *Théâtre complet*, J.-J. Thierry and J. Mélèze eds., (Paris: Gallimard, 1963), I, 1147.
35. *DA* [N], II, 56.

Tocqueville unfortunately did not make explicit—are not taken into account, then his reflections on the art and literature of democratic centuries will be found to be full of contradictions.

The Tocqueville scholar will be forced reluctantly to agree with the literary scholar. Indeed, Tocqueville's poetological reflections in the 17th chapter are determined by his orientation towards the genre of lyric poetry and his classical option in favor of the *beau idéal*. Thus his definition of the subject matter of "democratic literature" is determined by his idealistic conception of poetry:

> Equality does not merely turn men away from painting of the ideal; it diminishes the number of objects to paint.... I wish to examine if among the actions, sentiments, and ideas of democratic peoples there is not one which lends itself to the imagination of the ideal.[36]

Now it is well known, and it is in fact Tocqueville's central thesis on "democratic literature," that he declared "the human being" to be the central subject, or to express it in Hegel's words, elevated the "Humanus" to the status of a new saint. In the idealizing context of poetry, this abstract protagonist figures as people, nation, as the human race; it is in these forms, primarily as a collective subject, that Tocqueville makes "the human being" appear. He is evidently returning to the ideology and esthetics of the *siècle des lumières* and Romanticism, where "the human being" was presented as a member of the human species, as a member of a nation, as a bourgeois hero or as a sensitive individual.

Here Tocqueville is mixing the empirical and the theoretical, as he does so often, the literary scholar may critically object. But apart from the inspiration he took from literary tradition: how is his definition of democratic literature as anthropocentric literature derived from his political theory? As we shall see, Tocqueville is arguing here from his egalitarian-totalitarian concept of democracy:

> Variety disappears from the breast of the human species; the same manners of acting, thinking and feeling find themselves in all corners of the world...; men... come simultaneously to that which approaches most closely the constitution of man, which is everywhere the same. They thus become similar, although they have not imitated each other.[37]

The human condition is obviously no longer understood in the sense of the Enlightenment as emancipatory potential but rather in the sense of a decline of humanity. The "human being of the democratic centuries" is a living ab-

36. *Ibid.*, 72 et sq.
37. *Ibid.*, 191.

straction: "man, in general, is only the product of a social democracy; there are men who are different because of their difference in social status."[38]

It is the abstract figure of the human being in general which the writer takes as his literary subject from the universal uniformity conjured up by Tocqueville in apocalyptic visions[39]—a uniformity, which, Tocqueville said, made him sad and made him shudder.

> I am convinced that in the long run, democracy turns the imagination from that which is exterior to man himself, in order to fix it on nothing but man.[40]

Indeed it requires poetic idealization in order to make out of this protagonist the self-confident human being propagated by the Enlightenment or the individualistic hero of Romanticism. In the logic of Tocqueville's political theory and in particular of his egalitarian-totalitarian concept of democracy, this *Humanus*, *l'homme en général*, is *de facto* something completely different: an "interchangeable individual"[41] who likes to cloak himself as an individualist in order to conceal his loss of individuality, a "one-dimensional man" (Marcuse), the epitome of anonymity. Clearly a figure of this kind is unsuitable for classically inspired poetry:

> The poets who live in the democratic centuries will therefore never know to take a particular man for the subject of their portrait; for an object of a mediocre grandeur, and which one perceives distinctly from all sides, will never lend to the ideal.[42]

Democratic painters, on the other hand, are more prepared to devote themselves to the Real, "they copy from all sides small objects which overabound in nature."[43]

Fascinated by the esthetic implications of Tocqueville's ideas, the literary scholar will propose the following conclusion: if Tocqueville had not excluded literary realism from the outset, this transparent and abstract protagonist of "democratic literature " could have done without his travesties of *Humanus*, popular hero, romantic individual taken over from literary tradition. If the idealistic-classical component of Tocqueville's outline were dropped, then this protagonist would be predestined to become the reflecting being of modern literature: "In democratic societies, where men are all very

---

38. De Sanctis, *Tempo di democrazia*, 129.
39. A. Kaledin, "Tocqueville's Apocalypse: Culture, Politics, and Freedom in *Democracy in America*," *Tocqueville Review*, 7 (1985/86), 3-38.
40. *DA* [N], II, 75.
41. Seymour Drescher, *Dilemmas of Democracy: Tocqueville and Modernization* (Pittsburgh: University of Pittsburgh Press, 1968), 256.
42. *DA* [N], II, 74.
43. *Ibid.*, 56.

small and strongly similar, each, in envisaging himself, sees in an instant all the others."[44]

This is where the modern age of literature in our century starts—from Joyce to Beckett and including the Nouveau Roman: its heroes are reflecting beings without individuality—without the individuality which Baudelaire in a brilliant dictum described as *petite propriété*.[45] "*L'homme general*—typical man—exists: he is us, seen by us," Paul Valéry noted in his *Cahiers*.[46]

Let us conclude the reconstruction of Tocqueville's theory of literature with an important addition, the Tocqueville scholar will interrupt the literary scholar. Tocqueville has outlined alternative literary figures and alternative esthetic solutions to the idealizing travesties of the *homme en général*. Instead of the Ideal of Beauty and the Real, he has advised the Surreal: "Finding no more matter to the ideal in the real and the true, poets leave it entirely and create monsters."[47]

Due to the lack of the Ideal, democratic literature had to establish itself between the Real and the Imaginary. It created those modern protagonists who are familiar to the literary scholar: the reflecting beings and those "fantastic beings who sometimes make one regret the real world,"[48] as Tocqueville writes.

In these "fully imaginary regions" of which Tocqueville speaks,[49] I know my way around a little, the literary scholar will say in conclusion. One occasionally meets your Tocqueville there; in 1840, he left the world of theory a few times, gave up hypotheses, and betook himself into the world of speculation, imagination, fiction even.

(Text translated by Dermot McElholm)
(French quotations translated by Adam Schnitzer)

44. *Ibid.*, 74.
45. Charles Baudelaire, *Oeuvres complètes*, Claude Pichois ed., new edition, (Paris: Gallimard, 1976), II, 492 ("Des écoles et des ouvriers").
46. Paul Valéry, *Cahiers*, Judith Robinson ed., (Paris: Gallimard, 1974), II, 1359.
47. *DA* [N], II, 78.
48. *Idem.*
49. *Idem.*

[12]

Why Did Tocqueville Think a Successful Revolution Was Impossible?

Roger Boesche

Tocqueville had a lifelong ambivalence toward, and fascination with, the French Revolution. Although he called it the Great Revolution and the single most important event of the previous three centuries, he claimed that it brought about little substantial change; although one great-grandfather and two grandparents were killed in the Terror, and his own parents were imprisoned and barely escaped death, Tocqueville seldom repudiated even the violence of the Revolution in the harsh language one would expect; although he likened the Revolution to an ever-recurring illness that continued to infect France, he occasionally hoped for a new revolution to overcome the despotism of the Second Empire; and although he stated that no one in France "is less revolutionary than I," he repeatedly embraced as his own "the principles of the Revolution of 1789."[1]

In the second part of *Democracy in America*, Tocqueville wrote a chapter entitled "Why Great Revolutions Will Become More Rare." In this chapter

1. Alexis de Tocqueville, *Selected Letters on Politics and Society*, Roger Boesche ed., James Toupin and Roger Boesche trans. (Berkeley, Cal.: University of California Press, 1985), 113, 187, 215, 367-368. (Letters to Eugène Stoffels, October 5, 1836; to Paul Clamorgan, February 13, 1847; to Eugène Stoffels, July 21, 1848; and to Gustave de Beaumont, February 27, 1848). For Tocqueville's family's involvement in the Revolution, see André Jardin, *Alexis de Tocqueville 1805-1859* (Paris: Hachette, 1984), 9-17; and G. -A. Simon, *Histoire généalogique des Clérel, seigneurs de Rampan, Tocqueville, etc.* (Caen: Imprimerie Ozanne, 1954), 154-160. For an intriguing comparison of Tocqueville's view of the French Revolution with that of his father, see Palmer's Introduction to Robert R. Palmer ed., *The Two Tocquevilles* (Princeton, N.J.: Princeton University Press, 1987), 3-35.

he borrowed much from Aristotle in arguing that democracies produce a large middle class whose concern for property resists the tumult of revolution in two ways. First, "all revolutions more or less threaten the tenure of property," and thus the middle class, intent on maintaining property, has no interest in revolution. Second, concern for preserving one's property renders one little enchanted with grand and ennobling ideals. "Do not talk to him of the interests and rights of mankind; this small domestic concern absorbs for the time all his thoughts and inclines him to defer political agitations to some other season." Although a persuasive and idealistic leader will occasionally arouse this middle class, "to his vehemence they secretly oppose their inertia, to his revolutionary tendencies their conservative instincts,... to his poetry their prose."[2]

In his *Old Regime*, Tocqueville anticipated an argument later developed at great length by Weber. Revolutions rarely succeed, because revolutionaries must rely on the old administrative structure to govern the nation.

> For though in each successive revolution the administration was, so to speak, decapitated, its body survived intact and active. The same duties were performed by the same civil servants, whose practical experience kept the nation on an even keel through the worst political storms. These men administered the country or rendered justice in the name of the King, then in that of the Republic, thereafter in the Emperor's.... Whenever the initial shock had spent its force, one might have imagined that the nation had never swerved from the old groove.[3]

Although after a revolution it might appear that the old regime had fallen, the new regime, by relying on the existing bureaucratic structure, begins to rule suspiciously like the old.

In these analyses of the conservative nature of the middle classes and the resiliency of bureaucratic structures, Tocqueville clearly articulated his convictions that revolutions in modern democratic societies will be both rare and rarely successful. And yet woven throughout his writings is a more complicated argument suggesting that a violent and sudden revolution—which is what we ordinarily mean by the word *revolution*—can never be successful in attaining its goal. This contention that a revolution can never be successful, an argument more elusive because less developed and amply

2.   *DA* [B], II, 265-278, esp. 267-270.
3.   Alexis de Tocqueville, *The Old Regime and the French Revolution*, Stuart Gilbert trans. (Garden City, N.Y.: Doubleday, 1955), 202. Compare this to Max Weber's claim: "Even in the case of revolution by force... the bureaucratic machinery will normally continue to function just as it has for the previous legal government." *Economy and Society*, E. Fischoff et al. trans. (Berkeley, Cal.: University of California Press, 1978), 224. Tocqueville may well have invented the word *bureaucracy*. See George Wilson Pierson, *Tocqueville and Beaumont in America* (New York: Oxford University Press, 1938), 713.

dispersed in his writings, is more fascinating because it forces us to understand Tocqueville's broader thinking about how change comes about in history.

Three Types of Revolution

Tocqueville spent much of his life trying to understand the French Revolution in particular and the process of revolution in general. Despite such concern, however, he was notoriously imprecise in using the word *revolution*, just as he was with such words as *democracy* and *equality*.[4] Sometimes he used the word *revolution* to describe what we would call a *coup* and sometimes simply to indicate far-reaching change. Nevertheless, in general, Tocqueville did seem to recognize three distinct kinds of revolution: 1) political revolutions, 2) sudden and violent revolutions that seek not only new political institutions but an entire transformation of society, and 3) slow but sweeping transformations of an entire society that take at least many generations to bring about.

First, he was least interested in political revolutions that make changes in governance and political institutions, but leave the broader society comparatively unchanged. Perhaps erroneously, he claimed that the English Revolution of the seventeenth century "made sweeping changes in the political constitution of the country and even overthrew the monarchy, but it hardly affected the secondary laws or the customs and habits of the nation.... The apex was shattered, but the substructure stood firm." Similarly, the American Revolution was merely a "change of government."[5]

In one key passage analyzing England during his visit in 1833, Tocqueville outlined two other types of revolution: slow and relentless, or violent and sudden.

> If any fundamental change in the law, or any social transformation, or any substitution of one regulating principle for another is called a revolution, then England assuredly is in a state of revolution. For the aristocratic principle which was the vital one of the English Constitution, is losing strength every day, and it is probable that in due time the democratic one will have taken its place. But if one un-

4. For a fine discussion of the many meanings Tocqueville gave to the word democracy, see James T. Schleifer, *The Making of Tocqueville's "Democracy in America"* (Chapel Hill, N.C.: University of North Carolina Press, 1980), ch. 19.
5. *Old Regime*, 201-202. *L'Ancien Régime et la Révolution, OC*, II:2, 337. Contrast to Raymond Aron who claimed that Tocqueville talked only about political revolutions. See *Main Currents in Sociological Thought, I, Montesquieu, Comte, Marx, Tocqueville*, Richard Howard and Helen Weaver trans. (Garden City, N.Y.: Doubleday, 1968), 270.

derstands by a revolution a violent and sudden change, then England does not seem ripe for such an event.[6]

While an authentic revolution must involve "fundamental change" or some far-reaching "social transformation," this might occur in two different ways—either violently and suddenly, the kind of transformation attempted during the French Revolution, or slowly, as aristocratic society, for example, inexorably gave way to democratic principles.

The French Revolution of 1789-1799 was clearly Tocqueville's model for a sudden and violent revolution. In seeking not just a new government but an entirely new society, the revolutionaries of this period demanded a sudden and sharp "break with the past," and endeavored "to obliterate their former selves" in order to bring about "nothing short of a regeneration of the whole human race." The French Revolution attacked "political beliefs and religious beliefs, wanted to re-form at the same time both the individual and the state, tried to change ancient customs, accepted opinions, and fixed habits in all ways simultaneously." Only a total and rapid transformation of all aspects of society would suffice.[7]

Tocqueville discussed several examples of revolutions that slowly and relentlessly transformed European society. For instance, the "religious revolution" of the sixteenth century, which Protestants of course called the Reformation, gave increased political power to different nations and classes, while also gradually but substantially altering the fundamental habits and mores in key European countries. Similarly, but more importantly, he maintained that "the great Democratic Revolution"—in which the principle of equality was changing everything from political institutions to commercial production, from family relations to artistic creation—continued to transform Europe and even the world.[8] Examining the effects on society of this probably irresistible democratic revolution is, of course, the subject matter of the second part of *Democracy in America.*

6. Alexis de Tocqueville, *Journeys to England and Ireland,* Jacob-Peter Mayer ed., George Lawrence and K. P. Mayer trans. (Garden City, N.Y.: Doubleday, 1968), 51. See also Jean-Claude Lamberti, *Tocqueville et les deux "Démocraties"* (Paris: Presses Universitaires de France, 1983), 250-255.
7. *L'Ancien Régime et la Révolution, OC,* II:2, 275-276, 335. Like Marx, Tocqueville saw the Revolution of 1848 as, in many respects, a bad parody of 1789.
8. *Old Regime,* 187; *Selected Letters,* 101-102, 106-107 (letters to Mill, June 1835; and to Kergorlay, July 6, 1835). Melvin Richter attempts to distinguish, in Tocqueville's writings, among political revolutions, social revolutions, and total revolutions. See Richter, "Tocqueville's Contribution to the Theory of Revolution," in Carl J. Friedrich ed., *Revolution* (New York: Atherton Press, 1966), 75-121, esp. 90-91.

Tocqueville thought political revolutions comparatively unimportant, and thus he focused on these latter two kinds of revolution—sudden and violent, or slow and relentless. He regarded these as authentic revolutions, because they at least try to accomplish two things. First, they attempt to reduce (or occasionally increase) inequality and consequently bring new classes and groups to power, and second, they seek not just political change but social transformation.

The attempt to change the extent of inequality is the primary prerequisite of what Tocqueville regarded as an authentic revolution. The main achievement of the French Revolution, Tocqueville argued, was the suppression of so-called feudal institutions, and in doing so, the revolutionaries tried to replace feudal hierarchy and privilege with political institutions and some economic principles based on the elusive concept of equality for all men. Indeed, some "secret tie exists between the principle of equality itself and revolution," because a conflict about equality is at the heart of every revolution.

> Almost all the revolutions that have changed the aspect of nations have been made to consolidate or to destroy social inequality. Remove the secondary causes that have produced the great convulsions of the world and you will almost always find the principle of inequality at the bottom. Either the poor have attempted to plunder the rich, or the rich to enslave the poor.[9]

By depicting a fight about inequality as a struggle between rich and poor, Tocqueville certainly indicated that conflict among classes is one of many characteristics of a revolution.

Revolutions also attempt, not reforms and not minor changes in legislation, but a complete alteration of what Tocqueville called the "generating principle" of society. Tocqueville distinguished between two kinds of instability. On the one hand, all societies quarrel about proposed legislation, administrative decrees, and judicial decisions, but such quarrels are both expected and usually healthy. On the other hand, societies in the process of revolutionary transformation fight about "the very bases of society and the *generating principles* of the laws." These conflicts bring "trouble and upheavals," and a society enmeshed in such conflict is undergoing a revolutionary "state of violence and transition."[10]

Tocqueville made his argument clearest in the second part of *Democracy in America* when he talked about the concept of honor. Every society, he suggested, exhibits a "notion of honor" or "a system of opinions peculiar to

9. *DA* [B], II, 265-266; *Old Regime*, 19-20.
10. Alexis de Tocqueville, *Journey to America*, J. P. Mayer ed, George Lawrence trans. (Garden City, N.Y.: Doubleday, 1971), 170-171.

themselves as to what is blamable or commendable." Such a notion of honor develops from the needs of that society. Feudal aristocracies, for example, embraced a notion of honor based on military courage, because of the need for such virtues in a society constantly subject to war. By contrast, democracies embrace a notion of honor that praises commerce, industry, profit, and thrift, because commercial interests in democracies need to extol such virtues in order to legitimate their predominance. "The American lauds as a noble and praiseworthy ambition what our forefathers in the Middle Ages stigmatized as severe cupidity."[11] To alter the notion of honor—to replace courage with acquisitiveness—one needed to transform the generating principles of society. Aristocracy gave way to democracy, the leisured warrior disappeared in favor of the industrious businessman, and a defense of hierarchy yielded to a newly proclaimed equality. Such change was indeed revolutionary.

Such revolutionary change, however, took centuries to come about. And in fact, according to Tocqueville, this is always the case. Violent and sudden revolution—again, what we ordinarily think of when we use the word *revolution*—can never be successful, that is, can never quickly bring a far-reaching transformation of societies' generating principles. This can only be done slowly over a time span that includes many generations and perhaps even centuries. A political revolution that changes the rulers at the top can occur rapidly, and might even redress important grievances, but the developments that are authentically revolutionary need at least decades to ripen.

Historical Causes of Revolutions

In *Democracy in America* Tocqueville contrasted historians writing in aristocratic ages, who overemphasize the importance of single individuals in causing historical change, with historians living in democratic times, who focus too strongly on general causes in history and thus succeed, as he put it in his *Recollections*, "in banishing men from this history of the human race."[12] Tocqueville tried to stake out a middle position between these two caricatures. While human will plays some role in historical change, certainly impersonal historical forces set the historical stage and determine the kind of drama produced.

11. *DA* [B], II, 242-255.
12. Alexis de Tocqueville, *Recollections*, J. P. Mayer and A. P. Kerr eds., George Lawrence trans. (Garden City, N.Y.: Doubleday, 1971), 78; *DA* [B], II, 90-93.

Consider his attempts to explain the French Revolution. The French Revolution fascinated Tocqueville, not only because of its historical importance, but because it embodied all three kinds of revolution at once. It was simultaneously a political revolution, a sudden and violent attempt to break with the past, and part of "the great Democratic Revolution," the slow and irresistible democratic transformation of European society. No simple explanation was possible, because "to produce such important consequences, a concurrence of circumstances is required."[13] If we understand this "concurrence of circumstances," we will see that the French Revolution was "inevitable," that it was "prepared and announced necessarily by the work of centuries," and that "chance played no part whatsoever."[14] Tocqueville did not mean that every detail of the French Revolution was determined—a stage complete with Robespierre, Danton, and Napoleon—but that the aristocratic Old Regime had to give way to a more democratic society, while only the timing and the detailed characteristics of the birth of the new order were accidental. Chance, he wrote in his *Recollections*, is "a very important element" in historical change, but "chance can do nothing unless the ground has been prepared in advance" by more general causes. Or, as he wrote to Beaumont, "general causes... always end up dominating through particular accidents."[15]

Tocqueville mentioned at least eight of the circumstances, or secondary causes, that made up this particular "concurrence." First, the centralized administration of the Old Regime—both suffocating and inefficient—and "the absolute predominance of Paris," made a violent revolution easier, because to seize Paris was to conquer France.[16] Second, the ever-encroaching state was oppressive but also weak, because the French monarchy did not have the support of any single class, and hence was eventually, and quite easily, regarded as a government lacking all legitimacy. As a consequence, "the grandiose edifice built up by our Kings was doomed to collapse like a

13. Alexis de Tocqueville, "France Before the Revolution," in *Memoir, Letter, Remains*, (Boston: Ticknor and Fields, 1862), I, 215. The essay "France Before the Revolution" first appeared in the *London and Westminster Review*, April 1836, John Stuart Mill trans., under the title "Political and Social Condition of France."

14. *Old Regime*, 1; *Correspondance d'Alexis de Tocqueville et de Pierre-Paul Royer-Collard. Correspondance d'Alexis de Tocqueville et de Jean-Jacques Ampère*, André Jardin ed. (letter to Ampère, October 21, 1856), *OC*, XI, 351; *Old Regime*, 20.

15. *Recollections*, 78; *Correspondance d'Alexis de Tocqueville et de Gustave de Beaumont*, André Jardin ed. (letter to Beaumont, March 25, 1855), *OC*, VIII:3, 290.

16. *Old Regime*, 76-77; see François Furet, *Interpreting the French Revolution*, Elborg Forster trans. (London: Cambridge University Press, 1981), 140-145.

card castle once disturbances arose."[17] Third, the peasantry harbored genuine resentment toward an aristocracy that had few responsibilities but many privileges, while the peasants remained subject to a special tax (the *taille*) and occasional forced labor (the *corvée*).[18] Fourth, the improvement of the peasants' lot and the prosperity of the 1770s and 1780s contributed to the Revolution because of rising expectations, for "the most perilous moment for a bad government is one when it seeks to mend its ways."[19] Fifth, the growth of industry had created vast working class districts in Paris, so that "Paris had mastered France, and the army that was soon to master Paris was mustering its forces."[20] Sixth, "the development of industry" had created a new commercial class, which Tocqueville called a "democratic class," even within aristocratic France, with "separate instincts, opinions, and laws."[21] Seventh, the nearly total absence of practical political experience enabled many far-fetched ideas of the *philosophes* to take on great importance and astonishing believability.[22] Eighth, the poor harvest of 1788 led to a sharp economic crisis which, "in the French Revolution of 1789, as in modern revolutions, was one of the most effective among secondary causes."[23]

Two factors take on primary importance for Tocqueville, however, when he examined historical causality: class needs and the role of ideas. Tocqueville had learned from Montesquieu that institutions and customs, however strange, were the response to the needs of a given society or classes within that society. "It is the variety of needs in different climates," wrote Montesquieu, "that first occasioned a difference in the manner of living, and this gave rise to a variety of laws."[24] Tocqueville focused most intently on

17. *Ibid.*, 137.
18. *Ibid.*, 120-137. Tocqueville apparently thought that envy or resentment always plays a part in revolutions. For example, he related a story of a young servant girl who boasted, during the 1848 Revolution, that next week "it is we who will wear the lovely silk dresses." *Recollections*, 178.
19. *Old Regime*, 177. Or, "People did not fall from the excess of evil into revolution, but from the excess of progress into revolution. Having come to the middle of the staircase, they threw themselves out the window in order to arrive at the bottom sooner. Thus, moreover, does the world almost always go. It is almost never when a state of things is the most detestable that it is smashed, but when, beginning to improve, it permits men to breathe, to reflect, to communicate their thoughts with each other, and to gauge by what they already have the extent of their rights and their grievances. The weight, although less heavy, seems then all the more unbearable." *Selected Letters* (letter to Pierre Freslon, September 23, 1853), 296.
20. *Old Regime*, 76.
21. YTC, CVj, 2, 16-17 (in *DA* [N], II, 139).
22. *Old Regime*, 138-148.
23. *OC*, II:2, 89, 127.
24. Montesquieu, *The Spirit of the Laws*, Thomas Nugent trans. (New York: Hafner, 1949), bk. XIV, ch. 10. I have altered the translation slightly. For a discussion of

class needs. As classes arise, they need and seek to make use of new institutions, religions, laws, customs, and, as we saw earlier, notions of honor. New classes "contract certain peculiar needs, which give rise in their turn to special opinions." And before 1789, the Third Estate "had opinions, prejudices, and a national spirit of its own." Obviously the needs of different classes are not always in harmony, and the resulting tensions among the interests, ethics, and ideas of various classes frequently help propel historical change. France was in a revolutionary situation before 1789 precisely because "everywhere ancient institutions and old powers could no longer be adjusted exactly to the new condition and to the new needs of men."[25]

That Tocqueville employed a class analysis there can be little doubt. "I am dealing here with classes as a whole, to my mind the historian's proper study."[26] But what did Tocqueville mean by the word *class*? He certainly meant something different from what Marx meant, because, in Tocqueville's view, lawyers, the army, and domestic servants are all examples of distinct classes. Thus, an individual might belong to more than one class—for example, both the army and the aristocracy. Moreover, Tocqueville actually spoke of classes within classes. Not only was the Third Estate an autonomous class challenging the landed aristocracy, but it was "one portion of the aristocracy which revolted against the rest." This jumble, alas, becomes re-jumbled in his analysis of the United States, because in his writings on the United States, Tocqueville contradicted himself in claiming both that there were no classes in America and that there was indeed a class structure.[27]

Tocqueville apparently meant that the comparatively extreme social and economic mobility in the United States prevented the development of fixed classes as in Europe, classes to which one belonged almost exclusively because of birth. Most importantly, a class must perceive itself as having a common interest—as for example, lawyers have a common interest in remaining the only legitimate interpreters of the law—and a certain consciousness of itself as a distinct group which has "feelings or purposes..., traditions or hopes in common." Thus, although he perceived a powerful group of rich families in America, he could still conclude that "the class of rich men does

how Tocqueville used this notion of need, see my article, "Why Could Tocqueville Predict so Well?" *Political Theory*, 11:1 (February 1983), 79-104. Tocqueville apparently grounded his ethical theory on some enduring human needs. "Mankind is subject to general and permanent needs that have created moral laws." *DA* [B], II, 242.
25. *DA* [B], II, 254; "France Before the Revolution," 218; *OC*, II:2, 45.
26. *Old Regime*, 122.
27. "France Before the Revolution," 217, 222; *DA* [B], I, 288; *OC*, II:2, 291; *DA* [B], II, 4, 187, 298; *Journey to America*, 274.

not exist," because this group had no common prism of meanings through which to see the world and no common consciousness of itself as a class.[28]

Tocqueville's interpretations of European history always bear the unmistakable imprint of Guizot, whose lectures on European history and the philosophy of history Tocqueville attended during 1828-1830. Guizot sought to de-emphasize the importance of ideas in history, as if history changed because of some growing rationality, and to stress instead what he called "the material condition of society." The history of Europe during the previous several centuries, according to Guizot, had been distinguished by a movement toward greater equality, class conflict, the decline of the landed aristocracy, and the rise to prominence of the Third Estate, which included, of course, the bourgeoisie. "Modern Europe"—wrote Guizot—"was born from the struggle of the various classes of society." In Guizot's view, the French Revolution of 1789 was the culmination, and 1830, the conclusion, of a clash waged for centuries between classes defending either landed or commercial property.[29]

In Tocqueville's many analyses of European history, the influence of historians such as Guizot and Barante is apparent. The Third Estate, wrote Tocqueville, appeared in the twelfth century as a middle class standing between lords and serfs, and the subsequent history of Europe was the historical quest of this Third Estate for liberty and power. "The barbarian invasions brought into existence only two classes of men: nobles and serfs. The progress of civilization and the weakening of the feudal system soon allowed a third class to appear."[30] Six centuries later this simmering class conflict was the key cause of the French Revolution.

> At the same time that the wealth of the French *noblesse* was dwindling, and their political and social influence fading away, another class of the nation was rapidly acquiring moneyed wealth.... The new and encroaching class, which seemed to be elevating itself on the ruins of the other, had received the name *tiers-état*.[31]

28.   *DA* [B], II, 4, 170. See François Furet, "The Conceptual System of *Democracy in America*," in his *In the Historian's Workshop*, Jonathan Mandelbaum trans. (Chicago: University of Chicago Press, 1984), 167-196, esp. 187.
29.   François Guizot, *The History of Civilization in Europe*, William Hazlitt trans. (New York: A. L. Burt, n.d.), 80, 164. For a discussion of Guizot's influence on Tocqueville, see Jardin, *Alexis de Tocqueville*, 80-82. For a discussion of how Guizot's theory of history compares with Tocqueville's, see Furet, *Interpreting the French Revolution*, 135-139.
30.   *Journeys to England and Ireland*, 7. This is a translation of a long letter to Beaumont (October 5, 1828) on English history.
31.   "France Before the Revolution," 217; also *DA* [B], II, 328.

The French Revolution destroyed so-called feudal institutions, and eventually a government more suitable to the needs of the Third Estate emerged. "The true mother passion of the Revolution," according to Tocqueville, was "the passion of class," and he described the Revolution as eventually becoming a "struggle of the classes" and a "war among the classes."[32] Although initially timid and indecisive, "the bourgeoisie becomes excited, grows bolder, becomes animated, and passes ahead of the other classes, takes the leading role and does not give it up until the people itself climbs upon the stage."[33]

Four decades later this struggle persisted. "Our history from 1789 to 1830 appears to be forty-one years of deadly struggle between the Ancien Régime with its traditions, memories, hopes and men (i.e. the aristocrats), and the new France led by the middle class." The 1830 Revolution signalled the triumph of the bourgeoisie which used the government like "a trading company" or "a private business" for its own profit, and France became ruled by "the most selfish and grasping of plutocracies."[34] When Tocqueville warned in *Democracy in America* about a new and harsh "aristocracy of manufacturers," he was surely commenting on the bourgeoisie of the July Monarchy, a regime for which he hardly shared Guizot's enthusiasm. The 1848 Revolution also involved class conflict, but a new urban working class—a class not anticipated by Guizot—played a key role. Still, as late as 1853, Tocqueville maintained in a letter to Beaumont that this same revolution—*la grande révolution*—was continuing, that is, the attempted domination of "the bourgeois classes and the industrial element over the aristocratic classes and landed property."[35]

32. *OC*, II:2, 69, 100, 106; *Old Regime*, 63. See Irving M. Zeitlin, *Liberty, Equality, and Revolution in Alexis de Tocqueville* (Boston: Little, Brown, 1971), 122-127; and Pierre Gibert ed., *Alexis de Tocqueville: égalité sociale et liberté politique* (Paris: Aubier-Montaigne, 1977), Introduction, 19-21.

33. *OC*, II:2, 71. Certainly current, and generally accepted, scholarship about the French Revolution disputes this kind of class analysis usually associated with Marxist interpretations. [See Furet, *Interpreting the French Revolution*, 81-131, and Jack R. Censer ed., *The French Revolution and Intellectual History* (Chicago: The Dorsey Press, 1989.)] Because I am not an historian of the French Revolution, I bow out of this debate, but I do think Furet, in his efforts to dissociate Tocqueville from Marxist interpretations, understates the importance that Tocqueville—perhaps erroneously—attached to class conflict in his analyses of the many causes of the French Revolution. See Furet, 149-156.

34. *Recollections*, 5-6; *Correspondence and Conversations of Alexis de Tocqueville with Nassau William Senior*, M. C. M. Simpson ed., (New York: Augustus M. Kelley, [1872], 1968), I, 37, 134.

35. *Selected Letters*, 287 (letter to Beaumont, March 23, 1853). "Who among us doesn't see that human activity has changed its end, that the dominant passion, the mother passion, has changed? Instead of political, it has become industrial. Who fails to see

But doesn't this emphasis on classes and the growth of industry and the development of the state mean that history is caused, not by individual men and women, but by impersonal forces? Having angrily dismissed Gobineau's racial theory of history as not only wrong-headed but perniciously fatalistic because it abolished human freedom from history,[36] hasn't Tocqueville introduced a fatalistic doctrine himself with his claims of inevitability? Has Tocqueville succeeded, as he put it, in banishing men from the history of the human race? Not exactly. While the influence of men and women over their historical itinerary is limited, it is still important.

> When, after many efforts, a legislator succeeds in exercising an indirect influence on the destiny of nations, his genius is lauded by mankind, while, in point of fact, the geographical position of the country, which he is unable to change, a social condition which arose without his cooperation, customs and opinions which he cannot trace to their source... exercise so irresistible an influence over the courses of society that he himself is borne away by the current after an ineffectual resistance. Like the navigator, he may direct the vessel which bears him, but he can neither change its structure, nor raise the winds, nor lull the waters that swell beneath him.[37]

Providence, wrote Tocqueville, has not created humankind "entirely free," but has left both to individuals and to nations a very significant but limited freedom. For example, although no nation in the modern world can forever resist the principle of equality, each nation can determine whether this principle will lead to equality with democratic freedom or equality with democratic despotism.[38] As a consequence, the role of human will in the course of revolutions is circumscribed but significant—especially significant as time passes, because choices made at one moment in time that alter history slightly, become vitally important later. "Thus two lines starting out from

---

that our contemporaries are at present hardly concerned about liberties and government, and much more concerned about wealth and well-being?" In Seymour Drescher ed. *Tocqueville and Beaumont on Social Reform*, Seymour Drescher trans. (New York: Harper & Row, 1968), 195. From a letter to *Le Siècle*, January 3, 1843. As social historians point out, it is inaccurate to use the word *bourgeoisie* and the phrases "middle class" and "middle classes" interchangeably, but in an essay this short this jumbling is almost impossible to avoid, because Tocqueville and his contemporaries jumbled these labels. For a good discussion of these terms, see Peter N. Stearns, *Paths to Authority: The Middle Class and the Industrial Labor Force in France, 1820-1848* (Urbana, Ill.: University of Illinois Press, 1978), esp. 108-110.
36.   *Selected Letters*, 297-301 (letter to Arthur de Gobineau, November 17, 1853).
37.   *DA* [B], I, 171.
38.   *Ibid.*, II, 352; see Roger Boesche, *The Strange Liberalism of Alexis de Tocqueville* (Ithaca, N.Y.: Cornell University Press, 1987), ch. 12.

practically the same point but given slightly different directions diverge more and more, the more they are prolonged."[39]

One can see this in Tocqueville's discussions of the other key factor in revolutions—the role of ideas. On the one hand, Tocqueville claimed that "it is ideas that stir the world and not blind needs," that ideas were "one of the chief causes of the Revolution," and he devoted a whole chapter of his *Old Regime* to showing why the ideas of the *philosophes* could play such an important role in the Revolution. Indeed, the French Revolution was caused in part by something like a religion of equality that—"like Islam"—is attempting to "overrun the whole world with its apostles, militants, and martyrs."[40] Similarly, Tocqueville wrote that "not needs, but ideas brought about this great upheaval" of 1848, that decent men and women of the working class genuinely believed in misguided socialist doctrines, thereby creating a sort of "revolutionary religion that our bayonets and our cannons will not destroy."[41]

On the other hand, Tocqueville maintained that ideas are "the result of changes in [man's] material environment," that for revolutionary doctrines to have an effect, "certain changes must already have taken place in the living conditions, customs, and mores of a nation and prepared men's minds for the reception of new ideas."[42] Here Tocqueville seems to be contradicting himself in contending that ideas are not the cause of historical change, but rather the result of such change. In fact, there is no contradiction, because Tocqueville was saying that ideas are effective precisely to the extent that they address the problems of the time, and to the extent that they are useful to some group or class. For example, "the Third Estate... was obliged to profess the general principle of equality as a means of overthrowing" the aristocracy.[43] In other words, in eighteenth-century France the powerful idea of equality was often simply a soldier serving a deeper class interest.

In comparing the Reformation with the Revolution, Tocqueville saw in each instance a combination of interests plus ideals—in the former the material interests of the ruling classes and the ideals of the people, and in the lat-

---

39. *Old Regime*, 98. Compare to Weber. "Not ideas, but material and ideal interests, directly govern men's conduct. Yet very frequently the 'world images' that have been created by 'ideas' have, like switchmen, determined the tracks along which action has been pushed by the dynamic of interest." From *Max Weber: Essays in Sociology*, H. H. Gerth and C. Wright Mills eds. and trans. (New York: Oxford University Press, 1946), 280. From "The Economic Ethic of the World Religions."
40. *Journeys to England and Ireland*, 58; *Old Regime*, 6, 13, 138-148.
41. *Selected Letters*, 206, 216 (letters to Senior, April 10, 1848, and to Eugène Stoffels, July 21, 1848).
42. *Old Regime*, 13, 113.
43. "France Before the Revolution," 222.

ter, just the reverse. Indeed, Tocqueville concluded that the people alone could not make a revolution. Revolutions generally need the passionate energy of the people, the clarifying wisdom of the "enlightened classes," and the material interests of both. Every revolution exhibits just such a combination of class interests and passionate ideals. "Join to the passions born from self-interest the goal of changing the face of the world and of regenerating the species, and only then will you see all that man can accomplish. This is the history of the French Revolution."[44]

The key factors in revolutions, according to Tocqueville, are the material interests of classes and the human passions derived from ideals. In each case, however, in the actions of classes and in the nature of the ideals, there is some scope for human choice. Human freedom can never be unlimited, of course, because no one can force ideals on to an unready history.

Why Sudden and Violent Revolutions are Always Unsuccessful

In 1853 Tocqueville wrote to a friend that he was attempting to demonstrate in his *Old Regime* that "the greatest revolutions do not change peoples as much as we pretend, and that the principal reason for what they are is always in what they have been."[45] Both parts of his statement are linked. Violent and sudden revolutions change less than one would expect, precisely because we are creatures of the past, and a nation cannot cast off the traditions and mores of the past at will. In his Foreword to the *Old Regime* Tocqueville stated that the men and women who lived through the revolutionary years "had been shaped by the old order," and despite the upheavals of the Revolution, and "despite superficial alterations," when it ended "they remained the same essentially." Having unwittingly borrowed from the Old Regime their "customs, traditions, and modes of thought," the revolutionaries could not help but try to "use the debris of the old order for building up the new."[46] While using architectural ideas and building materials from the past, the revolutionaries predictably built a new edifice similar to the old.

Tocqueville certainly anticipated Valéry's famous maxim that we always back into the future. "Peoples like individuals," he wrote, "encounter the future by the past." Neither a nation nor an individual can easily "shake off the

---

44. *OC*, II:2, 349-350; *Old Regime*, 187; *Selected Letters*, 366-367 (letter to Beaumont, February 27, 1858); *OCB*, VIII, 442.
45. *OCB*, VII, 305 (letter to Léonce de Lavergne, October 31, 1853).
46. *Old Regime*, x, vii.

influence of the past," and if we seek to alter our world suddenly, we combat a formidable enemy armed with a tenacity tempered by centuries of experience. Just as Freud claimed that sons will rebel against authoritarian fathers, but ultimately rule just as they did, Tocqueville suggested that one generation may condemn previous generations and swear that they will be different, "but it is far easier to combat them than to avoid resembling them."[47]

Tocqueville's argument is frequently regarded as old-fashioned, because he is suggesting that nations develop a character—or, as Montesquieu would put it, a spirit—devilishly difficult to change. "I believe," he wrote in his notes for *Democracy in America*, "that nations just like men indicate in their youth the principal traits of their destinies." America, for example, will always be a nation seeking to conquer the world by commerce, much like Rome did by force of arms.[48] By the time he wrote *Democracy in America*, Tocqueville still argued that nations have characteristics in their youth that endure determinedly, just as "the entire man is, so to speak, to be seen in the cradle of the child."[49] Not only can we recognize key characteristics of modern Germany in Tacitus's *Germania*, we can discern an essential national character that survives countless secondary changes.

> In history all nations, like individuals, show their own peculiar physiognomy. Their characteristic traits reproduce themselves through all the transformations that they undergo. Laws, morals, religions, alter; dominion and wealth change hands; external appearances vary; the dress is different; prejudices vanish or are replaced by others. Through all these diverse changes you always recognize the same people. Something inflexible shows through.[50]

What constitutes and maintains this national character? *Les moeurs.* The word *mores*—and this is never an adequate translation—encompasses the customs, habits, manners, and day-to-day beliefs of a people. While Tocqueville expressly noted that he used the words *customs* and *mores* inter-

47. *OC*, VI:1, 143 (letter to Reeve, March 26, 1853); *DA* [B], I, 46; "France Before the Revolution," 204. Compare to Marx. "Men make their own history, but they do not make it just as they please; they do not make it under circumstances chosen by themselves, but under circumstances directly encountered, given, and transmitted from the past. The tradition of all the dead generations weighs like a nightmare [literally, "like an Alp"] on the brain of the living." 48. *The Eighteenth Brumaire of Louis Bonaparte* (New York: International Publishers, 1963), 15.
48. YTC, CVb, 23 (see *DA* [N], I, 310). Note a strong parallel. When Montesquieu examined Rome, he concluded that military discipline was its chief early characteristic, and he analyzed the long-term effects of this. When Tocqueville examined the United States, he concluded that commerce was one of its chief characteristics, and he sought to deduce—almost literally—possible long-term effects.
49. *DA* [B], I, 28.
50. *Journey to America*, 392.

changeably, he stated that these words referred to the manners of a people, to "the habits of the heart," and to the ideas and opinions that "constitute their character of mind." Thus the words *customs* and *mores* indicate "the whole moral and intellectual condition of a people." Indeed, Tocqueville declared that the "principal object" of *Democracy in America* was to show that neither physical abundance nor fertile plains on which to expand, neither enacted legislation nor the adopted *Constitution*, but rather customs and mores had created and sustained democratic habits and institutions. "Too much importance is attributed to legislation, too little to customs," or, as he wrote in the margin of a notebook, "Mores are the only tough and durable power among a people."[51]

Whereas in Europe people think they can establish a democracy by writing constitutions and convening parliaments, in fact one needs the habits of participation, discussion, and voting—habits that one cannot create with the stroke of a pen. Even the best constitutions and laws are "dead creations," if not supported by democratic mores.[52] Creating democracy in a society without democratic mores is consequently a nearly impossible political task. As Stendhal put it, "Besides, how is one to establish a Republic without republicans?"[53] Similarly, Tocqueville wrote in a letter to Beaumont, "But how difficult it is to establish liberty solidly among people who have lost the practice of it, and even the correct notion of it! What greater impotence than that of institutions, when ideas and mores do not nourish them!"[54]

Like Montesquieu, Tocqueville envisioned each society as a vast interrelated whole, one in which all the various components—social classes, political institutions, economic organizations, religious practices, family structure, moral beliefs, customs, laws, the means of communications, literature, entertainment, and so on—both reflect and reinforce one another. This notion does not mean uniformity, because within this whole there may be a variety of classes, dissenting groups, and subcultures. But it does suggest a fierce, conservative resistance to change, because to make one significant alteration in one part of the whole, one must make certain that this change ripples throughout the entire structure. If one genuinely wants to make women more equal, for example, then one must enact new laws, but also change women's political participation, employment opportunities, status within religious organizations, roles within the family, common attitudes toward women, and

51. *DA* [B], I, 310, 334; *Journey to America*, 305.
52. *Journey to America*, 42-45. Tocqueville was here recording a conversation with Francis Lieber.
53. Stendhal, *The Charterhouse of Parma*, Margaret R. B. Shaw trans. (Baltimore: Penguin, 1958), 415.
54. *Selected Letters*, 366 (letter to Beaumont, February 27, 1858).

the way they are depicted in the media, literature, and entertainment. To push one significant change forward, one must drag the entire baggage of society.

As a consequence, violent and sudden revolutions can redress immediate grievances, and they can change institutions, but they cannot transform society rapidly, precisely because they cannot quickly alter the long-established mores. Violent and sudden revolutions that attempt to transform all of society are thus fated to fail. Although the French Revolution indeed destroyed—or at least, as it continued into Tocqueville's time, was destroying—all that was connected with "aristocratic and feudal institutions," it could not rapidly alter the "host of ideas, sentiments, manners, and customs" that supported those institutions. (As he put it in a letter to Senior, the Revolution "could not enable the bourgeois to feel himself the equal of the *gentilhomme*."[55]) It is true that the aristocratic mores of the Old Regime were disappearing, although not because of the violent events of 1789-1799, but rather because the old social order was crumbling "bit by bit," and a new class was emerging and bringing with it increasingly commercial and democratic mores. "Even if [the Revolution of 1789-1799] had not taken place, the old social structure would nonetheless have been shattered everywhere sooner or later."[56]

In looking at the French Revolution as the violent culmination of a longer historical process of class conflict, Tocqueville offered an analysis of the events of 1789-1799 similar in one respect to that of Marx. These violent events of the French Revolution only signified the birth of a new society that had long been gestating within the womb of the old, an image of course made far more familiar by Hegel and Marx. The French Revolution grew out of "powerful and ancient causes" that had been "fertilized" over time. While "outwardly nothing had changed," in fact a "new substructure" had grown within the old society, and the Revolution was thus "the inevitable outcome of a long period of gestation."[57] Thus, the events of 1789-1799 were not the beginning of the revolution, but only the temporary culmination of a much longer process. By itself the Revolution of 1789-1799 created nothing of great importance, but rather "only developed the germs previously existing.

---

55. *Correspondence and Conversations of Alexis de Tocqueville with Nassau William Senior*, I, 93.
56. *Old Regime*, 20. Furet is right in saying, "Tocqueville suggests that the Revolution was above all a transformation in values and patterns of thought... [a] cultural (or, if one prefers, intellectual and moral) revolution." *Interpreting the French Revolution*, 157.
57. *OC*, II:2, 342; *Old Regime*, 20, 58, 143.

[The Revolution] regulated, arranged, and legalized the effects of a great cause, but was not itself that cause."[58]

Tocqueville's mentor was obviously not Marx, but rather Montesquieu, whose book on the greatness and decline of Rome was "the inimitable model" for Tocqueville's studies of the French Revolution.[59] Montesquieu argued that the needs of early Roman society had engendered frugality, austerity, unity, and military discipline, characteristics that propelled Rome to political and military greatness. Rome's very success, however, undermined the principles responsible for that success. With military victories, for example, came riches, which undermined the need for austerity and discipline. "Here, in a word, is the history of the Romans. By means of their maxims they conquered all peoples, but when they had succeeded in doing so, their republic could not endure."[60] From Republic to Principate to Empire, Rome had undergone far-reaching and revolutionary transformations in both political rule and in social mores, but the changes came slowly as new needs, classes, institutions, and mores developed. "To prepare great changes whole ages are sometimes requisite; the events ripen, and the revolutions follow."[61] For Tocqueville and Montesquieu, great and revolutionary change is always slow and gradual. "Politics is a smooth file"—wrote Montesquieu—"which cuts gradually, and attains its end by a slow progression."[62]

Tocqueville concluded that as a political revolution, the French Revolution had some success in eliminating abuses and institutions from the old feudal order, but as a sudden and violent revolution attempting to transform society and its mores rapidly—which is, to repeat, what we ordinarily mean by the word *revolution*—it was predictably unsuccessful. But Tocqueville also looked at the French Revolution as simply one violent moment in a centuries-long historical process of change. Referring to it as "this long revolution" and "the great revolution," he declared that he did not see it begin, and he would not see it end.[63]

> There are men who see in the Revolution of 1789 an accident and who, like the travellers in the fable, are sitting down to wait until the river has passed. What an empty illusion! Our fathers did not see the birth of this Revolution and we will not

58. "France Before the Revolution," 251.
59. *Selected Letters*, 257 (letter to Kergorlay, December 15, 1850).
60. Montesquieu, *Considerations on the Causes of the Greatness of the Romans and Their Decline*, David Lowenthal trans. (Ithaca, N.Y.: Cornell University Press, 1965), 169.
61. Montesquieu, *The Spirit of the Laws*, bk. XXVIII, ch. 39.
62. *Ibid.*, bk. XIV, ch. 13.
63. *Recollections*, 83; *Selected Letters*, 216 (letter to Eugène Stoffels, July 21, 1848).

see it end. It will roll along for more generations still with its unsettling floods. It has been more than six hundred years since it was given its first impulse.[64]

Obviously, Tocqueville linked the French Revolution in this broader sense to "the great Democratic Revolution," and as a slow and gradual revolution, it was destined to be successful in undermining feudal society, in bringing greater equality into the world, and in creating new mores appropriate to a new democratic and commercial world. This is why Tocqueville thought that Burke entirely misunderstood the French Revolution. Thinking that the revolutionaries only wanted to correct abuses, Burke urged them to reinvigorate "the ancient common law of Europe," but he was unable to understand "the new and universal event taking place," and could not see that the Revolution was one moment in a process steadily undermining the social structure on which that ancient common law rested.[65]

The process of revolution is always circular; one tries to travel to a new land in a carriage belonging to the old; one tries to teach a new way of thinking by talking in the language of the old. Sudden revolutionary change might be possible—and Tocqueville did not think it was—only with obliteration, a suggestion recalling Plato's lament that he could reform a polis only by banishing all who were older than ten and re-educating the remaining children. Similarly, Tocqueville claimed that India's customs constituted a hopelessly tenacious growth strangling all attempts to alter them. "*The impossibility of making the condition of the Indians good*, whatever the government. It would first be necessary to sweep away all these institutions and all these habits."[66] But one cannot change mores and habits by striking a sudden blow at the political institutions of society. Instead, an alternative must germinate and grow alongside the old order until it gradually stifles it, robbing it of sustenance by dominating soil and sun, until the old withers and the new blossoms. A revolution is never successful because of a sudden exertion of will; historical conditions must nurture and cultivate it patiently, like a garden.

In this sense, revolutionary change is possible. A nation that has long existed "under a system of castes and classes" can transform itself into a democracy only through a "long series" of critical events—"accomplished by violent efforts"—during which "property, opinions, and power" are transferred from aristocratic to democratic classes.[67] Similarly, American democracy might conceivably experience sweeping and revolutionary change,

64. YTC, CVh, 3, 23 (in *DA* [N], I, 7).
65. *Old Regime*, 21; *OC*, II:2, 341.
66. Alexis de Tocqueville, *L'Inde*, in *OC*, III:1, 540.
67. *DA* [B], II, 265.

although this could only happen slowly and gradually. "Nothing but a long series of events, all having the same tendency, could substitute for this combination of laws, opinions, and manners a mass of opposite opinions, manners, and laws."[68]

If we take the word *revolution* to indicate a process that slowly and relentlessly transforms society's institutions and mores, then Tocqueville certainly saw himself as living in the midst of a revolution—the on-going French Revolution—that was bringing greater equality, democracy, and industry to France, and of course new mores appropriate to this new society. While he and his contemporaries could not halt this revolution, they did have a some freedom to direct or channel it. "The nations of our time cannot prevent the condition of men from becoming equal, but it depends upon themselves whether the principle of equality is to lead them to servitude or freedom, to knowledge or barbarism, to prosperity or wretchedness."[69] France, unfortunately, was guiding this revolution badly, and Tocqueville likened France to a "sick man" and himself to a doctor attempting a desperate cure on this dangerously ill patient.[70]

This chronic illness, however, admitted of no quick cure, so Tocqueville was faced with the question of how to alleviate the malady. "Do you not see," he wrote in his notebooks, "that with equality and without liberty we are marching toward a singular servitude and toward inevitable barbarism. And if you see all this, what do you do?"[71] Tocqueville supported this "great Democratic Revolution," even though he did not regard it as the "Promised Land." France must proceed slowly but relentlessly to reshape its mores and customs so that they enhance democratic freedom. "In America free morals have made free political institutions; in France it is for free political institutions to mould morals." The country must "proceed slowly, with precaution, and with legality," extending "provincial liberties" until "the majority of the nation itself can be involved with its own affairs," that is, until almost all male citizens take an active part in political life. After selecting its destination, France must march toward it with determination. "I wish finally that people knew where they wanted to go, and that they advanced toward it prudently instead of proceeding aimlessly as they have been doing almost constantly for twenty years."[72] Knowing that no one could stop this democratic

---

68. *Ibid.*, I, 436.
69. *Ibid.*, II, 352.
70. *Correspondence and Conversations of Alexis de Tocqueville with Nassau William Senior*, I, 90; YTC, CVj, 2, 18.
71. YTC, CVd, 19 (in *DA* [N], II, 275).
72. *Selected Letters*, 102 (letter to Mill, June, 1835); *Journey to America*, 149; *Selected Letters*, 112-114 (letter to Eugène Stoffels, October 5, 1836).

revolution, he wanted his fellow citizens to guide it deliberately and properly.

It is in this sense that Tocqueville made the principles of 1789 his own. Although a violent revolution will not succeed in transforming society rapidly, it "cannot fail to give a sudden impulse to [a people's] feelings and ideas."[73] Despite all his misgivings about the Revolution, despite his analysis concluding that violent revolutions cannot succeed, Tocqueville never lost his admiration for the grandeur and the ideals of 1789. "The spectacle [of 1789] was short, but it was one of incomparable beauty. It will never leave the memory of men. All foreign nations saw it, all applauded it, all were moved by it."[74]

73. *DA* [B], II, 43-44.
74. *OC*, II:2, 134. Despite his love for 1789, Tocqueville also harbored a certain nostalgia for the Old Regime. See Wolin's essay, "Archaism, Modernity, and *Democracy in America*," in Sheldon Wolin, *The Presence of the Past: Essays on the State and the Constitution* (Baltimore: The Johns Hopkins University Press, 1989), 66-81.

[13]

Tocqueville and the Postmodern Refusal of History

Edward T. Gargan

In March of 1839 Tocqueville was elected to the Chamber of Deputies from Valognes. It was possible for him to take this step because the final volume of his *Democracy* was at last finished and would be published in 1840. In 1990 the one hundred and fiftieth anniversary of the *Democracy* invited and continues to encourage reflections on the significance of the *Democracy*'s place in serious efforts to understand the transition of our time from that of modernity to that of the postmodern. Anniversaries are indeed times to honor, to acknowledge obligations. This is especially so when time has not diminished our debts, but indeed may have increased our obligations. In a sense all of history is an account of indebtedness contracted between the present and the past. Claude Lévi-Strauss, however, in his essay on "History and Dialectic," a chapter in his *The Savage Mind*, insists that whatever the French have accomplished or failed to do in the past, time has the option eventually to break the connection between past and present.[1] He illustrates this proposition by proposing that the French Revolution still maintains a connection between the past and the present, but for our time the Fronde is out of focus, out of mind, without significance. "It suffices, therefore," he argues, "for history to move away from us in time or for us to move away from it in thought, for it to cease to be internalizable and to lose its intelligibility."[2] He gives, as an example of this kind of distance and loss, the little meaning or relevance that the *Mémoires* of the Cardinal de Retz about the Fronde have for our contemporary world.

1. Claude Lévi-Strauss, *The Savage Mind* (Chicago: University of Chicago Press, 1966), 254-255.
2. *Idem.*

Tocqueville was not unaware of the consequences when the passage of time wears away essential recollections pertinent to comprehension of one's own time. In the second volume of the *Democracy* he regrets that in the nineteenth century an understanding of the era of Louis XIV has not for the French been retained. And he concludes that this failure of memory damages and gravely lessens the present generation's ability to comprehend the choices it must make for its future. In essence, he argues that the capacity of a society to respond to the needs of its own time depends on its understanding of the linkage between time past, time present, time future. This interconnection permits Tocqueville in the *Democracy* to present a very positive account of the bondage between people and King in the age of Louis XIV. "The writers of that age," he proposes, "felt a species of genuine enthusiasm in raising the power of their King over all other authority"; and with a certain lack of restraint, he continues, "and there was no peasant so obscure, or who would not die cheerfully with the cry 'Vive le Roi!' upon his lips." To this Tocqueville adds, "these same forms of loyalty have now become odious to the French people."³ And only then does Tocqueville ask: "Which were wrong, the French of the age of Louis XIV or their descendants of the present day?"⁴ And while in this mode of counseling his readers of the *Democracy*, Tocqueville advises them to remember: "The love which a people may show for its laws proves only this: that we should not be in a hurry to change them."⁵

Tocqueville's intellectual openness and actual anxiety about the possible democratization of France is, of course, at the center of the *Democracy*. The burden of history pulls him in contrary directions. This vital tension creates the passion that sustains his great work. This anxiety and hesitation in his analysis requires him to appeal to his readers to enter into a dialogue with him as a fellow citizen of France. Beginning in the introduction to the *Democracy*, and continuing throughout it, Tocqueville asks his readers to recognize that his conclusions do not constitute assertions based on unquestionable judgments. The dialogue is possible between author and reader because Tocqueville as author seeks their confidence and participation by acknowledging: "I soon perceived," "I then turned my thoughts," "I observe," "I can conceive of a society," "I admit," "I cannot believe." In using this personal voice Tocqueville transfers to his readers of the generation of the 1840s and subsequent generations a grave responsibility. He has not presented to his readers assertions having the character of the axioms of

3. *DA* [B], appendix w, II, 225, 366.
4. *Idem.*
5. *Idem.*

Euclidian geometry and space. His readers having shared in his confessions of how he has arrived at the statements in the *Democracy* cannot plead that they are conscientious objectors in the face of this intense conflict for the future. It is this responsibility to decide again and again what kind of community and society is desired in the future that makes necessary the anniversary we celebrate and contributes to our confidence that other celebrants of the *Democracy* will gather in the next century. Tocqueville's *Democracy* cannot be dismissed in the fashion in which Claude Lévi-Strauss dismissed Cardinal de Retz's *Mémoires* as part of a past that does not make contact with our century.

Yet recent scholars have begun to note that academic attention to Tocqueville often accelerates and then is followed by a decreasing interest in what Tocqueville accomplished. Ronald G. Walters, in his valuable article of 1988, suggests that just as there are times when it is appropriate to speak of the "absent" Karl Marx in learned discourse, it is equally necessary to note there are also times when Tocqueville is notably absent.[6]

This accurate observation must be qualified by a recognition that where major discussions concerning the theory and practice of democracy are taking place then Tocqueville is seldom "absent." This is evident in the important recent work of Professor Robert A. Dahl in his *Democracy and its Critics*. Both Tocqueville and Marx are not absent from Dahl's exposition of the central issues in democratic theory. Among other observations, Dahl's work underlines the importance Tocqueville placed on "beliefs, mores, habits" as "more important than the [U.S.] Constitution" in making possible support and consent to the decisions of democratic societies.[7] Dahl also emphasizes the practical and theoretical significance Tocqueville assigns to an active associational life necessary to the health and well being of democratic systems.[8]

Yet we are not as readers of Tocqueville in the position of some critics of the theory of quantum mechanics who think it possible to determine the precise moment when a nucleus will decay. Our skills do not enable us to project the expected life of the *Democracy*. And here the implications of postmodern discourse raise the question as to whether or not it matters that we stress the continuing relevance of Tocqueville to understanding the problems of modernity. Today, philosophers such as Jean-François Lyotard

6. Ronald G. Walters, "Reforming Tocqueville," *The Tocqueville Review*, 9 (1987/88), 283-295.
7. Robert A. Dahl, *Democracy and its Critics* (New Haven: Yale University Press, 1989), 178.
8. *Ibid.*, 295.

and sociologists such as Jean Baudrillard insists that a decisive break has taken place separating irrevocably our existing moment in time from the period conventionally characterized as modern. For these most provocative of thinkers the decisive break that has occurred invalidates our inherited limits of language, methods of reasoning, possibilities of art and poetry. They see an accelerated process in time that has blasted away our received explanations of the human condition and the appropriate forms of human community.[9]

Here Jean Baudrillard, recently described in *Le Nouvel Observateur* as a *sociologue* become *métaphysicien*, insists that the best we can do is to locate ourselves in a fourth dimension beyond the disintegration of our intellectual world, our societal excesses, and the end of our history. There are no echoes here of the measured steps of Tocqueville.

So certain is Baudrillard of this process of disintegration that in 1975 he published his perturbing announcement "The Year 2000 Has Already Happened." Baudrillard dismisses our frantic efforts to keep records, to add to and protect our records of the modernity we erroneously think will continue. He asks:

> Isn't there here a symptom of our collective prescience of the end of the event and of the living time of history, so that one must arm oneself (as it were) with all of artificial memory, all the signs of the past in order to confront the absence of the future and of the glacial time which awaits us?[10]

Possessing ordinary intelligence and the conventional wisdom of our academic disciplines we are inclined to claim that Tocqueville at least was free of the terror experienced by our contemporary scholars dedicated to uncovering our nonfuture. We are inclined to rejoice that while projecting the future was paramount to the direction of the *Democracy* Tocqueville sanely believed that a knowledge of the difficulties to be encountered in the unfolding of democratic societies offered reasonable hope that disasters could be avoided. Comparing Tocqueville and Baudrillard we are likely to conclude that they do not belong in the same company, that their concerns do not connect across time. It is then that Baudrillard prepares an astonishing surprise for those following his career. In 1986, Jean Baudrillard published his

---

9.   Jean-François Lyotard, "Answering the Question: What is Postmodernism," in Lyotard, *The Postmodern Condition: A Report on Knowledge* (Minneapolis: University of Minnesota Press, 1984), 71-82.
10. Jean Baudrillard, "The Year 2000 Has Already Happened," in *Body Invaders Panic Sex in America*, Arthur and Marilouise Kroker eds., Geoff Bennington and Brian Massumi trans. (New York: St. Martin's Press, 1987), 35, 44.

Amérique, a shorter but unblushing imitation of Tocqueville's journey to America.

In his miniature imitation of the *Democracy*, Baudrillard describes America as "Astral," a Utopia achieved, facing the end of U.S. power and in a last reflection a "desert forever."[11] But this summary does not prepare us for the degree to which Baudrillard approaches Tocqueville in his response to the American experiment. In his chapter on New York, Baudrillard's predictions on the end of history seemed confirmed. In New York he is terrified to be amongst people who think alone, sing alone, eat alone and talk alone in the streets. He confesses that this is a "mind blowing" experience. Baudrillard finds in America a society where people do not make contact, where instead they "subtract from one another." As a sociologist he is appalled at the implications of the New York marathon. Baudrillard terms the marathon "the end-of-the-world show" where people freely enter into suffering "as to a state of servitude."[12] It is all a kind of suicide. Unlike Tocqueville, he decides that this stupid world is incapable of being understood "least of all" by "the American intellectuals shut away on their campuses."[13]

Then without any forewarning, Baudrillard in his chapter "Utopia achieved" surprisingly asserts "To land in America is even today, to land in that 'religion' of the way of life which Tocqueville described." [14] For Baudrillard, unlike Tocqueville, whatever crises confront America they are to be seen as distinct from the predicaments, disasters facing Europe. "Ours," he writes, "is a crisis of historical ideas facing up to the impossibility of their realization."[15] While of America he writes, "Theirs is the crisis of an achieved Utopia, confronted with the problem of its duration and permanence."[16] In a complicated way Baudrillard finds America's achievements accomplished independently from the Old World. He thinks, unlike Tocqueville, that in no way can the American experience be thought about or imitated by Europe.

Tocqueville, with his innate sense of restraint, would never have allowed himself to conclude that the two worlds were incapable of growing in wisdom by trying to understand one another. He would have rejected Baudrillard's assertion:

11.   Jean Baudrillard, *America*, Chris Turner trans. (London: Verso, 1984), 121-128.
12.   *Ibid.*, 19.
13.   *Ibid.*, 23.
14.   *Ibid.*, 75-76.
15.   *Ibid.*, 77.
16.   *Idem.*

We shall never enjoy the same freedom—not the formal freedom we take for granted, but the concrete, flexible fundamental active freedom we see at work in American institutions and in the head of each citizen.[17]

An American reader who has adjusted to Baudrillard's postmodern Domesday scenario cannot easily adjust to Baudrillard's denial of that plot for America. He hesitates before the exaggeration of Baudrillard's insistence that "American banality will always be a thousand times more interesting than the European—and especially the French."[18] Tocqueville's invocation to Americans and to Europeans to think upon their limits, their capacities to fail in the face of their opportunities does appear more appropriate advice to bring together all considerations at the end of this century concerning the American experience.

Finally, it is not amiss to conclude that in future years when the achievement of Tocqueville's work is again scrutinized that attention will be paid to his accomplishment as a student of the whole culture of a people, of a nation. It is to be hoped that when this takes place some recognition will be given to the way that the author Tocqueville succeeded in meeting Clifford Geertz's criterion for all who share the goals of anthropologists: they must convince their readers by their writing that they have been there, are here, were models at witnessing and successful at persuading their audience that it all matters very greatly.[19]

17. Baudrillard, *America*, 81.
18. *Ibid.*, 86.
19. Clifford Geertz, *Works and Lives. The Anthropologist as Author* (Stanford, Ca.: Stanford University Press, 1988).

[14]

How Many *Democracies*?

James T. Schleifer

At least since the appearance in 1964 of Seymour Drescher's brilliant article, "Tocqueville's Two *Démocraties*," scholars have debated how many *Democracies* Tocqueville wrote during the 1830s.[1] Are the 1835 and 1840 halves of the *Democracy* essentially two parts of a single work or two quite distinct books which happen to share the same title? Note that this is not the same issue which has been so well raised by Robert Nisbet and others about the many changing perceptions or interpretations of the *Democracy* since its appearance over one hundred and fifty years ago.[2] Of interpretations, there are many, especially when we recall the sustained international appreciation of Tocqueville's book over the years. But of judgments about the unity or disunity of the *Democracy*, there are essentially only two, what Seymour Drescher has recently labeled the "lumpers" and the "splitters".[3] Each group has perhaps as many individual variations as there are serious readers. But the basic approach remains bipolar: one *Democracy* or two?

The question is not a trivial dispute or empty intellectual game. It concerns the identification and continuity or disjuncture of basic themes in Tocqueville's work and involves answers to when and how some of his fundamental ideas emerged and developed.

1. Seymour Drescher, "Tocqueville's Two *Démocraties*," *Journal of the History of Ideas*, 25 (April-June 1964), 201-216.
2. Robert Nisbet, "Many Tocquevilles," *The American Scholar*, 46 (Winter 1976-1977), 59-75.
3. Seymour Drescher, "More Than America: Comparison and Synthesis in *Democracy in America*," 77-93, in Abraham S. Eisenstadt, ed., *Reconsidering Tocqueville's "Democracy in America"* (New Brunswick, N.J.: Rutgers University Press, 1988).

All Tocqueville's scholars and major interpretative works devoted to the
Democracy recognize, of course, both common features and significant differences between the two parts of Tocqueville's book. There are no abso-
lutists in this debate. Divisions of opinion arise from distinctive answers to
"which unities?" and "which diversities?" and from contending perceptions
about *why* the *Democracy* changed between the early 1830s and 1840. How
was Tocqueville's book reshaped by new experiences after 1835: travels,
readings, friendships, political involvements, innovations in methodology,
additional time for reflection and reconsideration, or the emergence of
different issues in contemporary France? Most essentially, the two groups
divide on the matter of emphasis. Are the 1835 and 1840 *Democracies* more
alike or more distinct?

Of the two basic approaches, the first, identified particularly with what
Jean-Claude Lamberti called the "Yale School," focuses on basic themes or
concepts by tracing each from the late 1820s to 1840.[4] This path to analysis
recognizes Tocqueville's background, readings, friendships and other
intellectual influences, travel experiences, political involvements, his habits
of thinking and writing, then follows the genesis and elaboration, the
twisting and turning, of Tocqueville's ideas, and ends by emphasizing the
unity of the two halves of the *Democracy*, despite obvious attention to
significant changes between 1835 and 1840.

The second approach also recounts the development of fundamental
concepts. Its special strengths, however, are examination of Tocqueville's
broadening experiences after 1835 (especially lessons learned from England
and from French political life) and careful comparison of the 1835 and 1840
Democracies. The two portions are set side-by-side to see what differences
emerge in the author's tone, methodology, ideas, emphases, and underlying
concerns. This path ends by proposing a definitive shift between the halves
of the *Democracy* despite the recognition that some fundamental threads are
present throughout Tocqueville's book.[5]

4. For the "lumpers," see especially George Wilson Pierson, *Tocqueville and
    Beaumont in America* (New York: Oxford University Press, 1938); and James T.
    Schleifer, *The Making of Tocqueville's "Democracy in America"* (Chapel Hill,
    N.C.: University of North Carolina Press, 1980). The term "Yale School" appears in
    Jean-Claude Lamberti, *Tocqueville et les deux "Démocraties"* (Paris: Presses
    Universitaires de France, 1983), 9-10. Lamberti's book has been translated into
    English: *Tocqueville and the Two "Democracies,"* Arthur Goldhammer trans.
    (Cambridge, Mass.: Harvard University Press, 1989).
5. For the "splitters," see especially Lamberti, *Deux "Démocraties"*; and the two
    articles by Drescher cited above. Also consult Seymour Drescher, *Tocqueville and
    England* (Cambridge, Mass.: Harvard University Press, 1964).

In his most recent formulation of this approach, Drescher carefully lists some of the major themes which link the 1835 and 1840 *Democracies*: the inevitability of democracy, the value placed on political liberty, and the effort to define the nature and future of democracy.[6] And he notes that the same comparative methodology characterizes both the 1835 and 1840 portions.

But his essential point is that we should recognize two separate works. A sharp break occurred after 1835, first, because of a fundamental change in Tocqueville's frame of reference, particularly "his extra-American experiences"[7], that is, his English journeys and French political involvements, and second, because of a drastic reversal in his expectations about the democratic future. Just as France eclipsed America as the leading example in Tocqueville's writing, so too did doubt and pessimism replace hope and optimism.

Drescher then examines two concepts to demonstrate his approach: centralization and individualism. According to his argument, not until after the publication of the 1835 work did Tocqueville realize that democracy lead to centralization and that democracy and centralization were dangerously and inextricably linked in the modern world. In 1835, he writes, Tocqueville showed a lack of concern about administrative centralization totally at variance from his profound worries in 1840. By then, centralization had, for Tocqueville, come "close to achieving full parity with democracy" as a fact for his and our times.[8]

The second example concerns the pattern of behavior which Tocqueville associated with democracy. In 1835 he focused on what Drescher calls the "'benign' egoism of the participatory citizen"[9], or enlightened self-interest, modeled on the American example. By 1840 his attention had shifted to the "pathological egoism of retreat"[10], or individualism, exemplified by the narrow behavior of his own countrymen. Both the word and most of the content of the individualism of 1840 are missing earlier. This change again reflects both Tocqueville's movement from America to France and the reversal of his prognosis for the democratic future. Drescher believes that there are "latent or overt contradictions"[11] between the 1835 and the 1840 books and concludes that we have a "Tocqueville problem [which] lies within the

---

6. Drescher, "Comparison," 77-93.
7. *Ibid.*, 88-89, 90.
8. *Ibid.*, 84-85.
9. *Ibid.*, 85-88.
10. *Idem.*
11. Drescher, "Comparison," 82.

confines of a single title".[12] In the end, he refers to "Tocqueville's separate but equally perceptive studies," the two *Democracies*.[13]

Despite heavy methodological debts to the Yale School, Lamberti, in his wonderful book, *Tocqueville and the Two "Democracies,"* also joins the splitters.[14] He concludes his long study by asserting that Tocqueville's book divides into two parts, but his version of the two *Democracies* is strikingly different from Drescher's. For Lamberti, the first *Democracy* includes the 1835 portion and the first three books of the 1840; the second *Democracy* consists of the last book from 1840 which looks ahead to the *Souvenirs* and the *Ancien Régime*. He sees 1838, when Tocqueville discovered the significance of the revolutionary spirit and undertook a major revision of his manuscript, as the critical moment or shift. The first *Democracy* (1835 and most of 1840) attempts (without success) to distinguish between democracy and revolution (Democracy *or* Revolution, as Lamberti labels it); the second (the last quarter of 1840) recognizes that the revolutionary spirit has survived revolution, that it encourages centralization and will coexist with advancing democracy (Democracy *and* Revolution).

This rupture, Lamberti contends, is more significant than that noticed by Drescher. His two *Democracies* are, therefore, not the same pair which Drescher earlier identified. Yet Lamberti still parallels Drescher by making the idea of centralization a principal player in disjuncture; he asserts that only after 1838 did Tocqueville see centralization as "characteristic of democracy itself".[15]

So we have the "lumpers," emphasizing unity (amidst change), and the "splitters," stressing division (amidst underlying ties). Perhaps a third basic approach, typified especially by the work of François Furet, should be added to our list. A key part of the more recent effort on the part of French scholars to recapture Tocqueville from the Americans and to remind us that Tocqueville was, after all, a French thinker who reflected the context of his own country, is Furet's essay entitled "Naissance d'un paradigme".[16] There,

12.   *Ibid.*, 92-93.
13.   *Idem.*
14.   Lamberti, *Deux "Démocraties,"* especially 173-189, 269-285, 296-313.
15.   *Ibid.*, 307.
16.   François Furet, "Naissance d'un paradigme: Tocqueville et le voyage en Amérique (1825-1831)," *Annales* 39:2 (March-April 1984), 225-239. Also see in *The Tocqueville Review*, 7 (1985/1986), the essay by Furet, "The Intellectual Origins of Tocqueville's Thought," 117-129. Concerning the French effort to "reclaim" Tocqueville, see especially, in addition to Furet's essays, Lamberti, *Deux "Démocraties,"* 9-12.
      Two other recent interpretations by French Tocqueville specialists present carefully balanced responses to the issue of How Many *Democracies*? See André Jardin's

we are told that before Tocqueville set foot in America or put pen to page, the essential elements of his doctrine were in place, including: the concept of advancing democracy as a triumphant force in the modern world; the effort to explore the consequences of democracy and to develop a theory of democratic society; the concern for the preservation of liberty; the separation of the ideas of democracy and revolution; and the use of an on-going tripartite comparison, France, England and America.

This conceptual framework was shaped largely in response to the intellectual atmosphere in France during the 1820s. To earlier studies of Tocqueville's American travels (1831-1832) and of his "second voyage" (the long process of the making of the *Democracy*, 1832-1840), Furet adds a third critical period: Tocqueville's intellectual journey between 1828 and 1831. On the one hand, this approach supports the emphasis of the Yale School on the unity of the 1835 and 1840 *Democracies*, for if Tocqueville's doctrine was set by 1831, surely the differences between the first and second halves of Tocqueville's book pale in significance. On the other hand, this perspective of Furet and others entirely transcends the debate about unity or disjuncture. Both the divisions between 1835 and 1840, highlighted by Drescher and Lamberti, and the evolutionary development—the twists, turns and variations which so fascinate the Yale School—recede into the background. What captures our attention is the marvel of a work derived from a conceptual framework already in place by 1831.

As we have noted, the three most significant themes cited by Drescher and Lamberti as fault lines between the 1835 and 1840 halves of the *Democracy* involve centralization, individualism and revolution. Both men argue that Tocqueville did not perceive the intimate link between democracy and centralization until he was writing the 1840 portion of his work.[17]

In the 1835 text, however, while presenting the distinction between governmental and administrative centralization, Tocqueville declared:

> I am also convinced that democratic nations are most likely to fall beneath the yoke of centralized administration, for several reasons, among which is the following. The constant tendency of these nations is to concentrate all the strength of the government in the hands of the only power that directly represents the people; because beyond the people nothing is to be perceived but a mass of equal individuals. But when the same power already has all the attributes of

ground-breaking biography, *Alexis de Tocqueville, 1805-1959* (Paris: Hachette, 1984), especially chapters 13-15. Also consult the introductory essays to the 1835 and 1840 parts of the *Democracy* by Françoise Mélonio in *Tocqueville* (Paris: Bouquins, 1986), 9-37, 397-425.

17. Drescher, "Comparison," 83-85; and Lamberti, *Deux "Démocraties,"* 306-307.

government, it can scarcely refrain from penetrating into the details of the administration.[18]

An earlier version in Tocqueville's working manuscript added here the telling sentence: "So we often see democratic nations establish at the same time liberty and the instruments of despotism [that is, a centralized administration]".[19]

Tocqueville, let us not forget, clearly recognized by 1835 that the concentration of power constituted one of the great threats to liberty in democratic nations. His 1835 volumes catalogue the dangerous places where excessive power might be gathered, including the legislature, the majority, the hands of a tyrant, and a centralized administration.[20] By 1840, it is true, power centralized in a pervasive and intrusive administration moved to the center of his anxieties. But in 1835 he had already perceived and written about the connection between advancing democracy and increasing administrative centralization as one focus of the consolidation of power. As he emphatically declared in a draft: "Moreover we must not be mistaken. It is democratic governments which arrive most rapidly at administrative centralization while losing their political liberty".[21] And as we shall see in a moment, he also offered in 1835 early sketches of his famous 1840 portrait of the soft, but suffocating despotism of the bureaucratic state.

The drafts of the 1835 *Democracy* even described the relentless European increase in administrative centralization which would become a significant theme in the final section of the 1840 volumes.

> Among most of the states on the continent of Europe the central government is not only charged with acting in the name of the entire nation, but also with regulating all matters which are general in nature. So therefore, in Europe we see that governments, instead of limiting their actions to this immense sphere, constantly move beyond [these limits] to encroach more and more on the rights of localities and tend to seize control of the direction of all affairs.[22]

A closer examination of Tocqueville's concept of individualism (what we might call privatism) and of his increasing fear of apathy and the decay of civic spirit also does not support the idea of disjuncture between 1835 and 1840. Although the word "individualism" does not appear in the 1835

---

18. *DA* [B], I, 99-100; cf. I, 158-162.
19. YTC, CVIa, 1, for the section entitled "Political Effects of Decentralized Administration in the United States," *DA* [B], I, 89-101. See *DA* [N], I, 79.
20. For elaboration, consult Schleifer, *Making*, especially part IV.
21. YTC, CVe, 57-60, and *DA* [N], 79-80.
22. YTC, CVh, 2, 82-84.

Democracy, in both parts of his book Tocqueville was troubled by the possible collapse of public life.

At least two passages from the 1835 *Democracy* foreshadow Tocqueville's 1840 discussions of individualism and of the type of despotism which democratic nations have to fear.[23]

> [A central government when united to centralized administration] accustoms men to set their own will habitually and completely aside; to submit, not only for once, or upon one point, but in every respect, and at all times.... It affects their ordinary habits; it isolates them and then influences each separately.[24]

And in the middle of a discussion about the political advantages of decentralization, he wrote:

> It profits me but little, after all, that a vigilant authority always protects the tranquillity of my pleasure and constantly averts all dangers from my path, without my care or concern, if this same authority is the absolute master of my liberty and my life, and if it so monopolizes movement and life that when it languishes, everything languishes around it, that when it sleeps, everything must sleep.[25]

In a draft he noted more succinctly that administrative centralization "brings about despotism and destroys *civic spirit*. People get used to living as strangers, as settlers in their own country, to saying: that doesn't concern me. Let the government worry about it."[26]

And in yet another draft, he declared:

> For my part, what I most reproach despotism for are not its rigors. I would pardon it for tormenting men if only it didn't corrupt them. Despotism creates in the soul of those who are submitted to it a blind passion for tranquillity, a type of depraved self-contempt, which ends by making them indifferent to their interests and enemies of their own rights. They are falsely persuaded that by losing all the privileges of a civilized man they have escaped from all his burdens and cast off all his duties. They then feel free and stand in society like a lackey in the house of his master, and think they have only to eat the bread given to them without worrying about the need to harvest. When a man has reached this point, I will call him, if you want, a peaceful inhabitant, an honest settler, a good family man. I am ready for anything, provided that you don't force me to give him the name citizen.[27]

All of these portrayals of the dangers of administrative centralization and of the growing threat of selfishness and withdrawal from public participation date from 1833 to 1835 during the making of the first part of the *Democracy*.

23. For the 1840 discussions, see especially *DA* [B], II, 104-113, 334-339.
24. *Ibid.*, I, 90.
25. *Ibid.*, I, 96.
26. YTC, CVb, 1-2 (*DA* [N], I, 76).
27. YTC, CVh, 1, 2-4 (*DA* [N], I, 185).

Moreover, in both halves of his book, Tocqueville not only linked this danger of apathy and the death of public life with administrative central-ization, but also offered his readers the same proposed solution: enlightened self-interest or self-interest properly understood, which he presented as an American contribution to social and political theory. He named and explained the concept in his travel diaries and early drafts, devoted a small sub-section to the notion in the 1835 *Democracy*, and expanded his discus-sion significantly in several chapters in 1840.[28]

It must be conceded, however, that in 1835 Tocqueville identified the major cause of the civic diseases of selfishness and apathy as excessive ad-ministrative centralization. By 1840 he realized much more clearly that they were also democratic illnesses. No bureaucratic intermediary was needed for infection. Here Drescher's sense of shift is correct.

Finally, the idea of revolution also fails to provide a persuasive example of a sharp rupture between the two *Democracies* as divided by Lamberti. Starting with the 1835 preface, Tocqueville combined the images of ad-vancing democracy and revolution by describing the great social revolution underway in Europe for centuries. Elsewhere in the 1835 text, he recognized that democracy and revolution were occuring simultaneously and struggled to distinguish their effects.[29]

Furet notes that one of Tocqueville's great originalities was precisely his recognition that democracy and revolution were separate phenomena too easily confused by his contemporaries.[30] They were two forces, distinct yet loose together in the world, both separate and conjoined. Most important, they each had consequences which needed to be recognized and reckoned with. Throughout the making of the *Democracy*, Tocqueville wrestled with both Democracy *or* Revolution and Democracy *and* Revolution, trying at the same time to identify the distinctive features of these two great currents and to understand their intimate interconnections.

Even if these three major examples, proposed to illustrate disjuncture, do not work, we must recognize that, as clusters of ideas, the concepts of centralization, revolution, and individualism (and the collapse of civic spirit) do undergo important changes for Tocqueville between 1835 and 1840. By 1840, administrative centralization became the concentration of power which most troubled Tocqueville; by then, he named as the most distinctive

28. For the drafts, see, for example, YTC, CVh, 2, 78-79 (*DA* [N], I, 286); and CVe, 66-67 (*DA* [N], I, 243). For the *Democracy*, see *DA* [B], I, 250-253, 408-410; II, 104-118, 129-135.
29. *DA* [B], I, 1, 7-8, 11-12, 14-15, 206.
30. Furet, "Paradigme," 233.

(democratic) despotism, the centralization of the bureaucratic state, rather than the brutal excesses of a tyrant in the Roman model or tyranny of the majority. The 1840 portion contains Tocqueville's discussion of "revolutionary spirit" and his more conscious effort to separate what was democratic from what was revolutionary. And only in the 1840 half did Tocqueville use the word "individualism" and declare that it was specifically a democratic phenomenon and danger; earlier sketches of withdrawal from public life were always linked to excessive administrative centralization.

Nonetheless, excerpts cited above from Tocqueville's drafts or text illustrate a characteristic of the *Democracy* which contradicts efforts to identify some fundamental disjuncture, wherever located. To a striking degree, phrases, sentences or paragraphs in the 1835 portion anticipate pages or even chapters in the 1840 *Democracy*. The germs of ideas often appear early in drafts or text and mature, over time and from constant reconsideration, into fully developed concepts. This is not to deny novelty, the appearance of new insights, unusual twists or reversals of opinion, or even the unexpected shrinking and disappearance of certain ideas. Yet Tocqueville's thinking and writing during the 1830s do reveal a strong evolutionary feature.

An especially fascinating example of this process of growth and maturation involves Tocqueville's understanding of the psychology, character or mentality of *homo democraticus americanus*. Here in particular, in the manuscripts and text of the 1835 *Democracy*, he scatters seeds of chapters which would appear five years later in 1840. In a draft about the future of American society, he mused:

> Bonds of American society. Find out what ideas are common to Americans. Ideas of the future. Faith in human perfectibility, faith in civilization which they judge favorable in all its aspects. Faith in liberty! This is universal. Faith in the *ultimate* good sense and reason of the people. This is general, but not universal.... *Philosophical and general ideas*. That enlightened self-interest is sufficient for leading men to do the right thing. That each man has the faculty to govern himself. Good is relative and that there is continuous progress in society; that nothing is or should be finished forever. *More specialized ideas*, advantages of equality. Omnipotence, ultimate reason of the majority. Necessity of religion. Truth, utility and sublime nature of Christianity.[31]

For many of the sentences in this description, a corresponding chapter appears in 1840.[32]

Other examples from the 1835 drafts or text include: the democratic desire for material well-being; the American dislike of general ideas and

31. YTC, CVh, 2, 78-79 (*DA* [N], I, 286).
32. See especially the chapters in the first and second books (on intellect and feelings) of the 1840 portion.

preference for practical rather than theoretical knowledge; the restlessness, envy and anxiety fostered by equality; the existence in America of small private circles which served the wealthy as retreats from a relentless social equality; and even references to manufacturing aristocracy and to the ability (or inability) of democratic nations to conduct foreign policy and wage war. Each of these germs would also flower in the 1840 *Democracy*.[33]

Two other illustrations of particular interest should also be cited, for they are among Tocqueville's most original insights. In an early draft of the introduction to the 1835 *Democracy*, Tocqueville declared: "I see that by a strange quirk of our nature the passion for equality, which should grow with the inequality of conditions, increases instead as conditions become more equal."[34] The desire for equality, Tocqueville realized, would not be satisfied; as the goal of equality came closer, even the smallest inequality became unbearable. The passion for equality was doomed to frustration.[35]

Very early, he also realized that among democratic nations the desire for equality surpassed the love of liberty. "The love of liberty is much greater and more complete feeling than the love of equality," he wrote in a draft for the 1835 *Democracy*, then noted with regret: "Democracy more favorable to the spirit of equality than that of liberty".[36] Once again, in separate chapters of the 1840 *Democracy*, Tocqueville would elaborate these insights and explore how in democratic societies the passion for equality became both all-consuming and unquenchable.[37]

If one measure of the unity of the *Democracy* is the evolution of certain central ideas, another indication which deserves notice is the similarity of remedies to democratic dangers which Tocqueville offered in the 1835 and 1840 halves of his work. Even if, over time, Tocqueville modified his evaluation of which democratic dangers threatened most acutely, the political program of safeguards which he presented to his readers in both 1835 and 1840 remained largely unchanged. In 1840, his answers to the underlying democratic dilemma—how to preserve liberty in the face of advancing equality—mirrored those of 1835: decentralization (or local liberties); associations; respect for individual rights; freedom of the press; broader rights

33. For these themes, respectively, compare *DA*, [B], I 169, 411 and II, 136-141; I, 308, 326, 408-411 and II, 3-20, 42-49; I, 208, 223-224, 260, 305, 336, 443-444 and II, 144-147; I, 187 and II, 226-227; I, 443 and II, 168-171; and I, 176, 235-245 and II, 279-302.
34. YTC, CVh, 3, 27-32 (*DA* [N] I, 7).
35. For 1835, see *DA* [B], I, 208. For 1840, see *ibid.*, II, 144-147.
36. YTC, CVh, 4, 36-37.
37. *DA* [B], II, 99-103, 144-147. For 1835, see *ibid.*, I, 208.

of political participation; and reawakened religion. The *Democracy* presents no disjuncture in solutions.

The last item—religion—bears emphasis. Throughout the *Democracy* Tocqueville tried to link the spirit of liberty and the spirit of religion. He believed that religion provided some of the moral and philosophical underpinnings which were essential to freedom in democratic ages. His role as a moral philosopher serves as another of the sustaining bonds between the two parts of his book.[38]

Even if several of the usual thematic examples of disjuncture between the 1835 and 1840 *Democracies* do not work, there is at least one difference— again brought to our attention especially by Drescher—which remains indisputable. The most compelling contrast between the halves of the *Democracy* is mood or sense of the future.[39] The 1840 portion is somber, worried, full of foreboding about the democratic future—in sharp contrast to the more enthusiastic and hopeful tone of 1835. During the late 1830s, Tocqueville's new involvements in the political arena as he wrote the 1840 *Democracy* profoundly influenced his thinking and writing. As Drescher points out, Tocqueville's extra-American experiences, along with his wider readings and the longer period of reflection, led to a profound shift in perspective. The *Democracy* became less and less American. His book moved from the New World to France and to democratic nations in general. And as Tocqueville's perspective changed, his confidence about the future faltered. As readers, we sense the disunity of tone.

In a draft of his 1840 Preface, Tocqueville wrote:

> Point out—to myself as well—that I was led in the second work to take up once again some subjects already *touched upon* in the first, or to modify some opinions expressed there. Necessary result of so large a work done in two parts.[40]

Here Tocqueville bows in the direction of both "lumpers" and "splitters." His reference to taking up once again subjects already touched upon supports the sense of evolution from germs of ideas—from phrases or sentences in 1835—into more fully matured concepts—in paragraphs or chapters in 1840. His recognition of modified opinions, on the other hand, supports the

38. On Tocqueville's ideas about religion and particularly his desire for a revival of religion, see James T. Schleifer, "Tocqueville and Religion: Some New Perspectives," *The Tocqueville Review*, 4:2 (Fall-Winter 1982), 303-321. The importance of religion in Tocqueville's thought and emotion is also one of the themes brought out in Jardin, *Tocqueville*.
39. Most commentators have remarked on this contrast, but see especially Drescher, "Comparison," 82, 88. Also consult Arthur M. Schlesinger, Jr., "Individualism and Apathy in Tocqueville's *Democracy*," in Eisenstadt, *Reconsidering*, 94-109.
40. YTC, CVk, 1, 50.

stress on a break between the 1835 and 1840 *Democracies*. That both these perspectives remain viable, fruitful and defensible indicates something about the character and complexity of Tocqueville's book. We as readers are able to pursue, over one hundred and fifty years later, the on-going re-examination which characterized the making of Tocqueville's work in the first place. And as we revolve the many facets of the *Democracy*, we repeatedly notice its striking unities and disunities.

Perhaps we should recall Tocqueville's own debate about the title of his book. By the fall of 1839 he was ready to publish the second part of the *Democracy* under a separate name: "On the Influence of Equality on the Ideas and Sentiments of Men." Why he considered this change, we do not know. Realization that issues of intellect, morals and values had replaced political and institutional concerns? Admission of his distance from America? Recognition that the very definition of democracy was changing? In any case, the last half of his work finally appeared as *Democracy in America*, volumes three and four.[41]

In a conversation some years ago about the various titles of the *Democracy* and the relationship between the 1835 and 1840 portions, George Pierson quipped that perhaps the 1840 *Democracy* was captive to the triumph of the 1835 work and was published under the same title for two simple reasons. Everyone expected a sequel, and the success of the earlier *Democracy* would guarantee a good reception for another work bearing the same name.

With this thought in mind, we should also note that for us as readers the 1835 part is captive to the 1840. This happens in two ways. First, we notice insights which Tocqueville touches on and slides over in sentences of the 1835 volumes and which we know will assume great importance in the 1840 volumes. We read knowing what will become of certain concepts, aware in advance of the fate of Tocqueville's ideas. This influences our perspective and our reading. Tocqueville's first readers didn't have this difficulty or advantage. Second, this reading with the second half of the *Democracy* in mind, as a background, becomes more problematic as the reputation and significance of the 1840 portion grows. The 1835 volumes can begin to fade from view; they can become almost irrelevant, too American, too specific, not "grand" enough in depth and sweep as the 1840 part assumes greater prestige as a study of modern society. We are presented with the irony of a reversal of a different sort. At the end of the twentieth century we tend to

---

41. On the changing titles of Tocqueville's book, consult Schleifer, *Making*, 3-34, 266-267, 270, 295-296, 301.

read and judge the two halves of Tocqueville's book precisely opposite to how they were read and judged in the nineteenth century.

Probably all readers recognize that the 1835 and 1840 *Democracies* are somehow profoundly different, most acutely in mood. Whether two parts of the same book or two nearly separate works, the *Democracy* was written by a man fascinated over time by the same set of ideas and questions. The book remains the personal reflection of someone who attempted to come to grips with fundamental issues which he believed faced his society and times.

Many scholars have attempted to define Tocqueville's essential thought, doctrine, convictions, fundamental idea, question or ideal type.[42] What are the implications of this on-going search, other than the elusiveness of the quarry? We apparently sense that behind the many uniformities and divisions which mark the *Democracy* there are certain themes which bind the two halves of Tocqueville's work irrevocably together.

42. See for example, in addition to essays already cited above, Francois Bourricaud, "Les 'convictions' de M. de Tocqueville," *The Tocqueville Review*, 7 (1985/1986), 105-115; and Robert Nisbet, "Tocqueville's Ideal Types," in Eisenstadt, *Reconsidering*, 171-191.

Notes on Contributors

Joseph Alulis is Assistant Professor of Politics at Lake Forest College. He is co-editor and a contributor to a collection of original essays on Tocqueville, *Tocqueville's Defense of Human Liberty*, Garland Press, forthcoming.

Pierre Birnbaum is Professor of Political Sociology at the Sorbonne and at the Institut d'études politiques (Paris). He is the author of *Sociologie de Tocqueville* (1969); *La Structure du pouvoir aux Etats-Unis* (1971); *La Fin du politique* (1975); *Les Sommets de l'Etat* (1977); *La Classe dirigeante française* (with Charles Barucq, Michel Bellaiche and Alain Marie) (1978); *Democracy, Consensus and Social Contract* (with Jack Lively and Geraint Parry) (1978); *Le Peuple et les gros* (1979); *La Logique de l'Etat* (1982); and *Sociologie de l'Etat* (with Bertrand Badide) (1984).

Roger Boesche is Professor of Politics at Occidental College, Los Angeles. He has edited and co-translated *Alexis de Tocqueville: Selected Letters on Politics and Society* (1985), and is the author of *The Strange Liberalism of Alexis de Tocqueville* (1987).

Hugh Brogan is Reader in History at the University of Essex. He is the author of *Tocqueville* (1973) and *The Longman History of the United States* (1985). He is joint editor, with Anne P. Kerr, of *Correspondance et Conversations d'Alexis de Tocqueville et Nassau William Senior* (Paris, 1991), tome VI, vol. 2, of the *Oeuvres complètes* of Alexis de Tocqueville.

Francesco M. De Sanctis is Professor of the Philosophy of Law at the University "La Sapienza" (Rome) and Professor of the History of Philosophy at the Istituto Universitario Suor Orsola Benincasa (Naples). He is the author of *Crisi e scienza. Lorenz Stein, alle origini della scienza sociale* (1974, 1976); *Le régime nouveau. Saggio su Tocqueville* (1979); *Tempo di democrazia. Alexis de Tocqueville* (1986); *Società moderna e democrazia* (Padua, 1986); and *Dall' assolutismo alla democrazia* (1989).

Herbert Dittgen is Assistant Professor at the Center for European and North American Studies at the University of Göttingen. He is the author of *Politik zwischen Freiheit und Despotismus. Alexis de Tocqueville und Karl Marx* (1986); and *Deutsch-amerikanische Sicherheitsbeziehungen in der Ära Helmut Schmidt. Vorgeschichte und Folgen des NATO-Doppelbeschlusses* (1991).

Edward T. Gargan is a Professor of History at the University of Wisconsin. He is the author of *Alexis de Tocqueville: The Critical Years 1848-1851* and *De Tocqueville* in the series *Studies in Modern European Literature and Thought*. He is co-author with Jerald Hage and Robert Hanneman of *State Responsiveness and State Activism*. He has co-edited with Marc Bertrand and Jacques Beauroy, *Popular Culture in France: The Old Regime to the Twentieth Century*, and edited, with an introduction, Hypollite Adolphe Taine's *The Origins of Contemporary France* in the series *Classic European Historians*.

Peter Augustine Lawler is Professor of Political Science at Berry College in Georgia. He has published widely on Tocqueville, and on the relationships between religion, philosophy, and politics in America. He is editor of *American Political Rhetoric* and *Tocqueville's Defense of Human Liberty*. His *The Restless Mind: Tocqueville on the Origin and Perpetuation of Human Liberty* will soon be published by Rowman and Littlefield.

Claude Lefort is Professor of Political and Social Theory and dean of the Ecole des hautes etudes en sciences sociales (Paris). He is the author (with Edgar Morin) of *La Brèche* (1968); *Eléments d'une critique de la bureaucratie* (1971); *Le travail de l'oeuvre. Machiavel* (1972); *Un homme en trop* (1976, 1986); *Sur une colonne absente* (1978); *Les formes de* *l'histoire* (1978); *L'Invention démocratique* (1981); *Essais sur le politique* (1986); and *Ecrire à l'épreuve du politique* (Paris, 1992).

Dalmacio Negro is Professor of the History of Political Ideas at the Universidad Complutense (Madrid). He is the author of *Liberalismo y socialismo, la encrucijada intelectual de Stuart Mill* (1975); *Comte: positivismo y revolución* (1987); and *Historia del liberalismo español* (1989).

Eduardo Nolla is Professor of Political Philosophy at the Universitas Nebrissensis (Madrid) and Visiting Professor at Yale University. He is the author of *Alexis de Tocqueville, 1805-1980* (1986); of the first critical edition of Tocqueville's *Democracy in America* (1990) and of a new edition of Gustave de Beaumont's *Marie, ou l'esclavage aux Etats-Unis* (1992).

James T. Schleifer is Professor of History and Director of the Gill Library at the College of New Rochelle. He is the author of *The Making of Tocqueville's "Democracy in America"* (1980), and the editor of the first volume of a new French edition of *Democracy in America* (1992).

Gisela Schlüter is Assistant Lecturer of Romance Philology at Hannover University. She is the author of *Demokratische Literatur* (1986) and has recently completed a book on the concept of tolerance in 17th and 18th-century France (in print).

Cushing Strout is emeritus Professor of American Studies at Cornell University. The most recent of his books on intellectual history are *The Veracious Imagination: Essays on American History, Literature, and Biography* and *Making American Tradition: Visions and Revision from Ben Franklin to Alice Walker*.

Catherine Zuckert is Professor of Political Science at Carleton College in Northfield, Minnesota. Her *Natural Right and the American Imagination: Political Philosophy in Novel Form* was named the most outstanding book in philosophy published in 1990 by the Association of American Publishers. She is the editor of *Understanding The Political Spirit: From Socrates to Nietzsche*.

Index

DATE DUE

DEMCO 38-297